Feng Shui Candle Lighting

By Tina Ketch

PSYCHIC EYE BOOK SHOPS
4810 Spring Mountain Road
Las Vegas, NV 89102
(702) 368-7785

Table of Contents

Table of Contents

We all have a multitude of possible destinies in this life.

The directions that we move will determine the destiny that we have chosen!

Tina Ketch

T he ancient practice of candle lighting to purpose, accomplished by the sages of long ago, has been brought back to life by Tina Ketch, in her series of books entitled the Candle Lighting Encyclopedias. The ancients mastered the effectiveness of lighting colored candles at certain times for different reasons. Many people throughout the ages accepted this practice as it was defined and refined. The Catholic Church acknowledged the importance of candle lighting, thus implementing this practice for ceremonial occasions such as: High Mass, Lent and Benediction. The Catholic Church was not the only religion to recognize the importance of lighting candles. The soothing abeyance of the candlelight, and the change of the demeanor of those who lit the candles, as well as those who observed the candles being lit, was dramatic. The effects were positive and uplifting.

Feng Shui, pronounced "Fung Shway", is a science developed in China over 4000 years ago. Feng Shui translates to wind, (which you cannot touch) and water, (which you cannot harness). Feng Shui is the harmony of the elements, and the placement of objects to enhance the positive flow of the elemental energy. There are two complementing aspects. One is "chi", which meanders, and the other is "shar chi", which travels very fast. The "chi" is the energy which flows freely, over hills and gentle valleys. The Chi does not go around sharp objects. This chi is referred to as the "cosmic dragons' breath", which promotes prosperity, happiness and good health. Chi is yang energy.

"chi"

When there are obstructions of this chi, the chi will encounter what is called "shar chi", or yin energy. Shar chi travels in straight lines and around straight corners. The shar chi is the killing breath, which will overcome the dragons breath, or chi. The shar chi is dangerous. It is the killing breath that solicits poor health and hostile emotions.

Chi will solicit positive changes in your life, the same as lighting certain candles at the appropriate times to obtain your hearts desires, or to manifest a change in your life. The shar chi is common to lighting the right candle, but at the wrong time, thus sending away that which you had hoped for.

"Shar Chi"

In this book, we will be combining these two ancient sciences, delving into an empowering aspect of our life. First, we will discuss Feng Shui. Second, we will discuss Candle Lighting, and third, we will be putting them both together for a powerful life-changing science.

The readiness of most people, and the willingness to learn, has brought us all to this point. Our journey will be short, but the destiny through which we will be traveling will be vastly rewarding. It no longer takes a lifetime to achieve a single goal. The chi has opened up for all to partake, with vast rewards and successful living. Open your hearts and minds, for it is time to begin.

When lighting candles and using Feng Shui, we will be taking both ancient practices, and modernizing them for simplicity. When you try to improve your life by making changes too fast, by lighting too many candles, you will find yourself becoming agitated. This is because the energy that you are creating is too strong. It took you a lifetime to get where you are now. Allow your candle lighting and Feng Shui time to work, without being obsessive with your new knowledge.

Remember, in all things, balance is vital. When you create the balance in your home, you are allowing positive Chi to flow. Positive Chi brings with it harmony. Balance and harmony are essential in a productive, successful life. You must create balance-soliciting harmony in all aspects of your life. When you come home and the children are running around, franticly seeking attention as you fix dinner, you know you have not created balance and harmony in your home. Establish routines that better suit your family's needs. This does not mean to quit your job, as that would solicit another type of imbalance.

Look at the area where your children sleep. Is that room balanced? Is it free from clutter? Is it peaceful? If the answer to any of these questions is, "No", then you have not done your job in effectively achieving balance and harmony. When your children are not balanced, you are not balanced. Feng Shui follows generations. When there is upset in the cycle, the energy trickles up, and it trickles down. There is a lot of common sense that follows both candle lighting and Feng Shui. Bigger is not always better, and more is not always best.

In this book, balance and harmony will be looked at as if under a microscope. We will be taking into consideration the elements, location, color and directions of many objects in our lives, including our home and the placing of the furnishings within the home.

The first thing that we need to know is, what kind of change are you looking for? What is it that you want, and most importantly, why do you think you do not have that now? Once these questions have been answered, you will be ready to begin.

First, we will be looking at how these essential elements play a role in our lives. We will be learning the differences in the diverse elements. It will be important to know, and to feel first hand, how water as an element, not just a glass of the wet stuff to quench our thirst, puts out the element of fire. It's easy to physically see how and why this happens, but can you conceptualize it?

When determining the balance of elements, there are simple rules to follow. We need all five elements to maintain balance, and balance will be the operative term. You want your elements to be balanced. When the elements are balanced, they are in harmony with one another.

For instance, when you have a vast amount of water, you will be putting out your fire energy. When you have a large amount of water, you will be turning your earth energy to mud, and so on. These are simple, easy-to-understand correlation's.

For years, people have lit candles, giving no thought or reason to the different color of candles that they were lighting. Often, some people would light candles when they were depressed, or when they had company for dinner. They gave no thought to the time of the day, or even the date, when they lit their candles. When the candles were lit at the proper time, and the right color of candle was lit, positive changes took place.

The same holds true for the practice of Feng Shui. Some people are sensitive to the vibrations of the energy emanated by different objects, furniture and even the pictures that they would hang on their walls. This is intuitive Feng Shui. When the person is in a good, positive mood they change things around to promote positive Feng Shui. When they are depressed and they move things around, they are moving the chi to match their mood. This is why when people get depressed, and argue and quarrel with others in the home, it is hard to break the cycle of aggression. They have moved the chi to promote shar chi, and the energy keeps going until they change the chi again to promote the positive chi.

Candle Lighting and Feng Shui are both very complex. We will be breaking both down in easy terms and simple applications so that it is easy to understand. Both use a basic premise, which is that energy moves. Color emanates energy, time solicits energy, the directions promote the existence of energy and the elements are energy.

We will be learning which sections in our homes each element represents. Then, we will be subdividing that information, allowing all five elements into each room. We will, then, learn how you can neutralize the elements so that they will be balanced, and how the elements can be used to fulfill your hopes and desires for the future. As we put this all together, your only remaining question will be, "Why didn't I learn about all of this earlier?"

When lighting candles and not using the Feng Shui methods, or when using the Feng Shui without the Candle Lighting, there will be different rules, principals and techniques that you will be following. The colors, times, directions and cures in this book have been established by implementing years of research in combining Candle Lighting and Feng Shui.

I came into this life with an unquenchable thirst for the truth. My trek has taken me 46 years, only to find that all I had to do was to pay attention. Like most others, I just knew it had to be an exhausting journey, and set out to make it as difficult as I possibly could. "Suffering is truth", right? Wrong! I just knew that, before I left this life, I wanted all of the answers. My problem came halfway through the journey, when I discovered I didn't have all of the questions. Thus, there was no way the answers would come. I stopped mid-stream and began to look around. The only reason that I told you this, is that I see you, too, have an inquiring mind!

I have passionately studied religion, psychology, astrology, numerology, chromo-therapy and candle therapy, if you get the gist, and it all came down to one thing - "To thine own self be true", and "thine own self", I have now found, to be the combination of Candle Lighting and Feng Shui.

When my own sister was dying, we used chromo-therapy to put her cancer into remission. When my son had an accident, I used a pyramid under his hospital bed. The next morning, when he was re-x-rayed, the doctors found that the crack in his skull appeared to have happened 30 years prior. He was six at the time.

When another son, in the hospital after a motorcycle accident, was told he must have his leg amputated, I asked the doctors for a few minutes alone with my son, before they performed the surgery. We did some past life releases. When the doctors came back into the room, I asked them to humor me by taking the x-rays again, to which they obliged. When this was completed, they remarked that there was a way to save my son's leg, and that the third pocket that had appeared torn was, in fact, not damaged. Hence, my son still has both legs.

These are just a few miraculous things that have happened to me in this life. However, nothing compares to the events that I have seen by using Feng Shui Candle Lighting cures.

I moved to the Atlanta area in 1984. Soon after, I began to hear about Feng Shui. It was supposed to be some kind of "wind, water, move-all-of-your-stuff-around" cure for everything. Believing in everything, and being convinced of nothing, I began to read a few books, take a few classes and become aware that something was up here, but I wasn't really sure what it was. Everything seemed to be so complicated - east, west, career, helpful people?

Then, all of a sudden, as I was writing The Candle Lighting Encyclopedia Volume II, I began to feel the "chi" that everyone had been talking about. I began to feel how the "chi" could change. It was one thing to know that there was an energy that could solicit happiness, peace of mind and success, and another energy that brought with it an antagonistic environment, sadness and poor health, but to actually feel it, see it and create situations and watch it change, really showed me that something was happening around me - and that something was Feng Shui.

After years of study, and as many involved in serious research, I am convinced that there is nothing in my life as powerful as I have found in combining the ancient art of Candle Lighting with the aged science of Feng Shui.

One excellent example of the Feng Shui Candle Lighting work must be when I began to work with a non-believing client. Several years ago, knowing that I was conducting research on this new system of knowledge, a client ask me to look at a new home that she had just bought. It was a beautiful, sprawling, U-shaped ranch, sitting on three acres of landscaped property.

I calculated the distance from the back of the property to the house, and then from the front of the house to the street. I knew from these measurements that everyone and his brother were going to be moving into this house with her. The house sat one acre off the street, with two acres remaining in the back.

I, also, calculated the vibrational color that was resonating with these calculations, and found them to be a death aspect. Before going any further, I told her what color of candle to light, at what time, and on what day of the month, to keep this death from entering her home. I could, also, see - without measurements - that the shape of her new home would lend to the suffering of her career. She was convinced this would never happen. So, with permission, I quickly hung two mirrors, closing in the missing section so that she would be right.

I continued with my work. Other than a missing "career section" in the house, her home was perfectly shaped. I measured the outside front dimension of her house, and then, by taking her height and weight into consideration, measuring each dimension with each other, I could see that the U cut out in the house was in the exact place as her heart in her body. Okay! So far, we have other people moving into the house, her

17

career suffering, death, and her heart failing her, and we hadn't even gone inside. Discouraged with the results thus far, she suggested we go to lunch and continue the rest of the work at another time. So, lunch it was, and we were off.

After that first attempt to cure her ailing home, we kept in touch, but it wasn't suggested that I come back to complete the work. Time passed, as I watch her parents move up from Florida, and in with her. As they did, finding that there was not enough privacy or room, they added on to her home, taking away from the otherwise perfectly shaped house.

By adding on, they took away two sections from the house. One was "the luck of children", and the other was "family and health". These are two sections I would not want to be without.

Nonetheless, it was about 9:30 p.m. on the 22nd of April when she called to ask me one simple question, "Am I going to die?". I told her that I didn't think so, but offered to take her to the hospital. She was checked out by the emergency room doctor for chest pains, and told to see her family care physician in the morning.

It was clear to me that the Feng Shui in her home had been activated, especially now, with her health section missing from her home. The next morning I rode with her to the doctor. He checked her out and gave her a mild sedative to calm her nerves.

I knew from the dimensions of her home, and that she had not lit her candles, that it was not her nerves, but her heart, and she was in trouble. It was on our way back home that she began to feel faint! She pulled over, and I took the wheel. She was going back to the emergency room! When we arrived, she was suffering full-blown cardiac failure. They were unable to stabilize her for several hours. The next day, she was taken by ambulance to another hospital, where they re-opened two veins in her heart.

After her recovery, she resumed a limited interest in my Feng Shui Candle Lighting work. She began to light the gray candles, to keep the death out of her house. We closed in her "health and family section" with an ornamental gazing ball on a blue pedestal. The reason that we used blue was that the distance from the house to close in that section vibrated on the same vibrational level as the color blue. We, then, activated the section by lighting one blue candle at 8:00 p.m., as the color blue and the vibration of 8:00 p.m. both resonate at the same color rate, and both represent good health.
When this was finished, she walked me back to her bedroom to show

me a new painting that she had recently purchased, and there it was - as big as life and staring me right in the face - two full-length, mirrored, closet doors facing her bed!

Hanging sheets over these doors, in this beautiful home, was not going to be an option. She was not interested in taking them down, but was receptive to painting over them with a new paint that emulates stained glass. After this was done, she was convinced that her health would be fine, and that she was finished with my work.

I knew that her health was fine, but still questioned the other missing section, "luck of the children." Since she had no children living at home, at the time, she was okay with that section being missing. My only thought was a sentence in my new book, which is "Feng Shui follows generations - that it trickles up and it trickles down". Even though her children were not living at home, I knew that they could still be affected.

Her next call came at about 5:00 a.m., July 6th. Her son had been in an accident. He was not seriously hurt, but there had been one fatality! She had been lighting her gray candles, and the death did not enter her home, but it was now time for me to go back to finish my work.

Although her son was not seriously injured in the accident, his car was totaled. He now had no way to get back and forth to work. His only option, in their minds, was for him to move in with her, so that she could drive him back and forth to work. Once again, someone else was going to be moving into her home.

With his first load of belongings, her son looked at the mirror previously placed on the wall, closing in her career section. First touching it, and then, as he walked by again, hitting the mirror, he knocked it off the wall, and sent it crashing to the ground, breaking it beyond repair. She quickly bought another, placing it in the same place where the first mirror had once hung. It wasn't long after he had disrupted the peaceful chi of the "career section" of the home, that he was let go from a job he had held for over ten years.

I needed to complete my work before anyone else could move in. I told her that, because there was more room in the back of her house than in the front, it provided an inviting "sheng chi", so that others would be drawn to live with her. We needed to change the dimensions of her lot. With a forlorn look on her face, I pulled several 1/4" wooden dowels out of my bag. Each dowel was 9" long, which represents the KWAN energy, exemplifying spectacular luck & happiness, speculation and money.

We were going to place these dowels into the ground at an even distance all around the home. The distance would be 10' apart and 10' from the house. The 10' which when calculated using Feng Shui Candle Lighting method represents Chai, which brings money that is secure, having money that will never be taken. Thus, by doing so, we have placed her house in the center of the property, with many blessings.

The next thing that we needed to do was to reshape one of her bed-rooms. She had noticed that everyone who had stayed in the room became very agitated and argumentative. I know that this sounds a bit strange, but nonetheless, because of the position of the closet, the room was shaped like a cleaver.

We placed a large mirror on the short wall, just as you walked into the room. Thus, with the mirror in place, it gave the illusion that it was pushing the wall back to square off the room.

As I was finishing, she asked me to see myself out as she was getting another one of her sick headaches. She was sitting at her desk. When I looked up, I could see the reason for her headache. There was a large, decorative beam directly above her head. We know that "chi" does not travel around sharp corners, so it was clear that the "shar chi" was gathering and swirling around the beam, and shooting down directly at her head. This was the reason for her headache.

There were several cures that we could choose from to solve this problem. In order to derive the most effective cure, we took the dimensions of the room, the placement of the room within the house, the color, her most auspicious directions and the elements that were being activated within the room, along with the time in which we would activate the cure, all into consideration. The best cure for this situation would be to hang flutes on the beam. However, her decor would not allow for me to do that. My next suggestion was for her to move her desk, still under the beam, but in a more auspicious direction for her personally, and for her to light a yellow candle once a month at 10:20 a.m., three days after the new moon. After the first month lighting her candle with the new desk position, her headache went away and never returned.

If we were only doing Feng Shui, or if we were only lighting candles, this cure would never work to eliminate her headaches. It is the combination of Feng Shui and Candle Lighting that creates the focus so that the cure will be effective. The Feng Shui Candle Lighting exercises and cures will not be the same if you were using one method or the other.

We still had the last missing section to work on, caused by her parent's new addition, which was the "luck of children". She had two children, both of which were air signs. We measured the distance from the house out into the yard, from both sides of the missing section, to square off this section, creating an invisible room. Since both children were air signs, we hung a wind chime in a tree, to close in the "luck of the children" section. The space that we closed in produced the element of water. We then lit a blue candle at 7:00 p.m. to activate the section, securing her children and their future endeavors.

My last task at this home was the front door. I remembered the night I had taken her to the hospital, that her house was easy to find because of the street light in front of her house. This, normally, is not a bad thing to have, as light solicits positive "chi energy". In this particular case, the street light was on a transformer pole. The transformer was sending yin energy directly toward this yang house. The simple cure for this will be to paint the front door of the house light blue. This will balance out the energy before it enters the home. In doing so we were deflecting any sha chi that had been directed toward the house.

The Candle Lighting and Feng Shui on this home took over 6 months, from start to finish. Ordinarily, it would not have taken this long, nor would the occupants have suffered the losses they incurred.

It is not uncommon for an extrinsic concept to take this amount of time to sink into ones' psyche to the point of acceptance. I know that it could be hard to understand how, or even why, such an abstract fundamental principle could change the life, or possibly even the death, of a human being. Yet, this did, and by using the techniques in this book, all of it could have been avoided.

When living in the Western world, as most of us do, we see that our lives are shrouded with gray, yet painted black and white. The common saying is that, " It either is or it is not", or "If I don't see it, it is not there". However, this concept is so diverse from that on which our culture was founded.

We have lived thousands of years with blind faith; the creed of God, the trinity for some, and the miracles of life, most of which are based on blind faith in our time. We did not see Moses come down from the mountain with the tablets of commandments from God, but we believe that he did, and live by that creed. We did not see the suffering of Christ, but feel his pain and live through his love. This belief allows us to embrace the doctrines of old, and through our passion, we will open our hearts and minds for yet another passage into a life of peace and happiness.

In this book, we are not suggesting that you set one righteous set of beliefs aside to pick up another, just to understand that in life and concept among this vast Universe that we all live, there are many things that have yet to be discovered. We take it for granted that, when we go to sleep at night, we will awake in the morning, and that the trees will turn green in the spring, and loose their leaves in the fall. We often take our lives for granted, complaining when things go wrong, but do little to change or to make any improvements to rectify our confusion or mistakes.

In this book, you will learn why things happen, and how, with clear steps to follow, to change the spiral that has grasped you into a life of assumptions. You will learn what to do, where to do it and when, and by doing this, you will have the life that you have created. There will be no assuming and no pain. Your life will be what you have created, and if it is love and passion, it is there for the asking. If you are looking for success, you will clearly see what you can do to summon that success.

Ti Lung symbolizes protection and guardianship

As we determined the importance of the elements that were emanating at the time of our birth, we will subdivide that information on a deeper level. The next charts will show the Chinese Calendar, which will reveal to you the significant element on the day that you were born.

When dealing with the elements, you will find greater insight into your life. This information will, also, answer questions that you have about your personality. It has always been interesting to see a person who has no earth in their astrological chart, but shows all the signs of an earth sign personality. Then, we find the time of their birth was an earth sign, as well as the day of their birth.

When you find the element of your birthday, compare it with the element of your birth time. Are these elements compatible? If they are, you will want to surround yourself with the other elements. This balances out your environment, remembering to exclude the two elements that your personality represents. In any case, you will be adding the missing elements to your environment, thus creating the balance.

For example, if you were born at an earth time, and in an earth year, you will not want to surround yourself with a terra-cotta collection. This would be too much earth.

Balance is, as we have discussed, vital. In the same way, if you were born during a fire year, you would not want to add an inordinate amount of water, because water destroys fire. Again, we must have balance. DO NOT overcompensate. A little more is more than enough. There will always be an element that will destroy another element. This cycle is called balance, and balance is essential in the cycle of life. The same as yin and yang has established a cycle, a balance. Yin and yang are not opposing forces. They are complementary to each other. Without one, the other cannot exist. The same as, without darkness (yin) there cannot be light (yang), without sun (yang) there would be no moon (yin), and without life (yang) there would be no death (yin).

We will be talking a lot about balance in this book. You will find that the word alone is not enough to create it being so. You must make sure that you are establishing the balance, not just talking about it. So many people talk about wanting something, but seldom do anything to achieve their desire. You must be a willing participant in these life-changing events.

As you begin to use Feng Shui Candle Lighting, the changes will occur. This is not about magic. It is about establishing the balance within your earthen environment. This will become a global issue for you. You will curtail the amount of negative influences in your life, as well as consume that which is good for you. You will be establishing a healthy balance, and this balance will change your life forever.

We have all heard that we must do the right thing. Feng Shui Candle Lighting is all about doing the right thing. If your house is a mess, if your billfold is disorganized, where do you think the balance is? You must clean a space for change to occur. There must be a place in your billfold for money to enter, i.e., balance, harmony and respect; for us, for our homes, for our belongings and for our life!

Year	From	To	Element
1900	1/31/1900	2/18/1901	Metal
1901	2/19/1901	2/17/1902	Metal
1902	2/18/1902	1/28/1903	Water
1903	2/29/1903	1/15/1904	Water
1904	2/16/1904	2/3/1905	Wood
1905	2/4/1905	1/24/1906	Wood
1906	1/25/1906	2/12/1907	Fire
1907	2/13/1907	2/1/1908	Fire
1908	2/2/1908	1/21/1909	Earth
1909	1/22/1909	2/9/1910	Earth
1910	2/10/1910	1/29/1911	Metal
1911	1/30/1911	2/17/1912	Metal
1912	2/18/1912	2/25/1913	Water
1913	2/26/1913	1/25/1914	Water
1914	1/26/1914	2/13/1915	Wood
1915	2/14/1915	2/2/1916	Wood
1916	2/3/1916	1/22/1917	Fire
1917	1/23/1917	2/10/1918	Fire
1918	2/11/1918	1/31/1919	Earth

Year	From	To	Element
1919	2/1/1919	2/19/1920	Earth
1920	2/20/1920	2/7/1921	Metal
1921	2/8/1921	1/27/1922	Metal
1922	1/28/1922	2/15/1923	Water
1923	2/16/1923	2/4/1924	Water
1924	2/5/1924	1/24/1925	Wood
1925	1/25/1925	2/12/1926	Wood
1926	2/13/1926	2/1/1927	Fire
1927	2/2/1927	1/22/1928	Fire
1928	1/23/1928	2/9/1929	Earth
1929	2/10/1929	1/29/1930	Earth
1930	1/30/1930	2/16/1931	Medal
1931	2/17/1931	2/15/1932	Metal
1932	2/16/1932	1/25/1933	Water
1933	1/26/1933	2/13/1934	Water
1934	2/14/1934	2/3/1935	Wood
1935	2/4/1935	1/23/1936	Wood
1936	1/24/1936	2/10/1937	Fire
1937	2/11/1937	1/30/1938	Fire

Year	From	To	Element
1938	1/31/1938	2/18/1939	Earth
1939	2/19/1939	2/7/1940	Earth
1940	2/8/1940	1/26/1941	Metal
1941	1/27/1941	2/14/1942	Metal
1942	2/15/1942	2/24/1943	Water
1943	2/25/1943	1/24/1944	Water
1944	1/25/1944	2/12/1945	Wood
1945	2/13/1945	2/1/1946	Wood
1946	2/2/1946	1/21/1847	Fire
1947	1/22/1947	2/9/1948	Fire
1948	2/10/1948	1/28/1949	Earth
1949	1/29/1949	2/16/1950	Earth
1950	2/17/1950	2/5/1951	Metal
1951	2/6/1951	1/26/1952	Metal
1952	1/27/1952	2/13/1953	Water
1953	2/14/1953	2/2/1954	Water
1954	2/3/1954	1/23/1955	Wood
1955	1/24/1955	2/11/1956	Wood
1956	2/12/1956	1/30/1957	Fire
1957	1/31/1957	2/17/1958	Fire
1958	2/18/1958	2/7/1959	Earth
1959	2/8/1959	2/27/1960	Earth
1960	1/28/1960	2/14/1961	Metal

Year	From	To	Element
1961	2/15/1961	2/4/1962	Metal
1962	2/5/1962	1/24/1963	Water
1963	1/25/1963	2/12/1964	Water
1964	2/13/1964	2/1/1965	Wood
1965	2/2/1965	1/20/1966	Wood
1966	1/21/1966	2/8/1967	Fire
1967	2/9/1967	1/29/1968	Fire
1968	1/30/1968	2/16/1969	Earth
1969	2/17/1969	2/5/1970	Earth
1970	2/6/1970	1/26/1971	Metal
1971	1/27/1971	2/15/1972	Metal
1972	2/16/1972	2/22/1973	Water
1973	2/23/1973	1/22/1974	Water
1974	1/23/1974	2/10/1975	Wood
1975	2/11/1975	1/30/1976	Wood
1976	1/31/1976	2/17/1977	Fire
1977	2/18/1977	2/6/1978	Fire
1978	2/7/1978	1/27/1979	Earth
1979	1/28/1979	2/15/1980	Earth
1980	2/16/1980	2/4/1981	Metal
1981	2/5/1981	1/24/1982	Metal
1982	1/25/1982	2/12/1983	Water
1983	2/13/1983	2/1/1984	Water

Year	From	To	Element
1984	2/2/1984	2/19/1985	Wood
1985	2/20/1985	2/8/1986	Wood
1986	2/9/1986	1/28/1987	Fire
1987	1/29/1987	2/16/1988	Fire
1988	2/17/1988	2/5/1989	Earth
1989	2/6/1989	1/26/1990	Earth
1990	1/27/1990	2/14/1991	Metal
1991	2/15/1991	2/3/1992	Metal
1992	2/4/1992	1/22/1993	Water
1993	1/23/1993	2/9/1994	Water
1994	2/10/1994	1/30/1995	Wood
1995	1/31/1995	2/18/1996	Wood
1996	2/19/1996	2/7/1997	Fire
1997	2/9/1997	1/27/1998	Fire
1998	1/28/1998	2/15/1999	Earth
1999	2/16/1999	2/4/2000	Earth
2000	2/5/2000	1/23/2001	Metal
2001	1/24/2001	2/11/2002	Metal
2002	2/12/2002	1/31/2003	Water
2003	2/1/2003	1/21/2004	Water
2004	1/22/2004	2/8/2005	Wood
2005	2/9/2005	1/28/2006	Wood
2006	1/29/2006	2/17/2007	Fire

As we get further into this book, you will see that determining your birth element will indicate to you the strongest corner of your home. Thus, by activating this corner, you will be stimulating the most positive Chi, which will have the most powerful effect on your psyche and well being. By activating this section of your house, it will give you the motivation to continue. Once the Chi takes over, success is on its way. Its force is strong and powerful. Chi energy can move mountains– its force is conclusive and convincing.

What is a Kau Number and Kau Formula

Each person has a number, which is personal to him or her. This number is based on the year of your birth as well as your gender. This personal number is called a kau number. Your Kau number will tell you what element resonates well with you, your compatible elements, as well as with whom you will be compatible, or incompatible. Your Kau number will be your first step in understanding yourself and others. As you begin to understand your personality, you will see how the different elements make up the world in which you live. Also, you will see how and why you act and react within your environment, and why certain things push your buttons, whether good or bad.

To determine your Kau number, first obtain your Chinese year of birth, based on the Chinese Element Calendar. Let's say that your birthday is 2/16/1965. Add the last two digits of your Chinese year of birth. Our example is 1965, so we will calculate it as 6 plus 5 = 11. If the total is higher than 10 reduce your total by adding the two numbers again. In this example, it will be 1 plus 1 = 2.

For a female, you will now add your total to the number 5. This will be 2 + 5 = 7. So for a female born in 1965 your Kau number is 7.

For a male, you subtract your total from the number 10. If you were born in 1965, your Kau calculation would be 6 plus 5 = 11, and 1 + 1 = 2. Now we subtract that total from 10, or 10 − 2 = 8. So your Kau number will be 8.

We will be using this Kau number to determine our compatibility with other people and places. It will be important to live in a harmonious environment determined by your Kau number, rather than in an inharmonious environment.

The applicable example here is the old saying, "Why do bad things happen to good people?" That is because they are not living in harmony with their compatible Kau number. They would, also, not be with other people from their same Kau group. Opposites do attract, but they can bring with them devastating effects if the oppositeness is incompatible.

Males	Females
Subtract from	Add
10	5
Thus	Thus
10 − 2 = 8	5 + 2 = 7
Thus, men born in 1965 the Kau number is 8	Thus, females born in 1965 the Kau number is 7

W hen calculating your Kau number using this formula, keep in mind that there is no Kau for the number 5. Thus, males with a number 5 should use the Kau number 2. Females with a number 5 should use the Kau number 8.

Your Kau number is one of the most important numbers that you will be using as you begin to light your candles and set up the Feng Shui in your home. Your Kau number will tell you which of four directions are the most favorable for you, and which four directions are not favorable for you. Your Kau number is, also, used as we touched on earlier, to determine your compatibility with your spouse, parents, children and even whether or not you are inherently compatible with coworkers.

Fung Shui is divided into two groups of people. There are the "East group" people, and the "West group" people. Using the table below, you can ascertain your Kau direction.

People with Kau numbers from the same group, East or West, are always compatible with each other. If you marry someone from your own group, you will be able to have a relationship that is not challenged by your partner. Your relationship will, also, not be challenged by your environment, if you both live in a house that is in that same group.

If two East group people live in a West group house, there can be problems in the relationship, but they will all be caused by outside interference. The chart below will tell you, depending on your Kau number, what direction group you will be most compatible with. People who marry outside of their group have a tendency not to be happy, and depending on the charts titled, "Compatibility Kau Numbers" and "Incompatibility Kau Numbers", you could be capable of causing not only damage to your own psyche, but physical harm to your partner. If your Kau number is the least possible combination on the incompatibility chart, you may want to avoid the relationship. Incompatible kau numbers can lend to an abusive relationship. At the very best, there will just be something that you don't like about them, feeling as if you can't put your finger on the reason.

There are controlling issues with these opposing relationships. Keeping in mind that the term abusive, or controlling, does not always mean life threatening, some people need, or want, to be controlled. An abusive relationship could be as minor as a free spirited person being married to someone who is controlling or domineering. In these instances, it will be helpful to light the appropriate candles to attract the relationship that will not stifle your creativity or spirit. To ascertain the best relationship energy and direction, you must consult the Lo Shu. We will be doing that next.

Kau	Direction
1	East
2	West
3	East
4	East
5	West
6	West
7	West
8	West
9	East

Feng Shui Candle Lighting is a powerful miracle of energy, and will change your life in a positive way forever. Lighting your candles in the most auspicious section of your home, and in the right direction for your Chi to flow, stimulates changes in your life. It is, also, important to note that Chi does not flow through or over clutter. When Chi encounters these messes, it is easily engulfed with the Sha Chi. When there is an inordinate amount of Sha Chi, the environment is confusing and hostile. Quarrels can ensue; along with jealousy, confusion and discontentment, all emotions that we would like to avoid.

Below, we have two tables. One is for the East Group People, and the other is for the West Group People.

The shaded areas on both represent the sections that will be best suited for you. People that are in the East Group are the people with the personal Kau numbers of 1, 3, 4, and 9. People that are in the West Group are those people with personal Kau numbers of 2, 6, 7, and 8.

The shaded areas on each table will show you with whom, and from which Kau number group, you will be compatible. If, for example, your personal Kau number is 1, you will be compatible with anyone whose personal Kau number was 1, 3, 4, or 9. If your personal Kau number is 8, then you will be compatible with those people with a Kau number of 2, 6, 7 or 8.

East Group

4	9	2
3	5	7
8	1	6

West Group

4	9	2
3	5	7
8	1	6

Next, we will be discussing which of the Kau numbers will be the four best in compatability, and which ones will be the four worst in compatability using the Lo Shu magic square in conjunction with their directions. This is not to say that you cannot be with anybody that you choose. It is merely a guide to whom you will, and will not, be compatible with when involving yourself in an intimate or business relationship.

This is the Lo Shu Grid. It is sometimes referred to as the magic square.

There are three rows of numbers and three columns. No matter how you add the numbers horizontally, vertically, or diagonally they all add up to 15. It is said that the 15 represents the number of days between the lunar cycle.

First, find your Kau number. Second, using the table below, you will be able to see your four choices of numbers, and corresponding directions, that will best suit your Kau, or personality. These numbers are called Lo Shu numbers.

Now, let's say your Kau number is 3, and that you are a female. Using the diagram (on page 33) we find that your best Lo Shu number is 9, the second best is 1, the third is 4 and the last is 3.

4	9	2
3	5	7
8	1	6

Now, let's shade this on our Lo Shu to get a better understanding of how it works. Please note there is, also, a corresponding direction, (diagram below), in each section of the Lo Shu. When activating these directions, your feng shui candle lighting will be brought into play, aiding you in finding the peace and success for which you have been looking.

To determine the chi flow in your home, always remember that the chi flows in the direction that you go. When your Kau number is 3, and your best direction is South (9), arrange your room so that you comfortably move about your room in a southerly direction.

Think about the direction that you travel as you normally enter your home and travel through the halls. Is this the best direction for you to go? If not, move your furniture so that your favorable directions are in a natural flow to your most auspicious directions. For instance, I naturally come in my home from the South and travel North.

Unless I park in the garage and walk around to the front of the house. The reason that I do this is that this is the flow of the chi. The chi will decide which direction you will follow.

4	9	2
Southeast	South	Southwest
3	5	7
East		West
8	1	6
Northeast	North	Northwest

Find your Kau number on the far, left-hand column in the diagram below. As you know the date and year of your birth, as well as your gender, determine your personal kau number. Once you have determined your personal kau number, you will be armed with a tremendous amount of Feng Shui knowledge, as everything else that we will be doing will be based on this number.

Your kau number will be the path that your innate personality will follow in order to fulfill your destiny. This kau number will give you an insight into the direction in which you must journey in order to determine your particular fortune in this life, whether this fortune is spiritual or monetary, or both.

As mentioned, the Lo Shu, or magic square, will give you an indication as to which Kau numbers represent a feasible direction for you to travel, and to which you may prosper, thus lending to favorable results. As well, the Lo Shu will represent which directions are not personally favorable for you.

The chart below will give you four chi energies that will favor your travel and prosperity . You will be given four energies that will favor your personal kau number from the best through to the fourth-best. All of them will be favorable, but since we have all grown accustom to options, the universe through Feng Shui offers them to us through this chart.

Best Lo Shu Numbers for Females				
Kau	Best Sheng Chi	2nd Best Tien Yi	3rd Best Nien Yen	4th Best Fu Wei
1	4	3	9	1
3	9	1	4	3
4	1	9	3	4
9	3	4	1	9
5	2	6	7	8
2	8	7	6	2
6	7	8	2	6
7	6	2	8	7
8	2	6	7	8

When using this chart if you are a male you will see the four Lo Shu energies that will be offering you opportunity for growth and success in this life.

Using the chart below we see that the row has been shaded in for the male kau number 9. This will represent from the best through to the forth best which Lo Shu energy is the most favorable for a man with the kau number of nine.

The kau numbers listed below from the Lo Shu will give you the corresponding Lo Shu direction in which you will need to activate in order to achieve this Lo Shu energy.

The first Lo Shu energy on this chart is called Sheng. Sheng chi represents money luck. (see page 41) When using the kau number 9 as the example, the Lo Shu Sheng chi number will be 3. The Lo Shu number three tells you that your money luck is in an easterly direction.

The second Lo Shu energy on the chart is that of Tien Yi, this chi represents upper-class-income and promises good health.

The third Lo Shu energy on this chart is the energy called Nein Yen. This energy for your kau number 9, represents the chi energy of longevity and stability, which if crossed referenced on the chart on page 32, is in the North section of your home.

The forth Lo Shu energy on our chart is that of Fu Wei. This is a very powerful energy as it represents our personal power and your ability to live a good life. (see pages 41-46 for definitions of Sheng through Fu Wei chi).

Best Lo Shu Numbers for Males				
Kau	Best Sheng Chi	2nd Best Tien Yi	3rd Best Nien Yen	4th Best Fu Wei
1	4	3	9	1
3	9	1	4	3
4	1	9	3	4
9	3	4	1	9
5	8	7	6	2
2	8	7	6	2
6	7	8	2	6
7	6	2	8	7
8	2	6	7	8

A gain find your Kau number on the far left hand column in the diagram below. If you are a female and your Kau number is 3, your very worst Lo Shu direction is Southwest. As well if you are a female and your Kau number is 9, your worst Lo Shu direction is Northeast.

Our example is that the Kau number was three, giving us the best Lo Shu numbers in order of; nine, one, four and three. Now, using the Lo Shu magic square we find that your worst Lo Shu directions are Southwest, second worst is Northwest, third worst is Northeast and the forth worst will be the direction of West.

When using this chart you will be made aware of your worst Lo Shu directions. In order to lessen the effects of the Ho Hai, through to the Chueh Ming energy you will need to keep these sections in your home neat and orderly.

When decorating and setting up your home you must take care that you do not place your home office, bedroom or any room of importance in these inauspicious direction.

When building a new home a storage room, laundry facilities or bathrooms would be good places for your worst Lo Shu directions.

In the event that you have a business meeting and your best location is

Worst Lo Shu Directions for Females			
Kau	4th to the worst Ho Hai	3rd to the worst Wu Kwei	2nd to the worst Lui Sha	very worst Chueh Ming
1	West	Northeast	Northwest	Southwest
3	Southwest	Northwest	Northeast	West
4	Northwest	Southwest	West	Northeast
9	Northeast	West	Southwest	Northwest
5	South	North	East	Southeast
2	East	Southeast	South	North
6	Southwest	East	North	South
7	North	South	Southeast	East
8	South	North	East	Southeast

not available you will need to, light your candles in your home, before the meeting, in the space that best represents what you are trying to accomplish.

Each Kau number has an energy that it resonates with, an energy that it is compatible with, an energy that it exemplifies and an energy that it will repel.

Each of these different energies will have a name, a definition, and direction that will illustrate its function in your life. When utilizing the information on these charts, showing you the worst compatible Kau numbers for your health and welfare, you will want to attune yourself to this information. You must empower the natural chi flow in your life. Participating in activities or even living in your worst directions will inevitably cause you harm.

Each Kau number has four directions that will complement you, and four Lo Shu directions that will not be to your advantage.

When you are in a position that you must be in one of the worst Lo Shu directions for your personal kau number, and have no choice as to being there, you can use this knowledge to your advantage. By being aware of your surroundings, and keeping your guard up so that you will not meet with the discomfort or confusion that may await you, by doing so you may escape adverse conditions.

You may think that it is not fair to have adverse directions or kau numbers, but you must bare in mind that not only do we grow through adversity, but also we must have balance in order to promote harmony.

Worst Lo Shu Directions for Males			
Kau	4th to the worst Ho Hai	3rd to the worst Wu Kwei	2nd to the worst Lui Sha	Very worst Chueh Ming
1	West	Northeast	Northwest	Southwest
3	Southwest	Northwest	Northeast	West
4	Northwest	Southwest	West	Northeast
9	Northeast	West	Southwest	Northwest
5	East	Southeast	South	North
2	East	Southeast	South	North
6	Southeast	East	North	South
7	North	South	Southeast	East
8	South	North	East	Southeast

Using the Kau Numbers to Understand Relationships

To determine your most favorable partner, use this chart to cross-reference your compatibility. If you are a woman, and your Kau number is 6, your most favorable partner will be someone with a Kau number 8. This compatibility will be the Sheng Chi energy. Using the Lo Shu definitions, you can see that this compatibility is suitable for financial success. Through this relationship, you will prosper.

You may want your bedroom in the Sheng Chi direction of your home. We all know that relationships are not based on money. However, prosperity comes in many other forms, and not just in cash. Thus, this would be a very prosperous and successful union.

Money is an exchange of understanding. It takes this much to get that much. Thus, the relationship will be one of conversation, compromise and understanding. To me, that spells success.

If you are a man, and your Kau number is 5, you will be using the Kau number 2. Your most compatible partner would be someone with the Kau number of 7. The second best would be 8. The third best would be 2, and last best will be 6.

We all know that understanding brings strength to relationships.

Compatibility for Men and Women Using Kau Numbers			
Kau	**Sheng Chi**	**Tien Yi**	**Nien Yen**	**Fu Wei**
1	3	4	1	9
2	7	8 male / 8 & 5 female	2 & 5 male / 2 female	6
3	1	9	3	4
4	9	1	4	3
5	7 male / 6 female	8 male / 2 female	5	6 male / 7 female
6	8 male / 8 & 5 female	7	6	2 & 5 male / 2 female
7	2 & 5 male / 2 female	6	7	8 male / 8 & 5 female
8	6	2 & 5 male / 2 female	8 male / 8 & 5 female	7
9	4	3	9	1

Sheng Chi Relationships: **If you are involved with a person that has a Sheng Chi relationship with you there will be an exquisite compatibility.** Aside from the fact that this could be a business or personal relationship the dynamics of this union will bring you a sense of satisfaction, trust and gratification. There will also be an immense consequence of luck. This is the basis for the saying of "when motive and opportunity meet" or "finding your soul mate". When a person has a Sheng Chi relationship with you they will take care never to say or do anything that will cause you physical or emotional pain or discomfort.

Tien Yi Relationships: **The Tien Yi kau relationships have a tendency to be the longest relationships that you will have in this life.** There will also be a sense of trust in this kinship that will give you the confidence that you can confide in the person whom you have a Tien Yi relationship with. As children we often bond through innocence. It will be the same innocence that we will experience in these relationships as adults. Anyone can be told information in confidence, but it will only be those with whom you have this kau compatibility that you will be able to trust to hold your coveted secrets. When we involve ourselves in relationships, we have a tendency to pass along guilt and stressful issues to those that we allow to get close to us. This is not the case with Tien Yi relationships. There will be an unspoken rule that you will not send and they will not receive stress or anxiety through the association and vise versa.

Nien Yen Relationships: **These relationships whether they are business or personal are almost nurturing in their significance.** Seldom will you find a relationship in the corporate world where people feel the need to take care of you, or that you feel the drive and desire to take care of them. Often these business relationships are misunderstood. Your desire to nurture and to take care can be misunderstood for something more than what it was intended to be. There is nothing said that would imply that these relationships could not be successful personal relationships. But one thing that you must remember when entering into this vibration of relationship is – some people are best left as friends! We live in a culture that is so desperate for love and attention that when we feel the slightest attraction to someone we want to make it more. More is not always best.

Fu Wei Relationships: **When you have this vibrational relationship with someone you will feel a great sense of satisfaction.** There will be a supporitve theme that will run the gamout of this relationship. There will be nothing that you will not do for the other person as they will be encouraging as well as supporitve of what ever your desires may be at the time. There will also be a feeling or need to step out of this influence from time to time so that you will be able to keep a keen perspective of the difference between what you want and what your relationship is telling you that is in your best interst.

Now that we have determined our favorable and unfavorable Lo Shu numbers and directions, we will be discussing incompatible kau numbers for personal and business relationships.

If your personal kau number is two, you will have a Ho Hai relationship with those people that have a kau number nine. The Ho Hai energy exemplifies that of accidents, problems, confusion and mishaps.

Have you ever met someone that you may have, at first glance, liked, only to find that in his or her company anything that could go wrong did go wrong? This is a classic example of one person with a personal kau number of two coupling with other person having a personal kau number of nine. This is the same for all Ho Hai relationships.

The second incompatible energy in conjunction with your kau number two, will be with a person with a personal kau number of one. This is the Wu Kwei energy. This energy is call the "five ghosts" by some people, others may refer to this energy as a black hole.

Anything that is in its space seems to get lost. If you are trying to date someone and your kau number is two and theirs is one, they will lose your telephone number.

This chart will give you your incompatible kau relationships.

Incompatibility for Men and Women Using Kau Numbers				
Kau Number	Ho Hai	Wu Kwei	Lui Sha	Chueh Ming
1	6	2 & 5 male	7	8 & 5 female
2	9	1	3	4
3	8 & 5 male	7	2 & 5 male	6
4	7	8 & 5 female	6	2 & 5 male
5	9 male / 3 female	1 male / 4 female	3 male / 9 female	4 male / 1 female
6	1	9	4	3
7	4	3	1	9
8	3	4	9	1
9	2 & 5 male	6	8 & 5 female	7

The next Lo Shu energy is that of Lui Sha. This energy is referred to as the 'six killings'. This energy can cause harm, illness and legal problems. The Lo Shu number that is associated with the Lui Sha energy is three, and we have already determined that the direction is East. If you are entertaining a relationship with someone whose kau number is three, and your kau number is two, I might suggest that you use caution in undertaking such a task.

The forth Lo Shu vibrational energy in our example is Chueh Ming. This inauspicious Lo Shu energy represents the most antagonistic of all Lo Shu energies. This is a vibration of death and destruction. If your kau number is two, and you are thinking about a relationship with someone with a kau number of four, you should expect this relationship to be disappointing from the onset.

Some people think that little mishaps are all right and that, perhaps, they would have happened anyway. This is not the case. The combined energy of both people brings the energy together for things to happen, or conversely, for things not to happen. These events happen through the combined vibrational energy of both of your kau numbers, and the directions of the Lo Shu vibrations.

Apart, you are both wonderful people. The combination between the two of you is something that you need to work hard to overcome. This does not mean that the two of you are not, or could not, be passionate and have a deep sense of love between you. It is just one of those relationships where effort must be enforced to maintain peace.

Not all relationships last, or are easy and not every relationship was meant to be. Now we know why.

Everyone can achieve great love in this life. And as you begin to understand why there are obstacles in your relationship, you understand how to safeguard your emotions. There can be long-range energy ramifications when combining two opposing Kau and Lo Shu vibrations. If you are convinced, still, that your opposing relationship will work, this will be the classic example of when and why Feng Shui Candle Lighting must be implemented for survival.

Another reason for the incompatibility of our example is that the Kau group that the kau number two belongs to is the West group and the Kau numbers one, three, four and nine are all from the East group.

Prince Charles and Princess Diana were an East and West combination. They went through all of the motions, but the end was inevitable.

Lo Shu Locations Defined

We have been discussing the auspicious and inauspicious Lo Shu numbers each of which represent a location in your home or direction, which will be favorable or unfavorable for you depending on your personal Kau number. As in all things, there must be balance, so both auspicious and inauspicious exists, and both are equally as important.

Auspicious Lo Shu Direction

Sheng Chi: This is the most auspicious Lo Shu energy. The luck associated with the Sheng chi is associated with money or prosperity. The direction of the sheng chi energy using your most auspicious direction chart and then by cross referencing with the Lo Shu, will show you which direction you need to go or to activate in order to prosper.

Place your bedroom, office or study in this corner of your home. This is, also, the direction that you should go to make money. This is the direction in which you would want the front entrance of your home. If it is not, you might want to take a picture of your front door and place it in the sheng chi section of your home.

Candles for money should be lit in this section. When you multiply the energy from the sheng chi with the candles that you will be lighting, you have a tremendous amount of prosperous energy flowing, and it will produce the money and success that you are looking for. This is a favorable direction. However, if you have your bathroom or kitchen in this section of your home, it can create negative results to the relationships that you have with your spouse and/or children.

The next chi energy is called Tien Yi and represents upper-middle-class income and all of the accouterments that accompany that **Tien Yi** lifestyle. It is, also, the direction in your home that you will need to activate if there is a family member that is ill or suffering from a prolonged illness.

In order to activate this section, you must first insure that there is no disorganization, so that the chi will flow freely. Once this is done, you will be able to light your candles in this section so that any health problems, or issues with your prosperity, will be unrestricted enabling the Tien Yi chi to flow freely and unencumbered. Light your candles in this direction, or section of your home, to bring money, and to assist in the recovery of an ailing family member.

The example here will be: if your Kau number is 9, then your Tien Yi direction will be 4, as seen on page 33. The direction on the Lo Shu for the number 4 is Southeast. When lighting your candles in this section of your home, or in any room in the Southeast corner, you will be activating the Tien Yi chi, thus assuring prosperity and good health.

41

Another example of this healing energy will be: if your daughter is ill, and her Kau number is 6, then her Tien Yi direction is the Lo Shu direction 8, which is Northeast. Light her healing candles in the Northeast section (or corner) of the South section of your home. The South direction represents your number nine kau number. The head of the household dictates the first Tien Yi energy, the second is determined by the Kau number of the ailing family member. We will be lighting the candles representative of both of you, as this will enable you the most beneficial healing energy.

Nien Yen The next auspicious Lo Shu energy, which is Nien Yen, which represents longevity. It is, also, the direction in your life and home that indicates a peaceful family, and calm and soothing energy. This is a place in your home, if free from confusion and clutter, that you would be able to do your best thinking, and easily find peace of mind.

If you are having problems with members of your family, you will need to lighting candles to activate the Nien Yen chi so that peace and tranquility will once again influence your home. Also, by stimulating this section, you yourself will have the ability to think clearly so that you can make the decisions that pertain to your own well-being, thus soliciting happiness in your life.

When you activate this section, you will see that the energy is strong, and the powerful chi here will create situations in your life and within your home so that everyone lives in peace and harmony. This section also extends itself so that with the free-flowing energy you will produce prosperous descendants.

If your Kau number is 6, using the table on page 29, and then on page 33, you will see that your Lo Shu direction representing this Nien Yen will be Southwest. In order to stimulate the Nien Yen energy you will need to lighting your candles in the Southwest section of your home.

Fu Wei The next auspicious Lo Shu energy represents a good life. This energy is called Fu Wei and represents personal power. By activating this section of your home, you will be protected from bad luck. By placing your bedroom in this section, you will have more boys than girls in your family, if you are of childbearing age and so inclined. This is the energy of happiness, but not necessarily prosperity. When you have good luck in your home, you will be carrying that energy into other aspects of your life, even outside of your home. Children with their bedrooms in this section will do well in school, and be really popular. Sense the Fu Wei is an energy of personal power, when activated in your home there will be powerful and exciting good luck for everyone who lives with you.

Happiness comes in several forms. Some people validate their existence by the amount of money that they have, or their ability to make it. Some people substantiate their existence through the value of their family, and the happiness that they derive from making them happy. The latter is the energy promoted by the Fu Wei Lo Shu energy. When it's happiness that you desire, or feel that you are missing, then this is the section that you will need to stimulate.

Again, using the tables on pages 33 and 34, find the Lo Shu number that corresponds to your personal Kau number. Next, find the direction which represents your Lo Shu number by using the Lo Shu on page 32. If your Kau number is 7, on page 33, you see that your Lo Shu Fu Wei number is, also, 7. On page 32, you will see that the Lo Shu number 7 represents the West direction.

For happiness and good luck, stimulate the West section in your home, by lighting your candles in this section, after you have assured yourself that this section is clean and free from clutter. This will also stimulate your personal power.

The term "free from clutter" is used often in this book. The reason for this is that, as you read in the introduction, sheng chi, which is the energy that enables us peace of mind, luck, success and happiness, among other positive verbs, only travels over smooth, clean, open spaces.

It is the shar chi that loves clutter, disorganization, straight lines and the corners of walls and furniture. Balance is harmony, and there must be balance in all things and never an inordinate amount of either shar or sheng energy.

A corner on your night stand pointing at you as you sleep will cause you a restless night. Sha chi will effect you more harshly than will the same amount of sheng chi energy. Sha chi will produce what is called poison arrows. These poison arrows come out of sharp corners, and the edges of walls or furniture.

Some of these arrows cannot be avoided, yet your use of them can be. Move any piece of furniture that has a sharp or pointed edge, that my be facing you as you sit to relax, or lie down to sleep. If there is a straight-edge corner protruding into any room, place a large, floor plant in front of the corners, as the sheng chi from the plant will lessen the effects of the shar chi poison arrow that has been causing you feelings of discontentment, anger or even hostility. In the event that there is a pointed corner facing your home from a neighbors house you will feel the effects of this poison arrow. Place a small eight sided mirror above your front entryway to absorb portions of this harmful Sha chi. As sha chi will lessen the effects of your Fu Wei chi or sheng chi coming into your home.

Ho Hai

Ho Hai is an inauspicious Lo Shu energy that signifies mistakes and accidents. This the most favorable of the four unfavorable Lo Shu energies.

This is the direction that you would not wish to have your bed facing. By sleeping in this section, or facing this direction, it could cause you to forget important points in conversation, commonly referred to as "brain fade", giving you the impression that you have a problem with your recollection. It is common for any of us to forget things; dates, times and even names from time to time. However, facing this Ho Hai energy in your sleep every night could cause you problems which could affect your livelihood.

If you have no choice but to sleep in this direction under this Ho Hai energy influence, there are cures or remedies that you can do to lessen the effects of this energy. As always, the first thing that you will need to do is to make absolutely sure that this room is clean, even under the bed, just because you cannot see clutter if it is there the effects of the Ho Hai will be felt. The second thing that you will need to do is to light your candles in your most auspicious section, but in the Ho Hai corner of that section. This will give you a combination of your best energy as it commingles with the Ho Hai.

The example will be: If your personal Kau number is 4, your most auspicious section, or Sheng Chi, will be in the North section of your home. You will be lighting your candles in the North section, and in the West corner of this room. The Ho Hai energy is being represented by the direction of the Northwest corner, but we do not light candles in the Northwest. The West is the alternative candle lighting direction for the Northwest. This is because if your Kau number is 4, then your Ho Hai section is Northwest.

However, often times the best offense is a good defense. Therefore, by keeping this section clean, and allowing the chi to flow without obstruction, you will not have a need to continually activate this section lessening the effects of the Ho Hai .

Wu Kwei

Wu Kwei is the Lo Shu number that translates to "five ghosts". It is important that you not place anything that is important to you in this section. If you were building a home, placing a bathroom in this section would be a good idea, thus sending the killing Shar Chi down the drain or toilet. This is the second of the four inauspicious directions.

A client found the perfect house. Upon moving in and setting up, his

44

wife inadvertently placed her office in this section. This direction also, represented the relationship section of the home. It was not a surprise when their relationship began to suffer shortly after moving in.

Nor was it hard to see that other traumatic events would soon come to pass. The second event was an IRS audit. The husband and wife filed joint returns thus the audit effected them both. The room was being activated everyday by its use.

When I suggested another room in the house for her office turning the first room into a storage room, and lighting candles lessening the Wu Kwei, the relationship began to go back together and the audit was over, successfully I might add.

The best protection is to make yourself aware of your inauspicious directions and use them as storage or other none essential rooms in your home.

For our example if your Kau number is 2 your Wu Kwei energy is in the Southeast section of your home. This is a section that you will need to be gentle with when activating. As we will see this may be a very important section in your home.

Lui Sha

Lui Sha is the third of the four inauspicious Lo Shu energy sections. It is referred to as the "Six Killings". This is the direction that causes harm to your family and your business. This Lui Sha direction can cause legal problems and illness to everyone living in the home. It is best not to place your bedroom or office in this section.

I might suggest again a toilet or storage room. Or at the very least a formal living room that you will not often use. If you are building a new home this is a great place for a bathroom.

The energy in this section is likely to cause injustice or violence to members of your family. Always be sure that this energy is neutralized by keeping the room clean and the elements well balanced.

When we stimulate this Lui Sha energy by neglecting our home, our families or ourselves we are only furthering the activation of this inauspicious energy. When this happens often this is the "why me" syndrome. You cause the problem and then whine that you then must deal with the consequences of your own actions.

If your personal Kau number is 1, using the table on page 35 your Lui Sha energy will be in the Northwest section of your home. This is a direction that we will use the West direction as an alternative when lighting candles. When your desire is to lessen the effects of harmful energy you must light your candles between the time of the full moon and before the next new moon.

Chueh Ming

This Lo Shu energy is called Chueh Ming, and its location is the worst of all four inauspicious Lo Shu directions. There is nothing good that will come from this energy.

You will not want to live in a home that faces your Chueh Ming direction. If you do, and cannot move, take a picture of your front door, and place it in one of your auspicious directions.

Do not place a room of importance in this section of your home, if it can be helped. There is a deadly force that can generate from your Chueh Ming direction, and should be avoided at any cost.

Make sure that this section is clean and the elements are balanced, so that the positive chi can flow. If your personal Kau number is 3, your Chueh Ming direction will be West.

There is a positive energy that will flow from the West direction, and it should be stimulated. We will learn about that in the following pages, but still, the Chueh Ming should be kept clean, and stimulated by lighting only small votive candles.

The only reason that you would stimulate an inauspicious energy is so that it will be neutralized so that the chi can flow and bring positive changes into your life.

When your front entryway is in this westerly direction you will be lighting larger candles if you wish as in this case you will be stimulating your chi entry and not necessarily the Chueh Ming.

It is not the West direction that is inauspicious, it is the Chueh Ming. If your personal kau number were 6, the West would be your Sheng Chi, which is the very best chi energy.

Shen Lung is an auspicious symbol of abundance.

46

Dividing Your Home Using the Lo Shu Directions

I have divided this house to give you a pictorial view of the eight sections in Feng Shui Candle Lighting. Again, all eight sections are governed by the different elements that emanate color and circumstances. These sections will represent aspects of our lives.

They are; Wealth and Prosperity in the Southeast, Fame and Recognition in the South, and Marriage and Happiness in the Southwest. The East is Health and Family, and in the West we have Luck of Children. The Northeast is our section for Education. North is your Career, and in the Northwest is the section for Helpful People.

As you can see, every aspect in your life can be encompassed within these eight categories. And there is a corresponding color representing the particular elements resonating within each section. For instance, a good color to paint a room in the Northeast corner of your house would be an earthen color, such as any shade of brown or yellow. By doing this, you are activating that part of your house that emanates the element of earth, which also represents stability and consistency. This is, also, the section of Education. Thus, by activating this section, you will attract the concentration you need to retain whatever you are studying.

This is the trigram for the Northeast section of your home it represents the Ken energy. Keeping in mind that this trigram, as do all the others, represents the operative section in every room. For instance, there will be a Northeast section of your house, and there will also be a Northeast section in every room of your house, and so on. This is a section soliciting meditation and contemplation. As we all know, success grows out of preparedness. We, also, have the front door of the house in the education section. This will tell you that the objective for the people living here will be on education, studying, getting ahead, and using the knowledge that they have to their advantage. They will value education and use their influence on others to drive that point home, i.e., education = success. So often we move into a new home or apartment and, by virtue of the move, we expect our lives to change, and they usually do! But not always the way we expect.

Southeast	South	Southwest
Wealth & Prosperity	Fame & Recognition	Marriage & Happiness
Green / Light Blue	Red / Purple	Brown / Yellow
East	Take your compass directions	West
Health & Family		Luck of Children
Green / Light Blue	from the center of your home.	White / Silver / Gold
Northeast	North	Northwest
Education	Career	Helpful People
Brown / Yellow	Black / Blue	White / Silver / Gold

Door

With this information, you will now know how and why your life will change, even before you make your move. Often times, we will change residences because we have gone up the ladder of success. After which only to find that the house we had moved from contained the energy that enabled us the success in the first place. We, then, awaken to find the new home will not lend to success that you once had. Also, through the energy in the home in conjunction with your personal kau number will not solicit for you an opportunity for your relationship to be nurtured. Who knows, perhaps the new home even has aspects that will make you ill. We will discuss each section so that your next move will be an educated one.

Now, lets look at the influence on the other parts of your house. We started with the Northeast, so we will continue to work ourselves around the house. The next section is East, represented here as health and family.

— — The trigram represented here is indicative of growth, happiness — — and vigor. It is the essence of spring. When this trigram is activated in the East section of your home, it promotes good health, ——— happiness and harmony it is the Chen energy. Now that we have determined what *health* is let's look at what effect this section will have on you personally, as well as the effects that it will have on your family, by not being activated.

Let's say your daughter has more than her share of earaches, and you begin having headaches. You quickly contribute your headaches to stress, and your daughters ear problems to something like wax buildup. Both of these are probably correct assertions on some level, but what about a deeper level into which you have yet to delve, i.e., Feng Shui Candle Lighting?

Let's say that you have your sewing room in the East section of your home. There are patterns all over the floor, the bobbin casing has fallen out of the machine and thread is everywhere. This clutter and disorganization is called Shar Chi, and the Shar Chi has manifested in you as headaches, and in your daughter as earaches. This example gives a simple solution. It is time to clean!

As you light your candles, (we will discuss this in our Candle section), and begin to clean, the stress at work begins to lift, and the headaches begin to subside. You continue to clean, and find that your daughter's ears have begun to drain, and the earaches are no longer keeping your child up at night. Life was not meant to be this hard!

This will, also, be the time when your son calls from college to tell you that he has passed his PE make-up test that he had failed miserably only last month. That's right, family is family. Even though your children move away from home, it does not mean that their parents' home ceases to be their family influence.

This is another classic example of how Feng Shui Candle Lighting energy trickles up and trickles down.

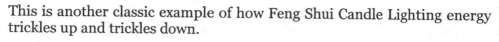 This is the trigram that represents the Southeast section of your home, which is represented by wealth and prosperity. This section is not just the 'get money' section, even though it could be used for that!

This direction or location is the Sun energy. Wealth and prosperity represent your ability to obtain, and retain, wealth. When you activate this trigram in your home, and especially in the Southeast section of the house, or the Southeast corner of any room, it will symbolize the germination and harvest of the wealth cycle. Thus, in doing so, all of your projects with be successful.

When you live from paycheck to paycheck, there is something wrong in this section of your home. The first question should be, "What room occupies this section?". Is it a bathroom? Bingo! That's the problem. Many Feng Shui persons feel that as you flush the toilet, you are, in a sense, flushing away all of your money.

One thing that you could do to stop this from happening in the future, might be to put a small mirror on the ceiling above the toilet. What you accomplish by doing this is that the mirror attracts the positive chi energy amusing it so that when the toilet is flushed this energy will not leave but continue to dance in the reflection of the mirror.

Another thing you can do is to always keep the seat closed on the toilet when it's not in use. By doing this, you will be holding onto your money, and it will not disappear.

We have talked about the Southeast section being governed by the wood element. You can attract money by putting a wooden toilet seat on the toilet. If this section is a bedroom, place plants that have room to grow. By placing plants that go to the ceiling, in a room that represents money, you are not allowing your money room to grow. The plants must have room to grow, i.e., put plants that grow out or down, rather than tall ones that grow up.

Also, make sure there are no mirrors facing the bed if this section is in the bedroom. This includes a television set. You do not want anything to reflect your image as you sleep. This creates shar chi, and will not allow your money to grow. It will also make you very ill. We will be lighting candles in this section of the house.

What condition is your bedroom in? Are there things under the bed, or are your drawers in disarray? Is this room pleasing to the eye, or is it where you throw everything from the living room that you don't want company to see? How do you feel when you walk into the room? Is it pretty? Is it comfortable and inviting, or is it just a place that you go when you are too tired to stay up any longer? Make whatever room occupies this Southeast section of your home pleasing to the eye, balanced and clutter-free. This is where your money comes from, and you want your money to be free-flowing, and not lost in the mess.

_____ This is the trigram that represents our next section which is the Li energy. The section that we will be discussing is South, which — — represents recognition and fame. This is the section that corre-_____ sponds with the way the world sees you. This trigram symbolizes a rise in prominence, perhaps just as the Phoenix that rises out of the flames; with honor, power, wisdom and dignity.

You may think that you live in a small town, and that no one really knows anything about you. You make think that there are really not enough people that you know who could view you at all. Yet, unbeknownst to you, there is an undercurrent out there with your name on it. Everyone that you have ever known, at one time or another, has spoken your name, and in the grand light of it all, you have gone everywhere that they have gone.

The world is smaller than we think, and the world is closing in on us. This is a good feeling to know that we are all still connected, but what does this section of your home tell you about what they think, and about what do they remember about you? What does this section tell you about the views that others have on who and what you are? If the views are good, and this section is pleasing to the eye, balanced and free from clutter, they remember and view you as a wonderful, competent person. If it is not, it will be anyone's guess what others will be thinking or saying about you. In our candle lighting section, we will be talking about all of the ways you can fix anything that could be causing you a problem, as well as how and when to attract what you want.

— — The next section is vitally important to anyone who wants a rela-— — tionship, and for all those who want to keep their relationship (s) — — going. This is the Southwest section of your home representing the Kum energy. The trigram represents the love, luck and nurturing, of not only humans, but of the earth, as well. This section represents the respect of the mother, the wife and the children. As it, also, represents the mountains that cradle the seas, it represents your marriage, happiness and your ability to nurture. The energy here is that of the mother, maternal feelings and the "stuff" that holds families together. This section of your home will radiate love, passion, compassion and the desire to have everything right.

Remember that the chi flows in and out of doors. For this reason, all of the doors in your home must, at all times, be in good working order so that the chi will refresh each room as it flows through them. So all of your doors to this and other rooms should be in good working order, and free to swing their full swing. Never put anything in the path of a door that must be walked over, as this will quickly turn the Chi flow into the harmful Shar Chi, causing distress, confusion and spiteful conditions in your home, as well as problems with in your relationships.

— — Our next section is West, Tui energy is emanating here. It is
     represented by the luck of children. The luck that is being re-
——— ferred to here is not just that of a competitive nature and the art
——— of winning. Luck is free-flowing, positive energy that keeps us
out of harm's way.

Luck is avoiding the chicken pox that all of the other children have contracted. Luck is being in the right place at the right time, so that the right thing can happen. Luck is the positive side of karma and destiny. Luck is, also, being successful in everything that you do.

This is a section that you would want to fill with your children's beautiful and sentimental memorabilia, but keep in mind this is not a section that is just about luck. This section, which represents the youngest child, brings joy and a bountiful amount of happiness.

——— The next of the eight sections is Northwest or Chien. This sec-
——— tion emanates the energy of helpful people. Three solid lines
——— represent the patriarch of the family, the father, and the power
     that emanates from this section of the home is said to assist the
father in his endeavors. You will find varying degrees and sources of power from this section, which transcends through the father figure, ancestors, etc. You might find it hard to think of just a few helpful people in your life, as they are probably plentiful. However, think about the people that have aided you in becoming who and what you are.

Your parents and grandparents would be among the list of helpful people in your life. If you live in the United States, you have the founding fathers to add to your list. If you are a writer, banker or engineer, think about what it took for you to gain the knowledge and the experience that you have.

When you put it in these terms, you can find a lot of helpful people that have influenced you in your life, and in your success. This would be a great place to hang pictures of your ancestors, and those minds that have aided you on your road to success.

If this section of your house is where your garage is, you will want to keep it clean and free from clutter. This would not be the best place for me to hang my mothers' picture, but I can show my respect by keeping my garage clean and free from clutter.

Remember that every room has all eight sections in it, so you can hang your ancestors' pictures in another room on the Northwest wall. Respect produces excellent Feng Shui Candle Lighting.

— — The last section that we have is North or Kan energy. It repre-
——— sents the career conditions in your life. There is, also, a hidden as-
— — pect to this section, which is hidden wealth.

Your career is anything that you do to produce money. Some may think they have a job and not a career. However, as we know, you achieve that which you believe.

There could appear to be a message of danger in this trigram. There are two open lines between one solid line which makes the trigram appear to be weak. Never let this fool you. There is strength in this trigram as, in fact, it is hidden. Yet it is, also, deceptive.

How many times have you thought that you have been stabbed in the back by a coworker? This is the trigram that could allow this type of thing to happen. But you can beckon the energy of this trigram to work for you. You may appear weak, that could causes people to take advantage of you, but with the assistance of this energy you will awaken the strength that you have inside of yourself.

If your livelihood is not your idea of your chosen profession, and you want to have more of a career, you will need to activate the chi flow in this section of your home. By using candles, which we will discuss later in the book, you can easily do this.

You can, also, stimulate this section by painting the walls blue. Another suggestion might be to place a fish tank on the North wall in the North section of the home. Be sure that the tank is clean and in good working order, and remember not to overcrowd your fish. More is not always better.

Water is a very emotional element, and we would never want to use too much, or to abuse it. Water also brings money. Always remember that there must be balance in order for harmony to exist. If you have plenty of money because you work all the time, there is not a balance in your life. Money is not hard to come by if there is balance in your life. If you have to work hard to create money, then there are problems elsewhere.

Money is not about effort, it is a product of balance and harmony. A well-balanced family has money and harmony in their relationships, along with successful children. A man or woman who must put excessive effort into everything that they do to make money will not have successful relationships, and may struggle with their children.

We have just discussed the eight directions of life. Now, we will talk about the eight directions, and the positive Chi that flows through the eight directions.

We know that four of the directions are Yin and four are Yang. As we discussed, there is positive Chi and the not-so-positive Shar Chi. Both compliment each other, and in order to complete the balance and harmony in all living things, both must exist.

We are now going to examine the same eight directions, yet this time we are going to look at the emotional aspects of each of these directions as dictated through the appropriate trigrams for each section.

The North direction, will produces a nurturing Chi, this is the energy that we will want to utilize for the protection of our home and family, as the North is typically the direction of the super power. When you want to "win" you must approach your adversary from the North. Clutter and disharmony would bring the opposite of this, which would be a lack in your ability to nurture or to protect your family. As well if you in fact approached your enemy from the South you would not win. The Shar Chi' would also bring a sense of procrastination, and a feeling of being lazy.

Have you ever stopped to reflect over your life to see that your home and family were the most important aspects of your life? Rewarding yourself for doing such a fabulous job through your success, you bought your family a new home, only to find, upon moving that you became flustered to the point that your family suffered?

This may have been because when you changed residences you also changed the direction of your front door. In your old house, your front door faced North, and in your new home, perhaps your front door faces Southeast. In doing this it changed your priorities from being nurturing to being creative.

Keep in mind that you would still be nurturing toward your family, but as your house has shifted in its chi flow priorities, you too have shifted in your priorities, establishing a more creative than nurturing outlook on life.

Remember as we begin to explore the aspects of our life, there will be simultaneous energies each functioning at the same time and in the same place, each with a specific cause, each guiding and directing us to our destiny. Each will express the purest form of its intent!

Southeast **4** **Creative** ————— ————— ——— ——— **Sun**	**South** **9** **Vigorous** ————— ——— ——— ————— **LI**	**Southwest** **2** **Soothing** ——— ——— ——— ——— ——— ——— **Kun**
East **3** **Stimulating** ——— ——— ——— ——— ————— **Chen**	**5**	**West** **7** **Calming** ——— ——— ————— ————— **Tui**
Northeast **8** **Flourishing** ————— ——— ——— ——— ——— **Ken**	**North** **1** **Nurturing** ——— ——— ————— ——— ——— **Kan**	**Northwest** **6** **Expansive** ————— ————— ————— **Chien**

North
1
Nurturing

This is the direction of North. This nurturing Kan energy provides the essence of what you will need to sustain life, as well, symbolizing problems. As there is one strong yang line between two weaker yin lines. This energy will take work to overcome the yang between the yin. This is not the most promising of the trigrams. As it can bring problems and confusion.

| Southwest |
| 2 |
| Soothing |

This soothing Chi' will allow you the rest and relaxation that you need to recharge yourself for the next day. It is not enough to get off work and watch a little television in order to relax. You must have this section in your home conducive for relaxation. The kitchen placed here will not give you the rest needed for your success.

A den, living room or sun room would be better placed in this section. This would, also, be an ideal section for a child's nursery. When a child has a soothing disposition, the whole family will benefit. Clutter in this section will create shar chi' in the form of irrational behavior, soliciting arguments and discontentment. If your child's room is in this section, and is in disarray, your child will appear as if he or she is hyperactive, destructive, or even non-communicative. Being defiant is another symptom of clutter in this section of your home. The Southwest section, will be the Southwest part of the house, or the Southwest corner of any room in your house.

| East |
| 3 |
| Stimulating |

The stimulating chi' emanating here is similar to that of motivation. Having the energy to accomplish projects that you had put off because of circumstances. This is not to be confused with procrastination, which is something that you put off because you don't want to do it.

This Chi' represents those things that you want to finish, but have not had the where-with-all and stimulating motivation, together at the same time, for completion. Regardless of what room you have in this section of your home, this stimulating East direction must be clean and free of clutter. This means clean drawers, closets and under the bed. By doing so, you will be allowing the positive chi' to flow so that you will successfully complete your projects.

When the chi is inhibited in this area, and the sha chi is flowing, you will feel as if you are in a wind tunnel in your mind, making it difficult to do anything.

| Southeast |
| 4 |
| Creative |

The creative energy here is that of a tender heart. It could, also, be denominated as your passion center. It is that driving force that allows you to be creative, as well as to be productive. This energy is passive and flexible, and it will produce the same energy possessed by writers and painters. This section would be a good place for your home office, as it allows you to get the job done, and the ability to deal with the distractions from the family without upset. The passion of this creative energy will produce success in your life. If you have an obsessive personality, place your home office in this section of your home. This will turn your obsessions into passions. Obsessions are typical of sha chi where passion is sheng chi, it will be the sheng chi soliciting success.

Northwest	This expansive energy is equivalent to that of Jupiter in astrology. The candles that you will light in this section, as well as the intentions that you create, will be magnified.
6	
Expansive	

You must, also, keep in mind that expansion will go both ways. The chi will expand the positive thoughts and intentions that you have, lending to success. Whereas, if the section is not free from clutter and the elements are not balanced, you are allowing an array of health issues to invade your physical body through the sha chi. These health issues indicated here could include such things as pulmonary problems, as well as problems with the neurological regions of the body.

When this happens the sha chi will not only vibrate through your body in the form of an illness, it will also pledge you with issues of illusions. These illusions will not just be bad dreams. You will lash out at your children, spouse and extended members of your family. This energy must be reckoned with through elimination.

When there is an inordinate amount of sha chi in this section of your home you will begin to turn your friends and family members into advisories. You will pick fights with them and become upset when they strike back. You have created illusions and you must deal with this chi before peace may be established with in the family.

West	This calming energy is helpful when you feel besieged from outside influences. You would have a tendency with this as a Kau number to be stressed and apprehensive if you do not have enough sheng chi to solicit relaxation in your life.
7	
Calming	

Often when sha chi is at play in this direction there is a tendency to distrust those around you. If the chi is not free to flow you may experience chest pains and, or problems with your teeth.

In women problems with your teeth and lower jaw pain may only be a precursor to chest and heart pain. Seek medical attention first. Then stimulate this section of your home so that the sheng chi will continue what your physician has started in aiding you in your recovery.

As you can see, it is of the utmost importance to keep a clean and clutter-free home, so that the chi will flow, thereby eliminating poor-health issues. It is equally important to have the elements in each section balanced, because if they are not, that, too, will attract sha chi.

If any one in the home becomes ill especially if their kau number is seven, this vibrational chi which is resonating in this section must be stimulated to assure sheng chi for the assistance of their speedy recovery. This is the section for calming relaxation – use it!

Northeast
8
Flourishing

The flourishing energy here is stable and consistent, but has conditions attached, that you will need to follow so that you will reap its rewards. This is the section in your home, or the direction that you will need to pay attention to, when you are studying for a test or learning anything new.

The element that resonates in this section is small earth. It is not only stable and consistent, this energy has a tendency to be stubborn and inflexible, giving you the comprehensible impression that you must get it right the first time around.

This is the energy that is equivalent to the task that you must accomplish before a harvest. If you have not gone through the steps to insure success you will at this juncture know that you have failed.

If in fact you have accomplished your task, dotted your "i's" crossed your "t's" you will at this point reap the rewards of a job well done.

Your determining factor will be – is this section in your home free of excess sha chi? Do you have an ample amount of sheng chi resonating in this Northeast section of your home? Are the elements balanced? When was the last time you used this section of your home for daily living? Have you activated the sheng chi in this as well as other sections in your home lately?

This is a checklist for the Northeast as well as all sections of your home. Once you become accustom to the flow of chi you will not need a list, these questions will become second nature in your attempts to live a successful, peaceful, and harmonious life.

South
9
Vigorous

This vigorous energy holds no hostages, and, at times, has no mercy. This is the section in your home that you will need to activate in order to be vigorous in your attempts to accomplish your objectives.

The element resonating here is fire, which at times can be dynamic and forceful, but only so that determination will prevail. Auspicious chi in this South section of your home will bring about recognition and fame.

In the event that you do not prepare yourself for positive recognition the observation of your accomplishments will not be favorable.

You cannot escape this or any other life emotional aspect. If you prepare yourself as well as activate the auspicious chi in this section of your home, others will view you in a positive light. In the event that you do not, you will experience the consequences. This is another classic example of "when you do the right thing – the right thing will happen".

I n every measurement there will be favorable and unfavorable dimensions. We are going to begin by taking a tape measure that is 17" long. Second we are going to divide the 17 inches into 8 equal sections. And thirdly we will divide each of the 8 sections into 4 sub-section. Giving us 32 different definitions within the 17" ruler. The first section will measure from 0 – 2 and 1/8 inches.

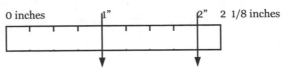

This first section is called **CHAI**. This first section is comprised of luck. Now this section will be divided into 4 more sections each 1/2 inch long.

0 inches			2 1/8 inches
1st	2nd	3rd	4th

Each of our sub-sections will represent a life aspect of luck.

First Section	Money luck – money coming from unexpected sources.
Second Section	Money that is secure – having money that will never be taken.
Third Section	Abundance of good luck – being at the right place at the right time.
Fourth Section	Abundance of good fortune – allowing good fortune to be free flowing.

The second section is from 2 1/8 inch to 4 2/8 inch.

2 1/8 inches   4 2/8 inches

This section is called **PI** which means sickness. When we divide this section into 4 sub-sections we find our first 4 sections representing ill-will.

| 1st | 2nd | 3rd | 4th |

First Section	Money loss – making money but not being able to keep it.
Second Section	Problems with authority – issues with police or government.
Third Section	Serious problems – being banished or incarcerated.
Fourth Section	Death or endings – the end of a relationship – without cause.

The third section will measure from 4 2/8 inches to 6 3/8 inch. This section is called **LI** representing separation.

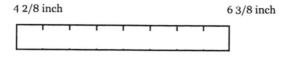

As we divide these two inches we find 4 sub-sections of various degrees of separation and loss. Each of these sections is approximately 1/2 inch.

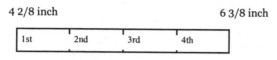

First Section	A host of bad luck – anything that can go wrong, will go wrong for you.
Second Section	A loss of income – someone you know will try and take your job.
Third Section	Association with people who will steal from you – people close to you.
Fourth Section	Everything will be lost or stolen – you allow this to happen.

The next or fourth section is from 6 3/8 inch to 8 1/2 inch. This is the second good aspect. It is called **YI** and pertains to luck that comes from others, or helpful people.

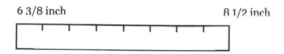

The four sections of YI will be various degrees of blessings and good for Fortune.

First Section	The blessing here is of good children – children helpful to others.
Second Section	Blessings of money – unexpected money income.
Third Section	The blessing here is of a very successful son – bringing honor.
Fourth Section	Blessings of many good fortunes – unlimited success.

The blessings here will prevail upon you unlimited success and happieness, to yourself and your family.

The next section on our ruler is from 8 1/2 inches through 10 5/8 inch. This section is called **KWAN** and it will represent the power that you have in your life.

8 1/2 inch   10 5/8 inch

Again we will divide this section into four sub-sections. Each will be equally powerful. Each section is approximately 1/2 inch.

1st   2nd   3rd   4th

First Section	Success – positive and enthusiasm passing test and lessons. Honors given.
Second Section	Spectacular luck & happiness – speculation and money. Opportunities.
Third Section	More money – unexpected income. A debt repaid from a past incarnation.
Fourth Section	Prosperity – money, success and honor. Good health and blessings.

The next section will be the sixth section on our ruler is going to be from 10 5/8 inch through 12 6/8 inches. This section is called **CHIEH** and refers to getting hurt or harmed. This as you can see is not one of the better sections.

10 5/8 inch   12 6/8 inch

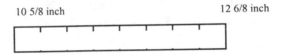

As we divide this section into our sub-sections we find four sections of harm, disgrace and bad news. Remember there must be a balance within the universe. And as there are positive aspects there are also harmful ones. Each section is approximately 1/2 inch.

1st   2nd   3rd   4th

First Section	Loosing something – through death or disappearance, emotional illness.
Second Section	Loss – of things you hold dear, such as income. Or the love of someone.
Third Section	Disgrace–loss of honor. A sense of dishonor (this is a perception and not a reality). A haunting vision that no one likes you. (self-imposed)
Fourth Section	Extreme – loss, of love or money. Putting too much energy into something that is not yours. This is a result of not minding your own business.

The loss that you could incur here is hard. Always remember that pain and disgrace is an emotional aspect of life and can be altered through your attitude, faith and candle lighting.

The seventh section will fall between 12 and 6/8 inch and 14 and 6/8 inch. This section is called **HAI** and represents pain and suffering. When working with anything within these dimensions caution should always be taken as not to cause harm to yourself and others.

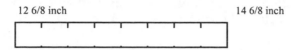

We will now subdivide this two inch section into four subsections, each approximately 1/2 inch. Each section will encompass varying degrees of loss and suffering.

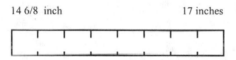

First Section	The destruction of what you hold dear – your home or family. Communication problems that you cause. Wind damage, or weather related problems.
Second Section	Death – the loss of someone you revere. The ending of something, closure.
Third Section	Illness – something that can not be diagnosed. Prolonged illnesses. Caffeine or acid related problems.
Fourth Section	Arguments – with people who matter to you. Arguments that cause emotional damage. (let go of the need to control others– get the facts)

The eighth and final section on our 17 inch ruler will be from 14 6/8 inch to 17 inches. The name of this two inch section is **PUN**. Pun represents abundance of money and happiness.

14 6/8 inch   17 inches

We will again divide this section into four subsections each approximately 1/2 inch each.

1st   2nd   3rd   4th

First Section	An abundance of money – free flowing money coming in.
Second Section	Your ability to test well – success in testing and scholastic interest.
Third Section	An abundance of monetary possessions – having the best of everything.
Fourth Section	Having more money than you can spend – financial success.

When you have come to the end of your 17 inch ruler, you start all over again. This cycle repeats itself over and over again.

W e are going to be talking about directions. When you begin to determine the direction of your home or room it may be a bit confusing. There will be two different terms. One is **facing** and the other is **sitting**.

This home is facing North but sitting South.

The front door faces North. To determine the direction of this house you will be standing at the front door facing out. This will show you how the house is facing North.

When you are standing looking into a room the direction will be a *sitting* direction.

When you are looking away from something such as looking out of the front door this will be a *facing* direction.

W e are going to begin by taking a tape measure that is 17" long, and
we are going to divide it into eight sections. Each section will be approxi-

mately two inches long. Every two inches of measurement will, again, be
divided into four 1/2 in sections. Each section will represent energy, and
within that energy-cycle you will have four more 1/2-inch cycle of energy. We will be using this child's room to show a few examples of how
you can use the Feng Shui measurements of the lengths and heights to
determine the auspicious and inauspicious chi.

First, we will start with the child's chair in the picture. The height is 30
inches. We have a 17 inch measuring tool, so we will subtract the height
of 17, to see that we have 13 inches remaining. For that reason, the measurement that we will be utilizing will be that of the remaining 13 inches.
Using the measurement table on page 61, we see that the 13 inches fall
along the ruler representing the section which is called HAI, and represents pain and suffering. And as we mentioned, each section has four
subsections.

Next, we will look to see which energy is functioning within the subsection of Hai. We see that, on this same chart, the 13 inches falls within
the first of the four subsections which represent "the destruction of what
you hold dear – your home or family" etc,.

This is only one dimension of the child's chair, and already we can see
that this is not the kind of energy that we want in our child's room. The
next measurement that you would want to do is the width of the chair.

The width of the chair is 22". Again, using the 17-inch ruler, we find that there are 5 inches remaining on our measuring tool. When we look on page 59 we see that the 5 inches falls along the section called **LI** representing "separation". We can, also, see that the 5 inches is within the second subsection that represents "a loss of income" meaning "that somebody you know will try and take your job".

Now, we might not think there is somebody else that might be trying to take your child-rearing job from you. But you might want to think about all of the times that you have cleaned your child's room, just so that it would look nicer than what your child is capable of doing. Or when you have cleaned the room because they have refused. You might need to take the chair out of your child's room. This simple change can transform the chi in the room.

Another thing that you would need to look at is the fact that the chair is sitting in front of the window, giving your psyche the impression that at any minute you could fall out. This is a very insecure feeling. The same principal would apply if you were to place the headboard of your bed up against the window. This would lend to a restless night, as well as bad dreams.

Now that you have taken the chair out of the room, lets look at some of the other objects that might be causing shar chi. Let's look at the bookcase along the wall. The dimensions are 52 X 70. The 52-inch width has a remaining one inch ($17 \times 3 = 51$ and $52 - 51 = 1$). One inch on page 58 is that of the **CHAI,** and is comprised of luck. One inch, also, falls within the second subsection that represents "money that is secure" – money that will never be taken away.

When we look at the length, and see that it is 70 inches, we will divide that by the 17 inches ($17 \times 4 = 68$ with 2 remaining), and find that we have a remaining 2 inches. The chart on page 58 shows us that the 2 inches falls within the same section as before, which is called **CHAI.** However, in this case, we will be using the 4th subsection, which represents "an abundance of good fortune" – allowing good fortune to be free flowing.

The bookcase will definitely be something that you will want to keep in your child's room.

There must be a balance of the chi and shar chi in each room and home, but you will not want to have an overwhelming amount of inauspicious dimensions in a child's room that may be a detriment to the child's health and welfare.

Before you decide to make the single most important investment in your life. You will want to determine what the home will be used for. Not just what you want to use it for but what the house has decided on its own that its use is. This might be a very strange question or even situation to think about.

Each house within its lot will hold a specific purpose of its own. In order to make sure that the home will serve the same purpose that you have in mind for it there are several measurements that you will need to make before investing your life into something that may not suite your needs.

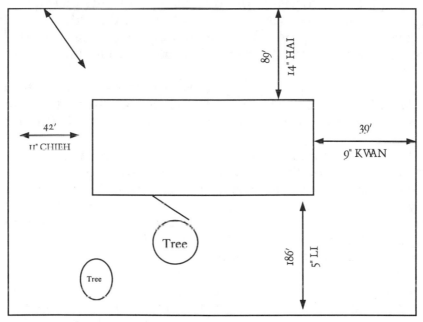

Keep in mind as you are making these measurements that a house and lot may be cured of its faults but at the same time a cure is not always the answer. It may be that the house was just not made for you.

When you are calculating the dimensions of your lot and home you will be using the calculation below and the definitions of each section and subsection on pages 58 through 61.

Calculations: Feet X 12 divided by 17 that answer X 17 and then subtract that answer from the first sum. So 42' X 12" = 504". 504" divided by 17" = 29.64. 29 X 17 = 493". 493" minus 504" = 11" which is CHIEN, see page 60.

We are going to pretend that our house is sitting South and facing North. We have forty-two feet on the East Side of the home, and thirty-nine feet on the West Side of the home. There is eighty-nine feet to the South, or the back yard, and one hundred and eighty-six feet in the North, or in the front yard.

By using the equation on page 65, we see that, on the East Side of the home, there is a remaining eleven inches, this is the Chieh energy. Chieh refers to harm, or the act of getting hurt. This eleven inches falls along the ruler in the first of the four sub-sections, making reference to losing something through death or disappearance.

As this is not an aspect that you want to have functioning around your home, you will have to change this dimension. I am sure that you are not going to be able to move your home over to make this side of the yard a more auspicious dimension, so there are other cures that you will have to do to defuse this energy from invading you and your family.

One thing that you can do to change the size of this side yard is to determine what kind of energy you want to function in this part of your lot. This is done by referring to the dimension chart on pages 58 through 61.

Let's take the total measurement that we had to start with, which was forty-two feet. Divide the forty-two feet into two sections, so that you will have a remainder of an auspicious dimension. We will divide this side yard into two sections; the first section will be thirty-two feet. When we calculate this dimension we get the remainder of ten inches (32 x 12 = 384, 384 divided by 17 = 22.59 and 22 x 17 = 374 and 374 – 384 = 10), which is the Kwan energy.

Ten inches is power in your life, and this remainder falls within the fourth subsection which is: prosperity, money, success and honor. The second section that we will have left from our original forty-two feet will be ten feet, which calculates down to a remainder of one inch (10 x 12 = 120, 120 divided by 17 = 7.06 and 7 x 17 = 119, 119 – 120 = 1). On page 58, we see that a remainder of one inch represents the energy of Chai, which exemplifies the luck in your life. The subsection which applies here is the second, which represents money that is secure, having money that will never be taken. Now that we have calculated this forty-two feet into two more auspicious sizes, we will have to do the work so that this energy will be activated.

First, we are going to take 1/4 inch wooden dowels. We are going to cut them into an auspicious dimension of eight inches, which will represent the Yi energy of blessings and good fortune. We are, now, going to drive our eight-inch dowels into the ground, ten feet apart, making an invisible energy fence of luck, blessings and prosperity.

To the West, there is a remaining inch measurement of nine inches, which is Kwan. The Kwan energy, as mentioned on page 60, measures from 8 1/2 inches to 10 5/8 inches, and represents the power that you have in your life. This is your ability to use this power mentally, spiritually or physically to obtain your wishes. As this dimension is subdivided into four sections, we see that nine inches falls within the first section, exemplifying success with a positive attitude and enthusiasm. Thus, the West side of the home is a very positive space in which you will draw strength and power.

The measurement in the North, or front, of the home has a remaining five inches, which has an energy of Li. Li is the energy of separation. The five inches, also, falls within the first subsection, representing a host of bad luck. Again, this is not an energy that you want in your front yard.

The beginning measurement for the front yard was 186 feet. We are going to take that measurement and divide it, so that we come up with an auspicious dimension that will bring us something better than a host of bad luck.

If we take the yard and divide in into two sections, with the first section being 142 feet and 11 inches, you will have a remainder of 15 inches, which represents Pun. Pun is the energy of abundance of money and happiness, and the 15 inches falls within the subsection representing <u>incoming, free- flowing money.</u>

The second section in the front yard will be the remainder of the 186 feet, or 43 feet and 1 inch. The remainder of inches is 7 inches which falls within the second section which is Yi. This Yi will exemplifies the luck that comes from others. The subsection that applies here is the first subsection, or <u>the blessing of good children, with children that are helpful to others.</u>

To change the dimension of your yard, you are going to take your 1/4 inch dowels, cutting them into eight inch sections, and drive them into the yard ten feet apart to make an invisible fence. The remainder of the 10 feet is the auspicious chi of Chai as we calculate it thusly, (10 x 12 = 120, 120 divided by 17 = 7.06 and 7 x 17 = 119, 119 – 120 = 1) representing again <u>money that is secure, having money that will never be taken.</u> Thus creating a new dimension for the front lawn.

The final measurement is the back yard, which is 89 feet from the house to the back lot line. Again, we will take the 89 feet and multiply that by 12, divide by 17 and so on. What we are left with, after the calculation, is 14 inches, which is Hai energy. Hai represents harm to yourself and others, and the 14 inches, also, falls within the fourth subsection, which represents arguments. These arguments, I might add, are with those people that mean something to you.

Now, I bet I would be safe in saying that this is not an energy that you would wish to have functioning around your home.

So, the calculations continue. The total number of feet that we will be working with is 89, and we will need to divide that number of feet so that we end up with an auspicious energy, and not one that will cause arguments or a potential divorce.

We will divide the yard into two sections. The first section will be 65 feet, which will have a reminder of 15 inches, or Pun energy, which is an abundance of money and happiness.

Also, the 15 inches falls into the first subsection of money flowing in to you.

The second section will be the remainder of the original 89 feet, or 24 feet. Twenty-four feet has a remainder of 16 inches. This 16 inches, also, exemplifies the Pun energy, but the subsection for 16 inches falls within the third subsection, which is not only abundance, but the best of everything. That is an energy with which we can live!

Again, you will need to claim this new energy by driving your eight inch dowels into the yard, placing them each ten feet from each other. Congratulations! You have taken a potentially dangerous plot of land and created abundance, prosperity and happiness for you and your family.

This North-facing house is a home that will work well with someone from the East group, since this is an East group home.

When you say this is an East group home, what you are referring to is that the home is facing a direction that is in the East group. With this in mind, the house would suit anybody with a personal kau number of one, three, four or nine.

If you were from the West group and lived in this home, you would need to take a picture of the front entrance and place it in one of your more auspicious sections within the home.

W e talked about how size and dimension played such an important roll in our lives. And how by having an inauspicious yard size could cause discomfort, disease or trauma in our life. We broached the topic of the chair in the child's room, which had been sending dangerous shar chi into the room. And consequently into the child's psyche thus emanating through his or her personality or disposition. We may not in the past been aware of how this chi had explicit ramifications through its vibrational force. Yet now consideration must be taken to those things that you may be holding on to for the sake of possession. Energy or chi exists in everything including the food that we eat. So would it not stand to reason that there is a dimensional chi or size chi emanating from your sofa, television, dining room table or even your bed, nightstand or desk?

I would not suggest that you toss a television that has an inauspicious dimension nor would I be inclined to throw out a Louis the XIII dining room set because the table is an inauspicious dimension. In the same vein I would not suggest that you light candles to release the sha chi of these pieces of furniture every month either. But there may come a time when this may need to be done. As mentioned often there must be balance in order for harmony to exist. You must have sha in order to effectively receive the blessings and rewards from the sheng chi.

How many times in your life have you heard that your thoughts have energy? Or even said "I'm not going to think about so-n-so because I am not going to give that situation energy"? This is the same concept. Things have energy and so do thoughts. Everything vibrates, everything is comprised of energy, thus also has chi. As we remember chi is energy.

On the next few pages you will find three charts pertaining to your specific kau number. The first chart will be the dimension chart, an example seen on page 70. This dimension chart, will contain the measurements from 0 through 17 inches. This chart has been broken down to .53125 of an inch long. This boils down to .53 of an inch for each section, or just a nudge over one-half inch each.

The second chart will be the color chart that will give you the color of candle or color of an object that you will need to use to stimulate the energy that you desire or conversely are sending away or releasing. The third will be the timing chart which will replace the size dimension with a time in which this energy is the most active.

Within each chart there will be a heading section, which will be the sections main influence which will be emanating for 2-inches, or 1 row of chi squares.

On the example here for kau number 1, we have a heading of "Hai". Second there will be the exact size or dimension of that section; our example has the dimension of 13.25 – 13.78. Thirdly you will have the subliminal energy that will be emanating with in the 1/2-inch section, shown here as "Ho Hai". These are the subsections that we talked about earlier. Fourth on the chart will be the section in which this energy will represent.

Heading	Hai
Dimension	13.25 - 13.78
Sub-heading	Ho Hai
Section	Southwest section
Corner	West corner

On the example this energy is resonating in the "Southwest section" of your home. And last will be the corner of the preceding section in which you will need to activate in order to stimulate this particular chi or conversely to lessen its effects. Our example shows that this Ho Hai energy is functioning in the "West corner" of the Southwest section of our home.

This example shows that there is "Hai, Ho Hai" energy functioning in the Southwest section of our home and in the West corner of that section. On page 44 we see that the Ho Hai energy is a source of mishaps and accidents. The first thing that you will want to do is to pinpoint where this energy is exactly. The chart says it is 13.25th to 13.78's of an inch from the West corner in the Southwest section of your home. Now in order for this energy to have been activated something had to activate it. Did you throw a book down in this section? Or did you leave something lying on the floor? Something was done in this space and by looking on the Timing Guide Chart it would have been activated between the time of 3:45pm and 4:30pm see page 80.

Depending on the amount of sha chi in your home this energy may be very weak or if there is not a significant amount of sheng chi in the home it could be very strong.

Sha chi is more active between the times of the full moon and until the next new moon. So if there is a problem in this particular section and corner it may take up to two weeks to manifest itself. An ounce of protection is worth a pound of cure, so keep the sheng chi stimulated in this room so that the sha chi will not be activated.

In the event that this sha has been activated to prevent it from manifesting in an adverse faction light a (see your personal kau color chart) white (if your kau number is one) candle in this section to lesson its effects. We can't keep life and karma from happening but we can by stimulating the sheng chi in our homes and with in ourselves, avoid harsh ramifications. This is a prime example of "when you do the right thing the right thing will happen."

Now this is not the only way that this chi can be activated. Another example might be if you have a piece of furniture that when measured has a remaining inch of 13.25th through 13.78s inch in dimension. There is no reason that if you appreciate this piece of furniture that you have to let it go. Simply place an object on it if possible that is the same color as that candle that you would be lighting to lessen the effects of the Ho Hai manifestation, which is white as per our example.

However be careful that you do not place anything to lessen the effects of this sha chi with something else that will also emanate the same energy. Make your decision as to what you will use to replace this sha chi with something with an energy dimension that you will want to manifest. Using your kau number dimension chart for your specific kau number to determine which energy you would like to manifest.

If your kau number is one and you want to manifest money through this inauspicious piece of furniture you might want to place a white 17 1/2 inch figurine in the space of your inauspicious section (that's assuming we are talking about a table or night stand).

The remaining 1/2 inch of this figurine will emanate the sheng chi which can be very prosperous for you.

The color white will lessen the effects of the Ho Hai and the 1/2 inch will resonate with the sheng chi that will manifest in your life as a good luck aspect for financial affairs.

Keep in mind that sha chi will manifest between the time of the full moon and next new moon. Where as the sheng chi will manifest in your life between the new moon and the next full moon. An important thing to remember is that both sha and sheng chi will always be vibrating or resonating. What we are talking about here is manifestation. The time period when something "happens".

If your desire is to light candles to stimulate the sheng chi in your home or personally you will light your candles between the new moon and the full moon. If your desire is to lessen the effects of sha chi you will light your candles between the full moon and the next new moon.

If you light the right color of candle to release or to lessen the effects of the potentially harmful sha chi, but you light it at the wrong time. Which would be between the new moon and the next full moon. You will be activating not stifling the sha chi. Chi energy is very real and the timing of your candle lighting will be imperative.

If you make a mistake— don't panic that is only the sha chi being activated, move your candle to the most auspicious section of your home as per your kau number - and then redo the exercise at the right time.

W hen timing is everything you will want to be assured that you get it right.

There will be a timing chart for each kau number. These charts are magical in the information that they possess. When you want to be assured that everything will be perfect you will need to be certain that the timing is well suited for the occasion.

On page 80 for instance under the Kau Number 1. Timing Guide there are eight rows. Each row is represented by a two-inch measurement. Within each row there are four squares. Each square represents a forty-five minute time period.

Starting on page 58 you will see that each two-inch measurement is subdivided into four subsections. Thus, each of our forty-five minute squares will also be divided into four subsections representing the same four sub-sections. Each subsection will last for eleven minutes and fifteen seconds each.

So let's use for example that you were born at 10:45AM., and your personal kau number is one. The square that you will be looking at will be the third square on the first row. The information that this square is giving us will be the karma that you came into this life to either experience or to reckon with and then to move on. Not everyone has come into this life with wonderful karma. However through our knowledge of our past we will experience a brighter tomorrow.

The title of this section is Chai, on page 58 we see that this Chai energy is comprised of luck. And the time that you were born was again 10:45AM. We can see also on page 58 that 10:45 AM would fall within the second subsection. The first subsection would be from 10:30:00AM until 10:41:15AM and the second subsection is from 10:41:15AM until 10:52:30AM the third subsection will be from 10:52:30AM until 11:03:45AM and the forth subsection will be from 11:03:45AM until 11:15:00AM. So the definition of your karma in this life and the definition for the time period from 10:41:15AM until 10:52:30AM which is <u>Money that is secure − having money that will never be taken away.</u> This will be your karma in this life.

Chai
10:30am11:15am
Nien Yen
Southeast section
South corner

We also see that there is a second energy that is resonating in this square. This is the Nien Yen luck, which represents a peaceful life and longevity. The directions represented in our square are Southeast and South. If we look on the bagua we see that the Southeast direction represents wealth and prosperity and the South direction represents fame and recognition.

So in effect what this little square told us is that if you were born at 10:45AM., and your personal kau number were one that you would have been born into this life to experience the aspects of wealth and fame.

Let's use another example to show how this chart works. Let's say that you are getting married and you have a personal kau number of three your plans are to get married at 5:50 PM. (I know this is not the traditional time for a wedding but one that will work for the example).

This is our square for our 5:50 PM., wedding. The title energy is Pi. On page 58 the Pi energy represents ill will, this is not a good energy for a wedding. But let's say you are a good person and you are convinced that the wedding will go off without a hitch. The time for the wedding is 5:50 PM. which falls within the third subsection on page 58 which represents Serious problems – being banished or incarcerated. The second energy resonating at this time is Chueh Ming on page 46, we see that there is nothing good that will come from this time energy and have been advised against it. Still persistent that everything is fine you go ahead with the wedding.

| Pi |
| 5:15pm-6:00pm |
| Chueh Ming |
| Southwest section |
| West corner |

When you look at the directions on this chart they will give you added information into what kind of problem that you might be looking at. As mentioned the Southwest direction represents marriage where the West direction represents Luck of children. Just because this chart was for the time that you got married it does not mean that the minute that the ceremony is over that the energy ceases to function. When you do something with conviction such as a wedding the energy of the time in which the ceremony took place will continue to function. This energy will continue to function until the end of the relationship. If the relationship does not end the energy will continue to resonate within the two of you. And it will be carried over if there are children.

I did know someone who did in fact have a personal kau number of three and did get married at 5:50 PM., They had one child that seemed to create one problem after another. Her child was also for a time confined in a state detention school. The energy does exist and it does continue to function.

The warning that she was given was that the problem would come from the Southwest. The Southwest direction represents relationships. The West direction indicated problems with children.

By the way the husband had a kau number of six which gave him an entirely different energy for the wedding. The husband and wife divorced the wife fought for custody – look up Yi Fu Wei – third subsection to find out what would have happened to her son had she not received custody. (page 59) These are just a few examples of how this timing guide section will work for you personally.

One important thing to remember is that with knowledge you may over come any obstacle – but you must heed its warning!

To give you some examples of how this can be accomplished, you would be wise to avoid directions or sections of your home that may cause potentially harmful consequence to your personal chi energy.

If your personal kau number is three and you were born at 5:50 PM instead of getting married at that time, this energy would had been resonating with you all of your life. This is the same concept as a recessive gene, something that you were born with that may or may not manifest in this life. Unless you activate that section of your home by keeping it clean and by lighting your candles, to lessen the adverse effects of the shar chi you will experience the plight of the Pi Chueh Ming.

We are all blessed in this life with the knowledge to defend ourselves and the wisdom to know when.

So let me explain this further. Let's say your kau number is two, and you were born at 6:12 AM. Look on page 83. There you will see the Kau Number 2 Timing Guide. Look down the page to find the time that you were born. The square representing the time that you were born is in the fifth row down the page and the first section, or square.

The energy title is Pi and the secondary energy is Ho Hai. On page 58 you will see the energy Pi listed. It states that this is an energy of sickness. You may had been ill as a child. Or perhaps there had been complications at the time of your birth. Nonetheless there will be issues for you in this life pertaining to your health.

Again if you were born at 6:12 AM. The section listed that we are referring is from 6:00AM – 6:45AM. We will now take this energy down one more time to find more detail about the conditions of your early childhood and birth that may be effecting you presently.

There are four subsections within each forty-five minute energy time frame. The first subsection will be from 6:00:00 AM – 6:11:15 AM.

On page 58 under the PI energy it states for the first subsection: <u>Money loss – Making money but not being able to keep it</u>. Had this been the subsection in which you were born under their may had been financial problems in the family. Or you may have been sensitive or effected by these types of issues during your early childhood. Perhaps as well there might have been financial conditions concerning your birth.

The second subsection is from 6:11:15 AM until 6:22:30 AM. We see that this is the subsection that was resonating at the time of your birth. Again referring to page 58, we see that under the PI energy the second subsection states <u>Problems with authority – issues with police or government.</u> I do have a friend that was born under this influence. Her mother worked for the Post Office, her father is a police officer. Her parents fought all the time, making her a nervous wreck. To this day she still cannot sleep through the night.

Just for the sake of the example lets continue to take this energy through its cycle. The third energy cycle will be from 6:22:30 AM until 6:33:45 AM. The third subsection on page 58 states that this section vibrates on the same level of vibration as <u>Serious problems – being banished or incarcerated.</u> Now people are seldom banished any more, but often they are what we call "disappeared". This is when you have people in your life that one-day you wake up and they are gone. People just disappear from your life. As we all know jail is not the only form of incarceration.

The forth subsection will be vibrating for the same time frame which is 11 minutes and 15 seconds and will be from 6:33:45 AM until 6:45:00 AM. This forth subsection on page 58 states that there are <u>Death or endings – the end of a relationship – without cause.</u> When this energy is resonating it does not always indicate a physical death, but you must keep in mind if conditions are right – it may.

Now that we have looked at how you can break down the vibrational time of 45 minutes into the vibrational cycles of time, we will look at the second energy that will be resonating during your birth-time, creating what we call the birth-time chi.

The second energy under the time line in our magical chi square is Ho Hai. This energy as stated on page 44, indicated mistakes and accidents. Now we all know that your birth was not an accident– but you may because of the time that you were born be accident prone. You may also have problems remembering things, peoples names, phone numbers etc,.

Lastly, as we dissect your birth-time chi we see that the directions indicated are the East section and the East corner. When ever you have a double direction there will be an immense amount of power in your life. As well this will also be a life of prominence for you to experience.

When you have a vibrational title that deals with health issues such as our example, you will want to reference the back of this book for health conditions relating to the direction indicated in your birth-time-chi square. The PI energy does deal with sickness but it will depend on your personal kau number as to which direction it represents. Thus, the illnesses will not be the same for each person.

When stimulating your birth-time chi by lighting your candles, often time's health issues are dealt with on an ethereal level and not necessarily manifesting in the physical body. Just as we were born with certain predisposed conditions there will also be environmental factors that will present similar situations thus inciting us to perhaps repeat a cycle or a life lesson that we may had thought we have concluded. Even though the initiation of these same conditions are environmental, it will be easy for you to see by using this timing method, that circumstances are in fact the same "chi conditions" that were present at the time of your birth.

As a result you will be able to witness first-hand how the chi energy resonating in your life or conversely sha chi, has moved you into position to once again experience or respond to environmental conditions, or life lessons via chi energy cycles. Thus the conditions or chi energy that was functioning at the time of your birth, when recycles back again will recreate conditions or situations that were an issue when you were born.

The condition will be the same but I would expect your response to be different. A classic example of how this happens might be; the three-year-old who gets himself locked in the bathroom. At three his first response is to panic. When you are 13 and you get locked in the bathroom your response is to get mad. When you are 23 and you getting locked in the bathroom your response is to be embarrassed. The environmental conditions are the same – the chi energy is the same yet your response to these stimuli is different.

As we go through the chi energy cycles we learn, grow and hopefully mature in our course of action. These cycles as viewed through the presence of sheng chi is called progressive developmental living. When sha chi is present stimulating the same issues, your response might be called habitual destructive behavior. By lighting your chi cycle candles you can avoid the destructive behavior.

Chi and environmental conditions come together to aid you in your development. Your reaction to these situations will tell you if you are functioning with sheng chi or Sha chi. It will be easy for you to distinguish between the two. Sheng chi is happy – Sha chi is angry and hostile.

I think we all may know by now that life and energy is comprised of a mathematical equation. In order to time the events in your life I will be giving you the equation to the second, so that you might determine which energy vibration will be resonating and when, so you may successfully light your candles for manifestation to occur. Each square will be

Chai	Chai	Chai	Chai
9:00:00am	9:11:15am	9:22:30am	9:33:45am
9:11:15am	9:22:30am	9:33:45am	9:45:00am
Sheng Chi	Sheng Chi	Sheng Chi	Sheng Chi
Southeast section	Southeast section	Southeast section	Southeast section
Southeast corner	Southeast corner	Southeast corner	Southeast corner
Chai	Chai	Chai	Chai
9:45:00am	9:56:15am	10:07:30am	10:18:45am
9:56:15am	10:07:30am	10:18:45am	10:30:00am
Tien Yi	Tien Yi	Tien Yi	Tien Yi
Southeast section	Southeast section	Southeast section	Southeast section
East corner	East corner	East corner	East corner
Chai	Chai	Chai	Chai
10:30:00am	10:41:15am	10:52:30am	11:03:45am
10:41:15am	10:52:30am	11:03:45am	11:15:00am
Nien Yen	Nien Yen	Nien Yen	Nien Yen
Southeast section	Southeast section	Southeast section	Southeast section
South corner	South corner	South corner	South corner
Chai	Chai	Chai	Chai
11:15:00pm	11:26:15pm	11:37:30pm	11:48:45pm
11:26:15pm	11:37:30pm	11:48:45pm	12:00:00pm
Fu Wei	Fu Wei	Fu Wei	Fu Wei
Southeast section	Southeast section	Southeast section	Southeast section
North corner	North corner	North corner	North corner

vibrating for 11 minutes and 15 seconds. Above I have done the first row for the kau number 1, giving you an example of how you can calculate your kau number into seconds to find the exact time for lighting your candles as to the precise chi energy that you want for manifestation. Using the subsection definitions on page 58 for the Chai energy you will see that the first square is resonating between 9:00AM – 9:11:15AM this is the first subsection; <u>Money luck – money coming from unexpected sources</u>. The heading for this square is Chai representing luck. The subsection is Sheng Chi which is also luck and prosperity. This would be a great time to light your candles for money. You will light them in the section and corner indicated, which is Southeast.

0 inches To 2 1/8 inch	Chai 0 - .53 Sheng Chi Southeast section Southeast corner	Chai .53 - 1.06 Tien Yi Southeast section East corner	Chai 1.06 - 1.59 Nien Yen Southeast section South corner	Chai 1.59 - 2.12 Fu Wei Southeast section North corner
6 3/8 inch To 8 1/2 inch	Yi 6.36 - 6.89 Tien Yi East section East corner	Yi 6.89 - 7.42 Sheng Chi East sections Southeast corner	Yi 7.42 - 7.95 Nien Yen East section South corner	Yi 7.95 - 8.48 Fu Wei East section North corner
8 1/2 inch To 10 5/8inch	Kwan 8.48 - 9.01 Nien Yen South section South corner	Kwan 9.01 - 9.54 Sheng Chi South section Southeast corner	Kwan 9.54 - 10.07 Tien Yi South section East corner	Kwan 10.07 - 10.60 Fu Wei South section North corner
14 6/8 inch To 17 inches	Pun 14.84 - 15.37 Fu Wei North section North corner	Pun 15.37 - 15.90 Sheng Chi North section Southeast corner	Pun 15.90 - 16.43 Tien Yi North section East corner	Pun 16.43 - 16.96 Nien Yen North section South corner
2 1/8 inch To 4 2/8 inch	Pi 2.12 - 2.65 Ho Hai West Section West corner	Pi 2.65 - 3.18 Wa Kuei West Section Northeast corner	Pi 3.18 - 3.71 Lui Sha West Section Northwest corner	Pi 3.71 - 4.24 Chueh Ming West Section Southwest corner
4 2/8 inch To 6 3/8 inch	Li 4.24 - 4.77 Wa Kuei Northeast section Northeast corner	Li 4.77 - 5.30 Ho Hai Northeast section West corner	Li 5.30 - 5.83 Lui Sha Northeast section Northwest corner	Li 5.83 - 6.36 Chuch Ming Northeast section Southwest corner
10 5/8 inch To 12 6/8 inch	Chien 10.60 - 11.13 Lui Sha Northwest section Northwest corner	Chien 11.13 - 11.66 Ho Hai Northwest section West corner	Chien 11.66 - 12.19 Wa Kuei Northwest section Northeast corner	Chien 12.19 - 12.72 Chueh Ming Northwest section Southwest corner
12 6/8 inch To 14 6/8 inch	Hai 12.72 - 13.25 Chueh Ming Southwest section Southwest corner	Hai 13.25 - 13.78 Ho Hai Southwest section West corner	Hai 13.78 - 14.31 Wa Kuei Southwest section Northeast corner	Hai 14.31 - 14.84 Lui Sha Southwest section Northwest corner

0 inches To 2 1/8 inch	Chai Orange Sheng Chi Southeast section Southeast corner	Chai Green Tien Yi Southeast section East corner	Chai Red Nien Yen Southeast section South corner	Chai Blue Fu Wei Southeast section North corner
6 3/8 inch To 8 1/2 inch	Yi Blue Tien Yi East section East corner	Yi Orange Sheng Chi East sections Southeast corner	Yi Red Nien Yen East section South corner	Yi Blue Fu Wei East section North corner
8 1/2 inch To 10 5/8 inch	Kwan Red Nien Yen South section South corner	Kwan Orange Sheng Chi South section Southeast corner	Kwan Green Tien Yi South section East corner	Kwan Blue Fu Wei South section North corner
14 6/8 inch To 17 inches	Pun Blue Fu Wei North section North corner	Pun Orange Sheng Chi North section Southeast corner	Pun Green Tien Yi North section East corner	Pun Red Nien Yen North section South corner
2 1/8 inch To 4 2/8 inch	Pi White Ho Hai West Section West corner	Pi Indigo Wa Kuei West Section Northeast corner	Pi Purple Lui Sha West Section Northwest corner	Pi Yellow Chueh Ming West Section Southwest corner
4 2/8 inch To 6 3/8 inch	Li Indigo Wa Kuei Northeast section Northeast corner	Li White Ho Hai Northeast section West corner	Li Purple Lui Sha Northeast section Northwest corner	Li Yellow Chueh Ming Northeast section Southwest corner
10 5/8 inch To 12 6/8 inch	Chien Purple Lui Sha Northwest section Northwest corner	Chien White Ho Hai Northwest section West corner	Chien Indigo Wa Kuei Northwest section Northeast corner	Chien Yellow Chueh Ming Northwest section Southwest corner
12 6/8 inch To 14 6/8 inch	Hai Yellow Chueh Ming Southwest section Southwest corner	Hai White Ho Hai Southwest section West corner	Hai Indigo Wa Kuei Southwest section Northeast corner	Hai Purple Lui Sha Southwest section Northwest corner

0 inches To 2 1/8 inch	Chai 9:00am-9:45am Sheng Chi Southeast section Southeast corner	Chai 9:45am-10:30am Tien Yi Southeast section East corner	Chai 10:30am-11:15am Nien Yen Southeast section South corner	Chai 11:15am12:00pm Fu Wei Southeast section North corner
6 3/8 inch To 8 1/2 inch	Yi 6:00am-6:45am Tien Yi East section East corner	Yi 6:45am-7:30am Sheng Chi East sections Southeast corner	Yi 7:30am-8:15am Nien Yen East section South corner	Yi 8:15am-9:00am Fu Wei East section North corner
8 1/2 inch To 10 5/8inch	Kwan 12:00pm-12:45pm Nien Yen South section South corner	Kwan 12:45pm-1:30pm Sheng Chi South section Southeast corner	Kwan 1:30pm-2:15pm Tien Yi South section East corner	Kwan 2:15-3:00pm Fu Wei South section North corner
14 6/8 inch To 17 inches	Pun 12:00am-12:45am Fu Wei North section North corner	Pun 12:45am-1:30am Sheng Chi North section Southeast corner	Pun 1:30am-2:15am Tien Yi North section East corner	Pun 2:15am-3:00am Nien Yen North section South corner
2 1/8 inch To 4 2/8 inch	Pi 6:00pm-6:45pm Ho Hai West Section West corner	Pi 6:45pm-7:30pm Wa Kuei West Section Northeast corner	Pi 7:30pm-8:15pm Lui Sha West Section Northwest corner	Pi 8:15pm-9:00pm Chueh Ming West Section Southwest corner
4 2/8 inch To 6 3/8 inch	Li 3:00am-3:45am Wa Kuei Northeast section Northeast corner	Li 3:45am-4:30am Ho Hai Northeast section West corner	Li 4:30am-5:15am Lui Sha Northeast section Northwest corner	Li 5:15am-6:00am Chueh Ming Northeast section Southwest corner
10 5/8 inch To 12 6/8 inch	Chien 9:00pm-9:45pm Lui Sha Northwest section Northwest corner	Chien 9:45pm-10:30pm Ho Hai Northwest section West corner	Chien 10:30pm-11:15pm Wa Kuei Northwest section Northeast corner	Chien 11:15pm12:00am Chueh Ming Northwest section Southwest corner
12 6/8 inch To 14 6/8 inch	Hai 3:00pm-3:45pm Chueh Ming Southwest section Southwest corner	Hai 3:45pm-4:30pm Ho Hai Southwest section West corner	Hai 4:30pm-5:15pm Wa Kuei Southwest section Northeast corner	Hai 5:15pm-6:00pm Lui Sha Southwest section Northwest corner

0 inches To 2 1/8 inch	Chai 0 - .53 Sheng Chi Northeast section Northeast corner	Chai 53 - 1.06 Tien Yi Northeast section West corner	Chai 1.06 - 1.59 Nien Yen Northeast section Northwest corner	Chai 1.59 - 2.12 Fu Wei Northeast section Southwest corner
6 3/8 inch To 8 1/2 inch	Yi 6.36 - 6.89 Tien Yi West section West corner	Yi 6.89 - 7.42 Sheng Chi West section Northeast corner	Yi 7.42 - 7.95 Nien Yen West section Northwest corner	Yi 7.95 - 8.48 Fu Wei West section Southwest corner
8 1/2 inch To 10 5/8inch	Kwan 8.48 - 9.01 Nien Yen Northwest section Northwest cornet	Kwan 9.01 - 9.54 Sheng Chi Northwest section Northeast corner	Kwan 9.54 - 10.07 Tien Yi Northwest section West corner	Kwan 10.07 - 10.60 Fu Wei Northwest section Southwest corner
14 6/8inch To 17 inches	Pun 14.84 - 15.37 Fu Wei Southwest section Southwest corner	Pun 15.37 - 15.90 Sheng Chi Southwest section Northeast corner	Pun 15.90 - 16.43 Tien Yi Southwest section West corner	Pun 16.43 - 16.96 Nien Yen Southwest section Northwest corner
2 1/8 inch To 4 2/8 inch	Pi 2.12 - 2.65 Ho Hai East section East corner	Pi 2.65 - 3.18 Wa Kuei East section Southeast corner	Pi 3.18 - 3.71 Lui Sha East section South corner	Pi 3.71 - 4.24 Chueh Ming East section North corner
4 2/8 inch To 6 3/8 inch	Li 4.24 - 4.77 Wa Kuei Southeast section Southeast corner	Li 4.77 - 5.30 Ho Hai Southeast section East corner	Li 5.30 - 5.83 Lui Sha Southeast section South corner	Li 5.83 - 6.36 Chueh Ming Southeast section North corner
10 5/8inch To 12 6/8inch	Chien 10.60 - 11.13 Lui Sha South section South corner	Chien 11.13 - 11.66 Ho Hai South section East corner	Chien 11.66 - 12.19 Wa Kuei South section Southeast corner	Chien 12.19 - 12.72 Chueh Ming South section North corner
12 6/8inch To 14 6/8inch	Hai 12.72 - 13.25 Chueh Ming North section North corner	Hai 13.25 - 13.78 Ho Hai North section East corner	Hai 13.78 - 14.31 Wa Kuei North section Southeast corner	Hai 14.31 - 14.84 Lui Sha North section South corner

0 inches To 2 1/8 inch	Chai Indigo Sheng Chi Northeast section Northeast corner	Chai White Tien Yi Northeast section West corner	Chai Purple Nien Yen Northeast section Northwest corner	Chai Yellow Fu Wei Northeast section Southwest corner
6 3/8 inch To 8 1/2 inch	Yi White Tien Yi West section West corner	Yi Indigo Sheng Chi West section Northeast corner	Yi Purple Nien Yen West section Northwest corner	Yi Yellow Fu Wei West section Southwest corner
8 1/2 inch To 10 5/8inch	Kwan Purple Nien Yen Northwest section Northwest cornet	Kwan Indigo Sheng Chi Northwest section Northeast corner	Kwan White Tien Yi Northwest section West corner	Kwan Yellow Fu Wei Northwest section Southwest corner
14 6/8inch To 17 inches	Pun Yellow Fu Wei Southwest section Southwest corner	Pun Indigo Sheng Chi Southwest section Northeast corner	Pun White Tien Yi Southwest section West corner	Pun Purple Nien Yen Southwest section Northwest corner
2 1/8 inch To 4 2/8 inch	Pi Green Ho Hai East section East corner	Pi Orange Wa Kuei East section Southeast corner	Pi Red Lui Sha East section South corner	Pi Blue Chueh Ming East section North corner
4 2/8 inch To 6 3/8 inch	Li Orange Wa Kuei Southeast section Southeast corner	Li Green Ho Hai Southeast section East corner	Li Red Lui Sha Southeast section South corner	Li Blue Chueh Ming Southeast section North corner
10 5/8inch To 12 6/8inch	Chien Red Lui Sha South section South corner	Chien Green Ho Hai South section East corner	Chien Orange Wa Kuei South section Southeast corner	Chien Blue Chueh Ming South section North corner
12 6/8inch To 14 6/8inch	Hai Blue Chueh Ming North section North corner	Hai Green Ho Hai North section East corner	Hai Orange Wa Kuei North section Southeast corner	Hai Red Lui Sha North section South corner

0 inches To 2 1/8 inch	Chai 3:00am-3:45am Sheng Chi Northeast section Northeast corner	Chai 3:45am-4:30am Tien Yi Northeast section West corner	Chai 4:30am-5:15am Nien Yen Northeast section Northwest corner	Chai 5:15am-6:00am Fu Wei Northeast section Southwest corner
6 3/8 inch To 8 1/2 inch	Yi 6:00pm-6:45pm Tien Yi West section West corner	Yi 6:45pm-7:30pm Sheng Chi West section Northeast corner	Yi 7:30pm-8:15pm Nien Yen West section Northwest corner	Yi 8:15pm-9:00pm Fu Wei West section Southwest corner
8 1/2 inch To 10 5/8inch	Kwan 9:00pm-9:45pm Nien Yen Northwest section Northwest cornet	Kwan 9:45pm-10:30pm Sheng Chi Northwest section Northeast corner	Kwan 10:30pm-11:15pm Tien Yi Northwest section West corner	Kwan 11:15pm-12:00am Fu Wei Northwest section Southwest corner
14 6/8inch To 17 inches	Pun 3:00pm-3:45pm Fu Wei Southwest section Southwest corner	Pun 3:45pm-4:30pm Sheng Chi Southwest section Northeast corner	Pun 4:30pm-5:15pm Tien Yi Southwest section West corner	Pun 5:15pm-6:00pm Nien Yen Southwest section Northwest corner
2 1/8 inch To 4 2/8 inch	Pi 6:00am-6:45am Ho Hai East section East corner	Pi 6:45am-7:30am Wa Kuei East section Southeast corner	Pi 7:30am-8:15am Lui Sha East section South corner	Pi 8:15am-9:00am Chueh Ming East section North corner
4 2/8 inch To 6 3/8 inch	Li 9:00am-9:45am Wa Kuei Southeast section Southeast corner	Li 9:45am-10:30am Ho Hai Southeast section East corner	Li 10:30am-11:15am Lui Sha Southeast section South corner	Li 11:15am-12:00pm Chueh Ming Southeast section North corner
10 5/8inch To 12 6/8inch	Chien 12:00pm-12:45pm Lui Sha South section South corner	Chien 12:45pm-1:30pm Ho Hai South section East corner	Chien 1:30pm-2:15pm Wa Kuei South section Southeast corner	Chien 2:15pm-3:00pm Chueh Ming South section North corner
12 6/8inch To 14 6/8inch	Hai 12:00am-12:45am Chueh Ming North section North corner	Hai 12:45am-1:30am Ho Hai North section East corner	Hai 1:30am-2:15am Wa Kuei North section Southeast corner	Hai 2:15am-3:00am Lui Sha North section South corner

0 inches To 2 1/8 inch	Chai 0 - .53 Sheng Chi South section South corner	Chai .53 - 1.06 Tien Yi South section North corner	Chai 1.06 - 1.59 Nien Yen South section Southeast corner	Chai 1.59 - 2.12 Fu Wei South section East corner
6 3/8 inch To 8 1/2 inch	Yi 6.36 - 6.89 Tien Yi North section North corner	Yi 6.89 - 7.42 Sheng Chi North section South corner	Yi 7.42 - 7.95 Nien Yen North section Southeast corner	Yi 7.95 - 8.48 Fu Wei North section East corner
8 1/2 inch To 10 5/8inch	Kwan 8.48 - 9.01 Nien Yen Southeast section Southeast corner	Kwan 9.01 - 9.54 Sheng Chi Southeast section South corner	Kwan 9.54 - 10.07 Tien Yi Southeast section North corner	Kwan 10.07 - 10.60 Fu Wei Southeast section East corner
14 6/8inch To 17 inches	Pun 14.84 - 15.37 Fu Wei East section East corner	Pun 15.37 - 15.90 Sheng Chi East section South corner	Pun 15.90 - 16.43 Tien Yi East section North corner	Pun 16.43 - 16.96 Nien Yen East section Southeast corner
2 1/8 inch To 4 2/8 inch	Pi 2.12 - 2.65 Ho Hai Southwest section Southwest corner	Pi 2.65 - 3.18 Wa Kuei Southwest section Northwest corner	Pi 3.18 - 3.71 Lui Sha Southwest section Northeast corner	Pi 3.71 - 4.24 Chueh Ming Southwest section West corner
4 2/8 inch To 6 3/8 inch	Li 4.24 - 4.77 Wa Kuei Northwest section Northwest corner	Li 4.77 - 5.30 Ho Hai Northwest section Southwest corner	Li 5.30 - 5.83 Lui Sha Northwest section Northeast corner	Li 5.83 - 6.36 Chueh Ming Northwest section West corner
10 5/8inch To 12 6/8inch	Chien 10.60 - 11.13 Lui Sha Northeast section Northeast corner	Chien 11.13 - 11.66 Ho Hai Northeast section Southwest corner	Chien 11.66 - 12.19 Wa Kuei Northeast section Northwest corner	Chien 12.19 - 12.72 Chueh Ming Northeast section West corner
12 6/8inch To 14 6/8inch	Hai 12.72 - 13.25 Chueh Ming West section West corner	Hai 13.25 - 13.78 Ho Hai West section Southwest corner	Hai 13.78 - 14.31 Wa Kuei West section Northwest corner	Hai 14.31 - 14.84 Lui Sha West section Northeast corner

0 inches To 2 1/8 inch	Chai Red Sheng Chi South section South corner	Chai Blue Tien Yi South section North corner	Chai Orange Nien Yen South section Southeast corner	Chai Green Fu Wei South section East corner
6 3/8 inch To 8 1/2 inch	Yi Blue Tien Yi North section North corner	Yi Red Sheng Chi North section South corner	Yi Orange Nien Yen North section Southeast corner	Yi Green Fu Wei North section East corner
8 1/2 inch To 10 5/8inch	Kwan Orange Nien Yen Southeast section Southeast corner	Kwan Red Sheng Chi Southeast section South corner	Kwan Blue Tien Yi Southeast section North corner	Kwan Green Fu Wei Southeast section East corner
14 6/8inch To 17 inches	Pun Green Fu Wei East section East corner	Pun Red Sheng Chi East section South corner	Pun Blue Tien Yi East section North corner	Pun Orange Nien Yen East section Southeast corner
2 1/8 inch To 4 2/8 inch	Pi Yellow Ho Hai Southwest section Southwest corner	Pi Purple Wa Kuei Southwest section Northwest corner	Pi Indigo Lui Sha Southwest section Northeast corner	Pi White Chueh Ming Southwest section West corner
4 2/8 inch To 6 3/8 inch	Li Purple Wa Kuei Northwest section Northwest corner	Li Yellow Ho Hai Northwest section Southwest corner	Li Indigo Lui Sha Northwest section Northeast corner	Li White Chueh Ming Northwest section West corner
10 5/8inch To 12 6/8inch	Chien Indigo Lui Sha Northeast section Northeast corner	Chien Yellow Ho Hai Northeast section Southwest corner	Chien Purple Wa Kuei Northeast section Northwest corner	Chien White Chueh Ming Northeast section West corner
12 6/8inch To 14 6/8inch	Hai White Chueh Ming West section West corner	Hai Yellow Ho Hai West section Southwest corner	Hai Purple Wa Kuei West section Northwest corner	Hai Indigo Lui Sha West section Northeast corner

0 inches To 2 1/8 inch	Chai 12:00pm-12:45pm Sheng Chi South section South corner	Chai 12:45pm-1:30pm Tien Yi South section North corner	Chai 1:30pm-2:15pm Nien Yen South section Southeast corner	Chai 2:15pm-3:00pm Fu Wei South section East corner
6 3/8 inch To 8 1/2 inch	Yi 12:00am-12:45am Tien Yi North section North corner	Yi 12:45am-1:30am Sheng Chi North section South corner	Yi 1:30am-2:15am Nien Yen North section Southeast corner	Yi 2:15am-3:00am Fu Wei North section East corner
8 1/2 inch To 10 5/8inch	Kwan 9:00am-9:45am Nien Yen Southeast section Southeast corner	Kwan 9:45am-10:30am Sheng Chi Southeast section South corner	Kwan 10:30am-11:15am Tien Yi Southeast section North corner	Kwan 11:15am-12:00pm Fu Wei Southeast section East corner
14 6/8inch To 17 inches	Pun 6:00am-6:45am Fu Wei East section East corner	Pun 6:45am-7:30am Sheng Chi East section South corner	Pun 7:30am-8:15am Tien Yi East section North corner	Pun 8:15am-9:00am Nien Yen East section Southeast corner
2 1/8 inch To 4 2/8 inch	Pi 3:00pm-3:45pm Ho Hai Southwest section Southwest corner	Pi 3:45pm-4:30pm Wa Kuei Southwest section Northwest corner	Pi 4:30pm-5:15pm Lui Sha Southwest section Northeast corner	Pi 5:15pm-6:00pm Chueh Ming Southwest section West corner
4 2/8 inch To 6 3/8 inch	Li 9:00pm-9:45pm Wa Kuei Northwest section Northwest corner	Li 9:45pm-10:30pm Ho Hai Northwest section Southwest corner	Li 10:30pm-11:15pm Lui Sha Northwest section Northeast corner	Li 11:15pm-12:00am Chueh Ming Northwest section West corner
10 5/8inch To 12 6/8inch	Chien 3:00am-3:45am Lui Sha Northeast section Northeast corner	Chien 3:45am-4:30am Ho Hai Northeast section Southwest corner	Chien 4:30am-5:15am Wa Kuei Northeast section Northwest corner	Chien 5:15am-6:00am Chueh Ming Northeast section West corner
12 6/8inch To 14 6/8inch	Hai 6:00pm-6:45pm Chueh Ming West section West corner	Hai 6:45pm-7:30pm Ho Hai West section Southwest corner	Hai 7:30pm-8:15pm Wa Kuei West section Northwest corner	Hai 8:15pm-9:00pm Lui Sha West section Northeast corner

0 inches To 2 1/8 inch	Chai 0 - .53 Sheng Chi North section North corner	Chai .53 - 1.06 Tien Yi North section South corner	Chai 1.06 - 1.59 Nien Yen North section East corner	Chai 1.59 - 2.12 Fu Wei North section Southeast corner
6 3/8 inch To 8 1/2 inch	Yi 6.36 - 6.89 Tien Yi South section South corner	Yi 6.89 - 7.42 Sheng Chi South section North corner	Yi 7.42 - 7.95 Nien Yen South section East corner	Yi 7.95 - 8.48 Fu Wei South section Southeast corner
8 1/2 inch To 10 5/8inch	Kwan 8.48 - 9.01 Nien Yen East section East corner	Kwan 9.01 - 9.54 Sheng Chi East section North corner	Kwan 9.54 - 10.07 Tien Yi East section South corner	Kwan 10.07 - 10.60 Fu Wei East section Southeast corner
14 6/8inch To 17 inches	Pun 14.84 - 15.37 Fu Wei Southeast section Southeast corner	Pun 15.37 - 15.90 Sheng Chi Southeast section North corner	Pun 15.90 - 16.43 Tien Yi Southeast section South corner	Pun 16.43 - 16.96 Nien Yen Southeast section East corner
2 1/8 inch To 4 2/8 inch	Pi 2.12 - 2.65 Ho Hai Northwest section Northwest corner	Pi 2.65 - 3.18 Wa Kuei Northwest section Southwest corner	Pi 3.18 - 3.71 Lui Sha Northwest section West corner	Pi 3.71 - 4.24 Chueh Ming Northwest section Northeast corner
4 2/8 inch To 6 3/8 inch	Li 4.24 - 4.77 Wa Kuei Southwest section Southwest corner	Li 4.77 - 5.30 Ho Hai Southwest section Northwest corner	Li 5.30 - 5.83 Lui Sha Southwest section West corner	Li 5.83 - 6.36 Chueh Ming Southwest section Northeast corner
10 5/8inch To 12 6/8inch	Chien 10.60 - 11.13 Lui Sha West section West corner	Chien 11.13 - 11.66 Ho Hai West section Northwest corner	Chien 11.66 - 12.19 Wa Kuei West section Southwest corner	Chien 12.19 - 12.72 Chueh Ming West section Northeast corner
12 6/8inch To 14 6/8inch	Hai 12.72 - 13.25 Chueh Ming Northeast section Northeast corner	Hai 13.25 - 13.78 Ho Hai Northeast section Northwest corner	Hai 13.78 - 14.31 Wa Kuei Northeast section Southwest corner	Hai 14.31 - 14.84 Lui Sha Northeast section West corner

0 inches To 2 1/8 inch	Chai Blue Sheng Chi North section North corner	Chai Red Tien Yi North section South corner	Chai Green Nien Yen North section East corner	Chai Orange Fu Wei North section Southeast corner
6 3/8 inch To 8 1/2 inch	Yi Red Tien Yi South section South corner	Yi Blue Sheng Chi South section North corner	Yi Green Nien Yen South section East corner	Yi Orange Fu Wei South section Southeast corner
8 1/2 inch To 10 5/8inch	Kwan Green Nien Yen East section East corner	Kwan Blue Sheng Chi East section North corner	Kwan Red Tien Yi East section South corner	Kwan Orange Fu Wei East section Southeast corner
14 6/8inch To 17 inches	Pun Orange Fu Wei Southeast section Southeast corner	Pun Blue Sheng Chi Southeast section North corner	Pun Red Tien Yi Southeast section South corner	Pun Green Nien Yen Southeast section East corner
2 1/8 inch To 4 2/8 inch	Pi Purple Ho Hai Northwest section Northwest corner	Pi Yellow Wa Kuei Northwest section Southwest corner	Pi White Lui Sha Northwest section West corner	Pi Indigo Chueh Ming Northwest section Northeast corner
4 2/8 inch To 6 3/8 inch	Li Yellow Wa Kuei Southwest section Southwest corner	Li Purple Ho Hai Southwest section Northwest corner	Li White Lui Sha Southwest section West corner	Li Indigo Chueh Ming Southwest section Northeast corner
10 5/8inch To 12 6/8inch	Chien White Lui Sha West section West corner	Chien Purple Ho Hai West section Northwest corner	Chien Yellow Wa Kuei West section Southwest corner	Chien Indigo Chueh Ming West section Northeast corner
12 6/8inch To 14 6/8inch	Hai Indigo Chueh Ming Northeast section Northeast corner	Hai Purple Ho Hai Northeast section Northwest corner	Hai Yellow Wa Kuei Northeast section Southwest corner	Hai White Lui Sha Northeast section West corner

0 inches To 2 1/8 inch	Chai 12:00am-12:45am Sheng Chi North section North corner	Chai 12:45am-1:30am Tien Yi North section South corner	Chai 1:30am-2:15am Nien Yen North section East corner	Chai 2:15am-3:00am Fu Wei North section Southeast corner
6 3/8 inch To 8 1/2 inch	Yi 12:00pm-12:45pm Tien Yi South section South corner	Yi 12:45pm-1:30pm Sheng Chi South section North corner	Yi 1:30pm-2:15pm Nien Yen South section East corner	Yi 2:15pm-3:00pm Fu Wei South section Southeast corner
8 1/2 inch To 10 5/8inch	Kwan 6:00am-6:45am Nien Yen East section East corner	Kwan 6:45am-7:30am Sheng Chi East section North corner	Kwan 7:30am-8:15am Tien Yi East section South corner	Kwan 8:15am-9:00am Fu Wei East section Southeast corner
14 6/8 inch To 17 inches	Pun 9:00am-9:45am Fu Wei Southeast section Southeast corner	Pun 9:45am-10:30am Sheng Chi Southeast section North corner	Pun 10:30am-11:15am Tien Yi Southeast section South corner	Pun 11:15am-12:00pm Nien Yen Southeast section East corner
2 1/8 inch To 4 2/8 inch	Pi 9:00pm-9:45pm Ho Hai Northwest section Northwest corner	Pi 9:45pm-10:30pm Wa Kuei Northwest section Southwest corner	Pi 10:30pm-11:15pm Lui Sha Northwest section West corner	Pi 11:15pm-12:00pm Chueh Ming Northwest section Northeast corner
4 2/8 inch To 6 3/8 inch	Li 3:00pm-3:45pm Wa Kuei Southwest section Southwest corner	Li 3:45pm-4:30pm Ho Hai Southwest section Northwest corner	Li 4:30pm-5:15pm Lui Sha Southwest section West corner	Li 5:15pm-6:00pm Chueh Ming Southwest section Northeast corner
10 5/8 inch To 12 6/8 inch	Chien 6:00pm-6:45pm Lui Sha West section West corner	Chien 6:45pm-7:30pm Ho Hai West section Northwest corner	Chien 7:30pm-8:15pm Wa Kuei West section Southwest corner	Chien 8:15pm-9:00pm Chueh Ming West section Northeast corner
12 6/8 inch To 14 6/8 inch	Hai 3:00am-3:45am Chueh Ming Northeast section Northeast corner	Hai 3:45am-4:30am Ho Hai Northeast section Northwest corner	Hai 4:30am-5:15am Wa Kuei Northeast section Southwest corner	Hai 5:15am-6:00am Lui Sha Northeast section West corner

0 inches To 2 1/8 inch	Chai 0 - .53 Sheng Chi West section West corner	Chai .53 - 1.06 Tien Yi West section Northeast corner	Chai 1.06 - 1.59 Nien Yen West section Southwest corner	Chai 1.59 - 2.12 Fu Wei West section Northwest corner
6 3/8 inch To 8 1/2 inch	Yi 6.36 - 6.89 Tien Yi Northeast Section Northeast corner	Yi 6.89 - 7.42 Sheng Chi Northeast Section West corner	Yi 7.42 - 7.95 Nien Yen Northeast Section Southwest corner	Yi 7.95 - 8.48 Fu Wei Northeast Section Northwest corner
8 1/2 inch To 10 5/8inch	Kwan 8.48 - 9.01 Nien Yen Southwest section Southwest corner	Kwan 9.01 - 9.54 Sheng Chi Southwest section West corner	Kwan 9.54 - 10.07 Tien Yi Southwest section Northeast corner	Kwan 10.07 - 10.60 Fu Wei Southwest section Northwest corner
14 6/8inch To 17 inches	Pun 14.84 - 15.37 Fu Wei Northwest section Northwest corner	Pun 15.37 - 15.90 Sheng Chi Northwest section West corner	Pun 15.90 - 16.43 Tien Yi Northwest section Northeast corner	Pun 16.43 - 16.96 Nien Yen Northwest section Southwest corner
2 1/8 inch To 4 2/8 inch	Pi 2.12 - 2.65 Ho Hai Southeast section Southeast corner	Pi 2.65 - 3.18 Wa Kuei Southeast section East corner	Pi 3.18 - 3.71 Lui Sha Southeast section North corner	Pi 3.71 - 4.24 Chueh Ming Southeast section South corner
4 2/8 inch To 6 3/8 inch	Li 4.24 - 4.77 Wa Kuei East section East corner	Li 4.77 - 5.30 Ho Hai East section Southeast corner	Li 5.30 - 5.83 Lui Sha East section North corner	Li 5.83 - 6.36 Chueh Ming East section South corner
10 5/8inch To 12 6/8inch	Chien 10.60 - 11.13 Lui Sha North section North corner	Chien 11.13 - 11.66 Ho Hai North section Southeast corner	Chien 11.66 - 12.19 Wa Kuei North section East corner	Chien 12.19 - 12.72 Chueh Ming North section South corner
12 6/8inch To 14 6/8inch	Hai 12.72 - 13.25 Chueh Ming South section South corner	Hai 13.25 - 13.78 Ho Hai South section Southeast corner	Hai 13.78 - 14.31 Wa Kuei South section East corner	Hai 14.31 - 14.84 Lui Sha South section North corner

0 inches To 2 1/8 inch	Chai White Sheng Chi West section West corner	Chai Indigo Tien Yi West section Northeast corner	Chai Yellow Nien Yen West section Southwest corner	Chai Purple Fu Wei West section Northwest corner
6 3/8 inch To 8 1/2 inch	Yi Indigo Tien Yi Northeast Section Northeast corner	Yi White Sheng Chi Northeast Section West corner	Yi Yellow Nien Yen Northeast Section Southwest corner	Yi Purple Fu Wei Northeast Section Northwest corner
8 1/2 inch To 10 5/8inch	Kwan Yellow Nien Yen Southwest section Southwest corner	Kwan White Sheng Chi Southwest section West corner	Kwan Indigo Tien Yi Southwest section Northeast corner	Kwan Purple Fu Wei Southwest section Northwest corner
14 6/8inch To 17 inches	Pun Purple Fu Wei Northwest section Northwest corner	Pun White Sheng Chi Northwest section West corner	Pun Indigo Tien Yi Northwest section Northeast corner	Pun Yellow Nien Yen Northwest section Southwest corner
2 1/8 inch To 4 2/8 inch	Pi Orange Ho Hai Southeast section Southeast corner	Pi Green Wa Kuei Southeast section East corner	Pi Blue Lui Sha Southeast section North corner	Pi Red Chueh Ming Southeast section South corner
4 2/8 inch To 6 3/8 inch	Li Green Wa Kuei East section East corner	Li Orange Ho Hai East section Southeast corner	Li Blue Lui Sha East section North corner	Li Red Chueh Ming East section South corner
10 5/8inch To 12 6/8inch	Chien Blue Lui Sha North section North corner	Chien Orange Ho Hai North section Southeast corner	Chien Green Wa Kuei North section East corner	Chien Red Chueh Ming North section South corner
12 6/8inch To 14 6/8inch	Hai Red Chueh Ming South section South corner	Hai Orange Ho Hai South section Southeast corner	Hai Green Wa Kuei South section East corner	Hai Red Lui Sha South section North corner

0 inches To 2 1/8 inch	Chai 6:00pm-6:45pm Sheng Chi West section West corner	Chai 6:45pm-7:30pm Tien Yi West section Northeast corner	Chai 7:30pm-8:15pm Nien Yen West section Southwest corner	Chai 8:15pm-9:00pm Fu Wei West section Northwest corner
6 3/8 inch To 8 1/2 inch	Yi 3:00am-3:45am Tien Yi Northeast Section Northeast corner	Yi 3:45am-4:30am Sheng Chi Northeast Section West corner	Yi 4:30am-5:15am Nien Yen Northeast Section Southwest corner	Yi 5:15am-6:00am Fu Wei Northeast Section Northwest corner
8 1/2 inch To 10 5/8inch	Kwan 3:00pm-3:45pm Nien Yen Southwest section Southwest corner	Kwan 3:45pm-4:30pm Sheng Chi Southwest section West corner	Kwan 4:30pm-5:15pm Tien Yi Southwest section Northeast corner	Kwan 5:15pm-6:00pm Fu Wei Southwest section Northwest corner
14 6/8inch To 17 inches	Pun 9:00pm-9:45pm Fu Wei Northwest section Northwest corner	Pun 9:45pm-10:30pm Sheng Chi Northwest section West corner	Pun 10:30pm-11:15pm Tien Yi Northwest section Northeast corner	Pun 11:15pm-12:00am Nien Yen Northwest section Southwest corner
2 1/8 inch To 4 2/8 inch	Pi 9:00am-9:45am Ho Hai Southeast section Southeast corner	Pi 9:45am-10:30am Wa Kuei Southeast section East corner	Pi 10:30am-11:15am Lui Sha Southeast section North corner	Pi 11:15am-12:00am Chueh Ming Southeast section South corner
4 2/8 inch To 6 3/8 inch	Li 6:00am-6:45am Wa Kuei East section East corner	Li 6:45am-7:30am Ho Hai East section Southeast corner	Li 7:30am-8:15am Lui Sha East section North corner	Li 8:15am-9:00am Chueh Ming East section South corner
10 5/8inch To 12 6/8inch	Chien 12:00am-12:45am Lui Sha North section North corner	Chien 12:45am-1:30am Ho Hai North section Southeast corner	Chien 1:30am-2:15am Wa Kuei North section East corner	Chien 2:15am-3:00am Chueh Ming North section South corner
12 6/8inch To 14 6/8inch	Hai 12:00pm-12:45pm Chueh Ming South section South corner	Hai 12:45pm-1:30pm Ho Hai South section Southeast corner	Hai 1:30pm-2:15pm Wa Kuei South section East corner	Hai 2:15pm-3:00pm Lui Sha South section North corner

0 inches To 2 1/8 inch	Chai 0 - .53 Sheng Chi Northwest section Northwest corner	Chai .53 - 1.06 Tien Yi Northwest section Southwest corner	Chai 1.06 - 1.59 Nien Yen Northwest section Northeast corner	Chai 1.59 - 2.12 Fu Wei Northwest section West corner
6 3/8 inch To 8 1/2 inch	Yi 6.36 - 6.89 Tien Yi Southwest section Southwest corner	Yi 6.89 - 7.42 Sheng Chi Southwest section Northwest corner	Yi 7.42 - 7.95 Nien Yen Southwest section Northeast corner	Yi 7.95 - 8.48 Fu Wei Southwest section West corner
8 1/2 inch To 10 5/8inch	Kwan 8.48 - 9.01 Nien Yen Northeast section Northeast corner	Kwan 9.01 - 9.54 Sheng Chi Northeast section Northwest corner	Kwan 9.54 - 10.07 Tien Yi Northeast section Southwest corner	Kwan 10.07 - 10.60 Fu Wei Northeast section West corner
14 6/8inch To 17 inches	Pun 14.84 - 15.37 Fu Wei West section West corner	Pun 15.37 - 15.90 Sheng Chi West section Northwest corner	Pun 15.90 - 16.43 Tien Yi West section Southwest corner	Pun 16.43 - 16.96 Nien Yen West section Northeast corner
2 1/8 inch To 4 2/8 inch	Pi 2.12 - 2.65 Ho Hai North section North corner	Pi 2.65 - 3.18 Wa Kuei North section South corner	Pi 3.18 - 3.71 Lui Sha North section Southeast corner	Pi 3.71 - 4.24 Chueh Ming North section East corner
4 2/8 inch To 6 3/8 inch	Li 4.24 - 4.77 Wa Kuei South section South corner	Li 4.77 - 5.30 Ho Hai South section North corner	Li 5.30 - 5.83 Lui Sha South section Southeast corner	Li 5.83 - 6.36 Chueh Ming South section East corner
10 5/8inch To 12 6/8inch	Chien 10.60 - 11.13 Lui Sha Southeast section Southeast corner	Chien 11.13 - 11.66 Ho Hai Southeast section North corner	Chien 11.66 - 12.19 Wa Kuei Southeast section South corner	Chien 12.19 - 12.72 Chueh Ming Southeast section East corner
12 6/8inch To 14 6/8inch	Hai 12.72 - 13.25 Chueh Ming East section East corner	Hai 13.25 - 13.78 Ho Hai East section North corner	Hai 13.78 - 14.31 Wa Kuei East section South corner	Hai 14.31 - 14.84 Lui Sha East section Southeast corner

0 inches To 2 1/8 inch	Chai Purple Sheng Chi Northwest section Northwest corner	Chai Yellow Tien Yi Northwest section Southwest corner	Chai Indigo Nien Yen Northwest section Northeast corner	Chai White Fu Wei Northwest section West corner
6 3/8 inch To 8 1/2 inch	Yi Yellow Tien Yi Southwest section Southwest corner	Yi Purple Sheng Chi Southwest section Northwest corner	Yi Indigo Nien Yen Southwest section Northeast corner	Yi White Fu Wei Southwest section West corner
8 1/2 inch To 10 5/8	Kwan Indigo Nien Yen Northeast section Northeast corner	Kwan Purple Sheng Chi Northeast section Northwest corner	Kwan Yellow Tien Yi Northeast section Southwest corner	Kwan White Fu Wei Northeast section West corner
14 6/8inch To 17 inches	Pun White Fu Wei West section West corner	Pun Purple Sheng Chi West section Northwest corner	Pun Yellow Tien Yi West section Southwest corner	Pun Indigo Nien Yen West section Northeast corner
2 1/8 inch To 4 2/8 inch	Pi Blue Ho Hai North section North corner	Pi Red Wa Kuei North section South corner	Pi Orange Lui Sha North section Southeast corner	Pi Green Chueh Ming North section East corner
4 2/8 inch To 6 3/8 inch	Li Red Wa Kuei South section South corner	Li Blue Ho Hai South section North corner	Li Orange Lui Sha South section Southeast corner	Li Green Chueh Ming South section East corner
10 5/8inch To 12 6/8inch	Chien Orange Lui Sha Southeast section Southeast corner	Chien Blue Ho Hai Southeast section North corner	Chien Red Wa Kuei Southeast section South corner	Chien Green Chueh Ming Southeast section East corner
12 6/8inch To 14 6/8inch	Hai Green Chueh Ming East section East corner	Hai Blue Ho Hai East section North corner	Hai Red Wa Kuei East section South corner	Hai Orange Lui Sha East section Southeast corner

0 inches To 2 1/8 inch	Chai 9:00pm-9:45pm Sheng Chi Northwest section Northwest corner	Chai 9:45pm-10:30pm Tien Yi Northwest section Southwest corner	Chai 10:30pm-11:15pm Nien Yen Northwest section Northeast corner	Chai 11:15pm-12:00am Fu Wei Northwest section West corner
6 3/8 inch To 8 1/2 inch	Yi 3:00pm-3:45pm Tien Yi Southwest section Southwest corner	Yi 3:45pm-4:30pm Sheng Chi Southwest section Northwest corner	Yi 4:30pm-5:15pm Nien Yen Southwest section Northeast corner	Yi 5:15pm-6:00pm Fu Wei Southwest section West corner
8 1/2 inch To 10 5/8inch	Kwan 3:00am-3:45am Nien Yen Northeast section Northeast corner	Kwan 3:45am-4:30am Sheng Chi Northeast section Northwest corner	Kwan 4:30am-5:15am Tien Yi Northeast section Southwest corner	Kwan 5:15am-6:00am Fu Wei Northeast section West corner
14 6/8inch To 17 inches	Pun 6:00pm-6:45pm Fu Wei West section West corner	Pun 6:45pm-7:30pm Sheng Chi West section Northwest corner	Pun 7:30pm-8:15pm Tien Yi West section Southwest corner	Pun 8.15pm-9:00pm Nien Yen West section Northeast corner
2 1/8 inch To 4 2/8 inch	Pi 12:00am-12:45am Ho Hai North section North corner	Pi 12:45am-1:30am Wa Kuei North section South corner	Pi 1:30am-2:15am Lui Sha North section Southeast corner	Pi 2:15am-3:00am Chueh Ming North section East corner
4 2/8 inch To 6 3/8 inch	Li 12:00pm-12:45pm Wa Kuei South section South corner	Li 12:45pm-1:30pm Ho Hai South section North corner	Li 1:30pm-2:15pm Lui Sha South section Southeast corner	Li 2:15pm-3:00pm Chueh Ming South section East corner
10 5/8inch To 12 6/8inch	Chien 9:00am-9:45am Lui Sha Southeast section Southeast corner	Chien 9:45am-10:30am Ho Hai Southeast section North corner	Chien 10:30am-11:15am Wa Kuei Southeast section South corner	Chien 11:15am-12:00am Chueh Ming Southeast section East corner
12 6/8inch To 14 6/8inch	Hai 6:00pm-6:45pm Chueh Ming East section East corner	Hai 6:45pm-7:30pm Ho Hai East section North corner	Hai 7:30pm-8:15pm Wa Kuei East section South corner	Hai 8:15pm-9:00pm Lui Sha East section Southeast corner

0 inches To 2 1/8 inch	Chai 0 - .53 Sheng Chi Southwest section Southwest corner	Chai .53 - 1.06 Tien Yi Southwest section Northwest corner	Chai 1.06 - 1.59 Nien Yen Southwest section West corner	Chai 1.59 - 2.12 Fu Wei Southwest section Northeast corner
6 3/8 inch To 8 1/2 inch	Yi 6.36 - 6.89 Tien Yi Northwest section Northwest corner	Yi 6.89 - 7.42 Sheng Chi Northwest section Southwest corner	Yi 7.42 - 7.95 Nien Yen Northwest section West corner	Yi 7.95 - 8.48 Fu Wei Northwest section Northeast corner
8 1/2 inch To 10 5/8inch	Kwan 8.48 - 9.01 Nien Yen West section West corner	Kwan 9.01 - 9.54 Sheng Chi West section Southwest corner	Kwan 9.54 - 10.07 Tien Yi West section Northwest corner	Kwan 10.07 - 10.60 Fu Wei West section Northeast corner
14 6/8inch To 17 inches	Pun 14.84 - 15.37 Fu Wei Northeast section Northeast corner	Pun 15.37 - 15.90 Sheng Chi Northeast section Southwest corner	Pun 15.90 - 16.43 Tien Yi Northeast section Northwest corner	Pun 16.43 - 16.96 Nien Yen Northeast section West corner
2 1/8 inch To 4 2/8 inch	Pi 2.12 - 2.65 Ho Hai South section South corner	Pi 2.65 - 3.18 Wa Kuei South section North corner	Pi 3.18 - 3.71 Lui Sha South section East corner	Pi 3.71 - 4.24 Chueh Ming South section Southeast corner
4 2/8 inch To 6 3/8 inch	Li 4.24 - 4.77 Wa Kuei North section North corner	Li 4.77 - 5.30 Ho Hai North section South corner	Li 5.30 - 5.83 Lui Sha North section East corner	Li 5.83 - 6.36 Chueh Ming North section Southeast corner
10 5/8inch To 12 6/8inch	Chien 10.60 - 11.13 Lui Sha East section East corner	Chien 11.13 - 11.66 Ho Hai East section South corner	Chien 11.66 - 12.19 Wa Kuei East section North corner	Chien 12.19 - 12.72 Chueh Ming East section Southeast corner
12 6/8inch To 14 6/8inch	Hai 12.72 - 13.25 Chueh Ming Southeast section Southeast corner	Hai 13.25 - 13.78 Ho Hai Southeast section South corner	Hai 13.78 - 14.31 Wa Kuei Southeast section North corner	Hai 14.31 - 14.84 Lui Sha Southeast section East corner

0 inches To 2 1/8 inch	Chai Yellow Sheng Chi Southwest section Southwest corner	Chai Purple Tien Yi Southwest section Northwest corner	Chai White Nien Yen Southwest section West corner	Chai Indigo Fu Wei Southwest section Northeast corner
6 3/8 inch To 8 1/2 inch	Yi Purple Tien Yi Northwest section Northwest corner	Yi Yellow Sheng Chi Northwest section Southwest corner	Yi White Nien Yen Northwest section West corner	Yi Indigo Fu Wei Northwest section Northeast corner
8 1/2 inch To 10 5/8	Kwan White Nien Yen West section West corner	Kwan Yellow Sheng Chi West section Southwest corner	Kwan Purple Tien Yi West section Northwest corner	Kwan Indigo Fu Wei West section Northeast corner
14 6/8 inch To 17 inches	Pun Indigo Fu Wei Northeast section Northeast corner	Pun Yellow Sheng Chi Northeast section Southwest corner	Pun Purple Tien Yi Northeast section Northwest corner	Pun White Nien Yen Northeast section West corner
2 1/8 inch To 4 2/8 inch	Pi Red Ho Hai South section South corner	Pi Blue Wa Kuei South section North corner	Pi Green Lui Sha South section East corner	Pi Orange Chueh Ming South section Southeast corner
4 2/8 inch To 6 3/8 inch	Li Blue Wa Kuei North section North corner	Li Red Ho Hai North section South corner	Li Green Lui Sha North section East corner	Li Orange Chuch Ming North section Southeast corner
10 5/8inch To 12 6/8inch	Chien Green Lui Sha East section East corner	Chien Red Ho Hai East section South corner	Chien Blue Wa Kuei East section North corner	Chien Orange Chueh Ming East section Southeast corner
12 6/8inch To 14 6/8inch	Hai Orange Chueh Ming Southeast section Southeast corner	Hai Red Ho Hai Southeast section South corner	Hai Blue Wa Kuei Southeast section North corner	Hai Green Lui Sha Southeast section East corner

0 inches To 2 1/8 inch	Chai 3:00pm-3:45pm Sheng Chi Southwest section Southwest corner	Chai 3:45pm-4:30pm Tien Yi Southwest section Northwest corner	Chai 4:30pm-5:15pm Nien Yen Southwest section West corner	Chai 5:15pm-6:00pm Fu Wei Southwest section Northeast corner
6 3/8 inch To 8 1/2 inch	Yi 9:00pm-9:45pm Tien Yi Northwest section Northwest corner	Yi 9:45pm-10:30pm Sheng Chi Northwest section Southwest corner	Yi 10:30pm-11:15pm Nien Yen Northwest section West corner	Yi 11:15pm-12:00am Fu Wei Northwest section Northeast corner
8 1/2 inch To 10 5/8inch	Kwan 6:00pm-6:45pm Nien Yen West section West corner	Kwan 6:45pm-7:30pm Sheng Chi West section Southwest corner	Kwan 7:30pm-8:15pm Tien Yi West section Northwest corner	Kwan 8:15pm-9:00pm Fu Wei West section Northeast corner
14 6/8inch To 17 inches	Pun 3:00am-3:45am Fu Wei Northeast section Northeast corner	Pun 3:45am-4:30am Sheng Chi Northeast section Southwest corner	Pun 4:30am-5:15am Tien Yi Northeast section Northwest corner	Pun 5:15am-6:00am Nien Yen Northeast section West corner
2 1/8 inch To 4 2/8 inch	Pi 12:00pm-12:45pm Ho Hai South section South corner	Pi 12:45pm-1:30pm Wa Kuei South section North corner	Pi 1:30pm-2:15pm Lui Sha South section East corner	Pi 2:15pm-3:00pm Chueh Ming South section Southeast corner
4 2/8 inch To 6 3/8 inch	Li 12:00am-12:45am Wa Kuei North section North corner	Li 12:45am-1:30am Ho Hai North section South corner	Li 1:30am-2:30am Lui Sha North section East corner	Li 2:30am-3:00am Chueh Ming North section Southeast corner
10 5/8inch To 12 6/8inch	Chien 6:00am-6:45am Lui Sha East section East corner	Chien 6:45am-7:30am Ho Hai East section South corner	Chien 7:30am-8:15am Wa Kuei East section North corner	Chien 8:15am-9:00am Chueh Ming East section Southeast corner
12 6/8inch To 14 6/8inch	Hai 9:00am-9:45am Chueh Ming Southeast section Southeast corner	Hai 9:45am-10:30am Ho Hai Southeast section South corner	Hai 10:30am-11:15am Wa Kuei Southeast section North corner	Hai 11:15am-12:00pm Lui Sha Southeast section East corner

0 inches To 2 1/8 inch	Chai 0 - .53 Sheng Chi East section East corner	Chai .53 - 1.06 Tien Yi East section Southeast corner	Chai 1.06 - 1.59 Nien Yen East section North corner	Chai 1.59 - 2.12 Fu Wei East section South corner
6 3/8 inch To 8 1/2 inch	Yi 6.36 - 6.89 Tien Yi Southeast section Southeast corner	Yi 6.89 - 7.42 Sheng Chi Southeast section East corner	Yi 7.42 - 7.95 Nien Yen Southeast section North corner	Yi 7.95 - 8.48 Fu Wei Southeast section South corner
8 1/2 inch To 10 5/8 inch	Kwan 8.48 - 9.01 Nien Yen North section North corner	Kwan 9.01 - 9.54 Sheng Chi North section East corner	Kwan 9.54 - 10.07 Tien Yi North section Southeast corner	Kwan 10.07 - 10.60 Fu Wei North section South corner
14 6/8 inch To 17 inches	Pun 14.84 - 15.37 Fu Wei South section South corner	Pun 15.37 - 15.90 Sheng Chi South section East corner	Pun 15.90 - 16.43 Tien Yi South section Southeast corner	Pun 16.43 - 16.96 Nien Yen South section North corner
2 1/8 inch To 4 2/8 inch	Pi 2.12 - 2.65 Ho Hai Northeast section Northeast corner	Pi 2.65 - 3.18 Wa Kuei Northeast section West corner	Pi 3.18 - 3.71 Lui Sha Northeast section Southwest corner	Pi 3.71 - 4.24 Chueh Ming Northeast section Northwest corner
4 2/8 inch To 6 3/8 inch	Li 4.24 - 4.77 Wa Kuei West section West corner	Li 4.77 - 5.30 Ho Hai West section Northeast corner	Li 5.30 - 5.83 Lui Sha West section Southwest corner	Li 5.83 - 6.36 Chueh Ming West section Northwest corner
10 5/8 inch To 12 6/8 inch	Chien 10.60 - 11.13 Lui Sha Southwest section Southwest corner	Chien 11.13 - 11.66 Ho Hai Southwest section Northeast corner	Chien 11.66 - 12.19 Wa Kuei Southwest section West corner	Chien 12.19 - 12.72 Chueh Ming Southwest section Northwest corner
12 6/8 inch To 14 6/8 inch	Hai 12.72 - 13.25 Chueh Ming Northwest section Northwest corner	Hai 13.25 - 13.78 Ho Hai Northwest section Northeast corner	Hai 13.78 - 14.31 Wa Kuei Northwest section West corner	Hai 14.31 - 14.84 Lui Sha Northwest section Southwest corner

0 inches To 2 1/8 inch	Chai Green Sheng Chi East section East corner	Chai Orange Tien Yi East section Southeast corner	Chai Blue Nien Yen East section North corner	Chai Red Fu Wei East section South corner
6 3/8 inch To 8 1/2 inch	Yi Orange Tien Yi Southeast section Southeast corner	Yi Green Sheng Chi Southeast section East corner	Yi Blue Nien Yen Southeast section North corner	Yi Red Fu Wei Southeast section South corner
8 1/2 inch To 10 5/8inch	Kwan Blue Nien Yen North section North corner	Kwan Green Sheng Chi North section East corner	Kwan Orange Tien Yi North section Southeast corner	Kwan Red Fu Wei North section South corner
14 6/8inch To 17 inches	Pun Red Fu Wei South section South corner	Pun Green Sheng Chi South section East corner	Pun Orange Tien Yi South section Southeast corner	Pun Blue Nien Yen South section North corner
2 1/8 inch To 4 2/8 inch	Pi Indigo Ho Hai Northeast section Northeast corner	Pi White Wa Kuei Northeast section West corner	Pi Yellow Lui Sha Northeast section Southwest corner	Pi Purple Chueh Ming Northeast section Northwest corner
4 2/8 inch To 6 3/8 inch	Li White Wa Kuei West section West corner	Li Indigo Ho Hai West section Northeast corner	Li Yellow Lui Sha West section Southwest corner	Li Purple Chueh Ming West section Northwest corner
10 5/8inch To 12 6/8inch	Chien Yellow Lui Sha Southwest section Southwest corner	Chien Indigo Ho Hai Southwest section Northeast section	Chien White Wa Kuei Southwest section West corner	Chien Purple Chueh Ming Southwest section Northwest corner
12 6/8inch To 14 6/8inch	Hai Purple Chueh Ming Northwest section Northwest corner	Hai Indigo Ho Hai Northwest section Northeast section	Hai White Wa Kuei Northwest section West corner	Hai Yellow Lui Sha Northwest section Southwest corner

0 inches To 2 1/8 inch	Chai 6:00am-6:45am Sheng Chi East section East corner	Chai 6:45am-7:30am Tien Yi East section Southeast corner	Chai 7:30am-8:15am Nien Yen East section North corner	Chai 8:15am-9:00am Fu Wei East section South corner
6 3/8 inch To 8 1/2 inch	Yi 9:00am-9:45am Tien Yi Southeast section Southeast corner	Yi 9:45am-10:30am Sheng Chi Southeast section East corner	Yi 10:30am-11:15am Nien Yen Southeast section North corner	Yi 11:15am-12:00pm Fu Wei Southeast section South corner
8 1/2 inch To 10 5/8inch	Kwan 12:00am-12:45am Nien Yen North section North corner	Kwan 12:45am-1:30am Sheng Chi North section East corner	Kwan 1:30am-2:15am Tien Yi North section Southeast corner	Kwan 2:15am-3:00am Fu Wei North section South corner
14 6/8inch To 17 inches	Pun 12.00pm-12:45pm Fu Wei South section South corner	Pun 12:45pm-1:30pm Sheng Chi South section East corner	Pun 1:30pm-2:15pm Tien Yi South section Southeast corner	Pun 2:15pm-3:00pm Nien Yen South section North corner
2 1/8 inch To 4 2/8 inch	Pi 3:00am-3:45am Ho Hai Northeast section Northeast corner	Pi 3:45am-4:30am Wa Kuei Northeast section West corner	Pi 4:30am-5:15am Lui Sha Northeast section Southwest corner	Pi 5:15am-6:00am Chueh Ming Northeast section Northwest corner
4 2/8 inch To 6 3/8 inch	Li 6:00pm-6:45pm Wa Kuei West section West corner	Li 6:45pm-7:30pm Ho Hai West section Northeast section	Li 7:30pm-8:15pm Lui Sha West section Southwest corner	Li 8:15pm-9:00pm Chueh Ming West section Northwest corner
10 5/8inch To 12 6/8inch	Chien 3:00pm-3:45pm Lui Sha Southwest section Southwest corner	Chien 3:45pm-4:30pm Ho Hai Southwest section Northeast section	Chien 4:30pm-5:15pm Wa Kuei Southwest section West corner	Chien 5:15pm-6:00pm Chueh Ming Southwest section Northwest corner
12 6/8inch To 14 6/8inch	Hai 9:00pm-9:45pm Chueh Ming Northwest section Northwest corner	Hai 9:45pm-10:15pm Ho Hai Northwest section Northeast section	Hai 10:15pm-11:15pm Wa Kuei Northwest section West corner	Hai 11:15pm-6:00pm Lui Sha Northwest section Southwest corner

I n determining also which chi energy is vibrating in the place where you live as well as within you, you must first go back to where this life began. Your birthplace, will be your starting point.

The distance between where you were born and where you live now will give you the underlining chi energy that will be functioning in your life.

We have determined that each of our squares is .53 of an inch and that each resonates for 45 minutes. As well, each square will be subdivided into 4 subsections each resonating for exactly 11 minutes and 15 seconds. We may also be interested to know that a second is the basic unit of time. It is the length of time taken for 9192631770 periods of vibration of the ceasium-133 atom to occur.

The distance between the hospital where I was born and where I live now is 994 miles. There are 5280 feet in one mile. First we will convert the miles into feet 994 x 5280 = 5248320 feet. Now we will convert the feet into inches. There are 12 inches in one foot. So this calculation will be 12 x 5248320 = 62979840 inches.

| 6 3/8 inch |
| To |
| 8 1/2 inch |

Next we will use our Chinese ruler to see what the remaining inches will be for our chi formula. When we divide 17 inches by 62979840 inches we get 3704696 with a remainder of 8 inches. So our total is 8 inches. My kau number is three, so the 8 inches falls within the measurement section of 6 3/8 inch to 8 1/2 inches. The 8 inch remainder then falls within the Yi title in the North section which on page 59, resonates with luck and helpful people.

The subsection which represents 8 inches is the forth subsection of Yi which is Fu Wei luck, this subsection represents Blessings of many good fortunes – unlimited success. Thus, this Yi square gives me at my residence an underlining chi energy of Yi Fu Wei luck. For my kau number 3 using the color chart on page 85, I will be lighting a green can-

| Yi |
| 7.95 - 8.48 |
| Fu Wei |
| North section |
| East corner |

dle. The timing square that I will use is Yi Fu Wei on page 86. The time that this square is resonating is from 2:45 AM until 3:00 AM. When using the timing guide for my personal kau number, I will be lighting my candle between 2:48:45 AM and 3:00:00 AM, because the 8 inches represents the forth subsection on the measurement chart on page 59. In order to stimulate this Yi Fu Wei chi luck I will be lighting my green candle between the time of the new moon and before the next full moon.

This same principal may be applied to trips that you take and even your jaunts to the grocery store.

When using the example of going to the grocery store or any daily jaunt you must be armed with two valuable pieces of information. The first will be your kau number and the second will be the time that you commence the trip. The chi energy that is resonating at the time that you leave will be in-a-sense just like an astrological birth-chart. As the birth-chart will dictate your life characteristics the chi energy resonating at the time that you leave in-conjunction with your personal kau number will be the chi energy that will effect your entire trip.

The same principal applies when you go to work – you leave at the same time every day and drive the same distance. The chi energy at the time that you leave your home will incite certain things to happen during the day, by the same token, by calculating the distance that you drive will incite chi energy to resonate with you during the day until you return home again.

Now lets look at this chi cycle in a little different light. How many times have you heard – "break your habits, drive a different way to work or go to a different grocery store"? When you break out of your routine you are adding or subtracting chi energy to your trip.

Let's say you leave every morning at 6:45 AM to go to work and you are going to drive 6 miles. And by the way your kau number is 4. You will begin your trip with pretty good chi energy, as the chi resonating at 6:45 AM is Kwan and the subsection is Nien Yen (page 89).

Lets calculate your miles. There are 5280 feet in one mile, you are driving six miles, that will equal 31680 feet. This total divided by 17 will give you a remaining total of 9 inches. On your Kau Number Dimension chart on page 87 for your kau number 4, nine inches resonates with the chi vibration of the same vibrational energy that was vibrating at the time that you left. This chi is the Kwan Tien Yen luck. This would be a great day at work or a fabulous trip.

But let's say you changed the distance to work by going two additional miles by taking a different route. In doing so you will be changing the chi energy cycle of your trip and if you were going to work – it would change the chi energy of your entire day.

The original 6 miles gave you the chi energy of Kwan, Nien Yen, by adding two miles you are in essence adding another 3 inches which will change your day from Kwan Nein Yen which represented power, to Chien and Wa Kuei which are both harmful chi energies. In changing your route you changed the chi cycle for the entire day. Combining both the time chi and the distance chi will give you your overall chi energy during your day. This chi will be activated– up until you return home again.

A s there is a progression in life, there is also a progression of birth-time chi luck.

This progression will be as follows: 3 hours on the timing chart = 1 year of life. 4 subsections will = one year of life. Each subsection will be 91 days of lifetime. And each minute of time in the square will equal 48 hours and 15 seconds of life. Each 91-day cycle will be divided into 4 – 22 day and 18 hour subsections.

So! If you were born on June 10th 1948, and you are a female your personal kau number will be 8. If you were born at 10:20:00 AM your birth-time chi would be, as seen On page 98, Hai, Ho Hai.

Hai
9:45am-10:30am
Ho Hai
Southeast section
South corner

Let's say today is June 5th 1999. That gives you a total number of days in this life of 18559. Divide that number by 91 days as there are 91 days in each square cycle. So, 18559 divided by 91 = 203.9. This tells us that you have completed 203 square cycles thus far, and are in the 9th day of the 204th cycle. There are 32 cycles in an 8-year time frame.

Pun
5:15am-6:00am
Nien Yen
Northeast section
West corner

There are four cycles in one year. So 4 divided by 203 = 50.75. Thus indicating that you are 50 years old with 5 days until your 51st birthday. Okay, you have been in this cycle for the past 86 days, and had been experiencing the chi of Pi – Nien Yen. On page 58 we see that the Pi energy represents illness, and if you look on page 42 under the sub-energy of Nien Yen you see that this energy is representative of a peaceful family, and calm and soothing energy.

Pi
12:00pm12:45pm
Ho Hai
South section
South corner

By the same token if you do not regard the advice offered by the heading chi, by stimulating the chi in your home there will be an illness. More often than not illnesses that are represented in this subsection are stress related.

This cycle will continue for the next 5 days until your birthday. At which time the cycle that you will be going into will be Pi – Ho Hai that will again last for 91 days.

On page 58 we see that there is ill- will and sicknesses connected to the Pi energy. This cycle square also falls along the third subsection. Thus, you will be dealing with serious problems that you have in your life, as well, there will be problems with someone leaving your life. This could be as minor as the ending of a relationship, or an issue with friends or neighbors. Banishment or incarcerated in the 1990's takes on a whole new meaning than it did years ago when this energy was first termed. There is a possibility during this cycle that a neighbor that you thought to be a friend could move away – and for you leaving no forwarding address.

This could also be an indication of a hospital stay due to a physical health related issue, (emotional illness will be resonating with the energy of CHIEN, and the first subsection). The reason that this could be considered as a form of incarceration is that when admitted into the hospital we are not permitted to leave without punishment of having to pay the entire bill without the assistance of medical insurance.

This could also be a feeling of being trapped within your own home or a situation work. This also is a cycle of feeling that you are out of control or at the very least not in control and at the mercy of others, in other words they are not taking you seriously enough.

So what we have seen here is that our lives are progressive. We will always emanate the chi that we were born with – as well, we will be influenced by our progressive chi.

When you begin to progress your birth chi the first thing that you will need will be your personal kau number.

Once this has been determined, find your birth chi on the timing chart under that kau number.

Progress your birth chi by using the calculations mentioned. Each square represents 91 days. There are 364 days in one year. So if you were 19 years old you would have lived 6916 days. You will now divide 6916 days by 91, to see how many chi energy squares you have experienced, to know where you are in your life cycle. Therefore, 91 divided by 6916 days equals 76 cycle squares. Okay, now you will need to count from your original chi energy birth square, 76 squares.

There are 32 chi energy squares, so 32 divided by 76 equals 2 with a remainder of 12. So, you would have concluded two complete cycles of 32 chi-squares each, and are 12 chi energy squares into the third cycle.

Count 12 squares from your original birth chi-square. This will give you your progressed chi energy for right now. You will be counting from left to right and not up and down on your kau number timing chart.

If your kau number is eight and your original birth chi energy square were Li-Lui Sha, then 12 chi squares from that point would be Chai-Nein Yen. To determine where within this cycle you are, calculate the days from your last birthday and divide that number of days by 91 days.

| Chai |
| 4:30pm-5:15pm |
| Nien Yen |
| Southwest section |
| West corner |

There are 91 days in each square. The remaining days from that total will tell you where within this chi cycle you are.

When we count 12 chi squares from the birth-time chi square we get Pun-Tien Yi. On page 61, we see that the Pun energy is resonating on the

| Pun |
| 4:30am-5:15am |
| Tien Yi |
| Northeast section |
| Northwest corner |

same vibrational level as an abundance of money and happiness. This may correlate to your age. As often at this age there is an abundance of happiness, graduating from High School, contemplating or beginning college or starting in a new career.

The second energy represented in this progressed chi energy square is Tien Yi. This is the energy as stated on page 41, mentions that it represents an upper-class income. This would not be a bad place to start out from.

Next we see that there are two directions represented on this square. The first is Northeast and the second is Northwest. If your desire is to move away from home, I would first look to the Northeast section of the city or town that you are interested in, second focus on the Northwest direction of that area.

Regardless as to whether you move, you will need to stimulate the chi energy in both of these directions. If you have only one room that you occupy in your home you will need to stimulate the chi in the Northeast section and in the Northwest corner. This will be the space in which this chi is resonating and effecting you at this time.

To be even more precise with your progressed cycle, there are four subsections within each 91 day chi energy square. Each subsection will last for 22 days and 18 hours. If you are 26 days into this progressed cycle you will be experiencing the second subsection of the Pun energy.

Again we will reference page 61. The second subsection under the Pun energy states: <u>Your ability to test well – success in testing and in scholastic interest.</u> There is a strong indication that you will be learning something new and with the aid of this Pun energy you will do very well.

Your next subsection will begin in 18 days and 36 hours. At which time your next cycle of progressed energy will be the third subsection on page 61. Which represents: <u>An abundance of monetary possessions – having the best of everything.</u> As you learn through your progressions you will begin to understand how this progressive chi luck can help you.

The five elements represent the productive and destructive cycles of all living things. There will never be an ending that does not signal a rebirth of something new. Understanding this cycle of life will give you a greater understanding of how life functions, and how the cosmic breath of the dragon, or Chi, will illicit positive changes in your life. It will, also, aid in your understanding of how shar chi will melt optimism. As this melting of optimism happens, you will develop poor health and a destructive, pessimistic outlook on life.

Below is the Element / Season chart. You will see that each season has a corresponding color and direction. Additionally, each direction will produce an element and destroy an element. This balance is called the cycle of life and the harmony that exist within the universe.

The element for summer is fire. The colors that correspond with summer are red and purple. The direction is South. Fire produces earth and destroys metal.

We will be using this chart as we begin to light candles to enhance and stimulate the positive Chi in our lives.

Element / Season	Color	Direction	Produces	Destroys
Fire Summer	Red Purple	South	Earth	Metal
Water Winter	Black Blue	North	Wood	Fire
Wood Spring	Green Light Blue	East (big wood) Southeast (small wood)	Fire	Earth
Metal Autumn	White Silver Gold	West (small metal) Northwest (big metal	Water	Wood
Earth Third month of each season	Brown Yellow	Southwest (big earth) Northeast (small earth)	Metal	Water

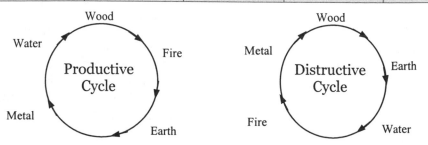

Your Strengths as Determined by Birth Element

U sing the timing chart on page 111, light the color of candle, representing the element resonating at the time that you were born, to honor your birth-time element. This honor is important, because if it were not for the time of your birth there would be no life for you to experience, and if it were not for your birth element you would not have the basis for your strengths in this life.

If your personal kau number falls in the West group, you will be using the first direction and the first color listed on the chart. If your personal kau number falls in the East group, you will be stimulating, or activating, the direction and lighting the color of candle listed second on the same timing chart.

If you were born between 9:00AM and 12:00PM, the elemental influence of your birth-time is small wood. If you have a personal kau number of one, three, four or nine, you belong to the East group. If your personal kau number is two, six, seven or eight then you were born in the West group.

East group people will be lighting different colored candles then will those born in the West group as seen on page 111.

We have investigated which chi energies were resonating at the time of out birth, as well which measurement energies were vibrating during our birth soliciting karma (cause and effect) in this life. We will now look at the elements that were resonating at the time we were born that have assisted in forming our innate personality.

The element resonating at the time of your birth, which was between 9:00AM and 12:00PM, was the element of small wood. The direction in which this element was resonating was Southeast. When referring back to the Lo Shu, the Southeast direction resonates with the life aspect dealing with wealth and prosperity. Thus, one of your strengths in this life will be your ability to make, invest and to amass a fortune.

You will, need to light the color of candle indicated on page 111 as per your kau group to stimulate your own personal birth-time chi or inherited luck. Just to make this example simple the color of candle that you will be lighting will be light blue if you are in the East group and green if you are in the West group. Your birth element is small wood, the direction resonating is Southeast and the aspect, or life lesson for you in this life is to experience the conditions of wealth and prosperity.

By lighting this candle giving distinction to your birth-element you will be activating your personal chi, as you stimulate the chi flow within you and within your home.

It is important when determining the strength of your personality, that you recognize which of the five elements were resonating at the time of your birth, and how this information plays such an important roll in your life. This knowledge can assist you in your understandings of the mechanics of your intrinsic personality. Also guiding you in the direction of your inherent destiny in this life.

When combining this birth-time element chart (page 111) with the five-element chart (page 107), you will see which of the other elements will stimulate your personal chi. You will, also, see which elements, by virtue of the production and destruction chart, will allow you to grow, as well, which elements will depress you, threatening the success that you are trying to accomplish in this life.

When lighting candles to stimulate your personal birth-element chi you will also be paying homage to your parents, grandparents and all other ancestors that have walked this earth before you.

If you look at your life from a scientific standpoint you will be looking at the genetic traits which make up your total DNA. This is the molecular contribution between your parents, which when combined produce you. You will also understand the genetic traits of their parents and your parents, parents. As all of this scientifically will make up who and what you are.

This is the same information you will find in the element and birth-time chart.

Let's say that your grandfather was a tenacious individual who would succeed through all odds. One might think that you might have this same tenacity because you had an observation of this personality or that it was learned by your father and then passes onto you through learned behavior.

If in fact you are scientific minded you would have to say "yes" that this is how it works and that this is how your personality was developed.

But lets look at one more possibility, and then you make your determination as to whether your innate personally is based on learned behavior, osmoses, or feng shui candle lighting.

Now, let's say your birthday is September 6th, 1945 that you are a male, and were born at 6:12 PM. First you will take the year that you were born 1945, add the 4+5=9. Men subtract that number from 10, thus 10-9 = 1.

So your personal kau number is one!

The element resonating during your kau number year is wood (page 26). You were born at 12:25 PM this is a fire element (page 111). We can see on the bottom of page 107 in the productive cycle that wood produce fire, so these two elements produce a productive complimentary aspect in your life.

Your personal kau number is one which resonates in the North section on the Lo Shu chart as seen on page 32. And when we confer with the timing chart on page 80 we see that the time of your birth which again is 12:25 PM resonates with the Kwan energy which is the energy of power as seen on page 60. Thus, stimulating your innate personality with the power for success, the determination to prevail and the will to achieve your objectives.

So what this is all telling us is that with your birth element you will have the propensity for consistency, giving you the perseverance to stay with a project until it has been completed. Your birth-time element is fire that will give you a passion to complete what you start. As you have also been blessed with the birth-time chi of Kwan which insures you of a healthy harvest and rewards for a job well done.

You will be lighting a purple candle on any day between the time of the new moon and before the next full moon at 12:25 PM. Thus, representing the time of your birth. Giving honor to your birth and your life, therefore stimulating your personal chi. You will light this candle in the South section of your home as indicated on page 80 on the timing guide for birth-time kau number chart.

As we have seen through our example, as a result of your birthday, the time of you birth, your gender, (which make up your kau number) the direction that your kau number resonates which is North indicating career, and the elements resonating at the time of your birth you have inherited the same "tenacious success through all odds" personality as your grandfather.

So the question is, how did you acquire these tendencies? Was your personality and tendencies formed through genetics by succession? Or was it through the birth elements and personal kau number, interpreted through the Lo Shu and Kwan chi that has determined them?

As you know some of these questions will always remain in the same category as "which came first the chicken or the egg"! Regardless of the conclusion we are now armed with some valuable as well powerful information for self-discovery.

The colors of candles and directions used in this section will only be used to honor your birth-time and not for other exercises in this book.

North 12:00am – 3:00am	**Water** 	West group – light black East group – light blue
South 12:00pm – 3:00pm	**Fire** 	West group – light red East group – light purple
East 6:00am – 9:00am	**Big Wood** 	West group – light green East group – light blue
West 6:00pm – 9:00pm	**Small Metal** 	West group – light white East group – light gray
Northeast 3:00am – 6:00am	**Small Earth** 	West group – light brown East group – light yellow
Northwest 9:00pm –12:00am	**Big Metal** 	West group – light white East group – light silver
Southeast 9:00am – 12:00pm	**Small Wood** 	West group – light green East group – light lt. blue
Southwest 3:00pm – 6:00pm	**Big Earth** 	West group – light brown East group – light yellow

Life Aspects as Seen Through the Bagua

Feng Shui has divided life into eight sections. These sections depict aspects of our everyday life. The areas of life in which they encompass are: wealth and prosperity, recognition and fame, marriage and happiness, family, health, the luck of your children, education, your career and a section that references the helpful people that you have in your life. Each of these life categories has a corresponding direction, in which both resonate equally. What this means is that both the "direction" and the "life situation or aspect" vibrate on the same vibrational level, thus making them the same in vibrational energy yet distinct in definition.

The map below is referred to as a Bagua. The bagua is an eight-sided map of life. This map, or bagua, will serve as an overview for everything that we do and experience. The North section is KAN, which represents the aspect in your life resonating with our career development and evolvement. Follow the map around to acquaint yourself with the directions and life experiences, as you correlate these directions to situations in your life.

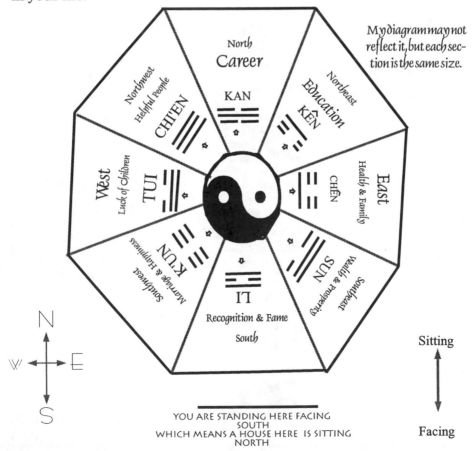

My diagram may not reflect it, but each section is the same size.

YOU ARE STANDING HERE FACING SOUTH WHICH MEANS A HOUSE HERE IS SITTING NORTH

Sitting

Facing

The Northeast direction as well as the Northeast section of your home will resonate with the life experiences relating to your education and your ability to retain information. The energy also resonating in this direction is called KEN. This energy when stimulated will give you the fortitude, concentration or motivation that will be needed in order for you to be enlightened or to be self-instructed.

The next energy direction is East. This direction relates to your health and your ability to be healthy, in addition to your ability to abolish ailments from your body. The vibrational energy that is needed to accomplish this is called CHEN.

The next direction is Southeast. The Southeast direction and as mentioned the Southeast section in your home would resonate with the vibrational energy called SUN. This SUN energy resonates on the same level of vibration as your aspirations for wealth and prosperity. Your ability to become prosperous or to maintain your financial status will be vibrating on this same level. If your desire is to increase your ability to be prosperous you will need to stimulate the chi in this section of your home.

Next we have the direction of South. This southerly direction is governed by the vibrational energy called LI. When your desire is to become famous or to gain recognition for you or an accomplishment you will need to activate the LI energy in the South section of your home.

Our next direction on the bagua is Southwest. The Southwest direction will be resonating with the vibrational energy called KUN. This KUN energy will insure you when stimulated or activated that conditions pertaining to your marriage, happiness and or relationships will be successful.

The next direction on the bagua is West. The energy resonationg in this direction is called TUI. The TUI energy will aid you in your ability to insure the luck and safety in your childrens lives.

The last direction on the bagua is Northwest. The Northwest direction will govern the energy of helpful people in your life. When you are in need of asistance from others you must activate the chi flow in the Northwest direction or section in your home. The energy resonating in this section is called CHIEN.

To activate the energy in these directions stimulating the bagua in your life you must insure that there is minamial clutter in each of these sections of your home, as well as to light the right color of candle at the right time to activate this chi energy.

E ach person will have eight power chi days a year representing the life aspects as mentioned on the bagua. These power days will be determined by the day that you were born. If you were born on the 1st day of any month the first chart will pertain to you, and so on.

This will be the one-day of each year when the vibrational energy of the sheng chi and your psyche will come together evaluating your life position as compared to your ambitions. It will be at this time that changes or choices in your life will be exhilarated. The balance or lack of balance that you have in your life will determine these subconscious choices.

There will be eight power days. There will be eight directions and there will be eight life aspects. Also listed on these charts will be the color of candle and a designated time to light that candle based on whether you are a West group person or an East group person. When lighting your candle you will be strengthening the energy resonating within your psyche for the purpose of manifestation. Through this exercise positive changes will manifest for you during the coming year pertaining to each particular life aspect that you have enhanced. You will light these candles in your most auspicious direction as seen on the "Best Compass directions for your Kau number" chart on page 236.

Career	January 1.	West group – Black East group – Blue	12:00AM-12:45AM
Education	March 1.	West group – Brown East group – Yellow	3:00AM-3:45AM
Health	April 1.	West group – Green East group – Blue	6:00AM-6:45AM
Wealth and Prosperity	June 1.	West group – Green East group – Lt. Blue	9:00AM-9:45AM
Recognition and Fame	July 1.	West group – Red East group – Purple	12:00PM-12:45PM
Marriage and Happiness	September 1.	West group – Brown East group – Yellow	3:00PM-3:45PM
Luck of the Children	October 1.	West group – White East group – Gray	6:00PM-6:45PM
Helpful People	December 1.	West group – White East group – Sliver	9:00PM-9:45PM

The **second** day of any month.

Career	January 2.	West group – Black East group – Blue	12:00AM-12:45AM
Education	March 2.	West group – Brown East group – Yellow	3:00AM-3:45AM
Health	April 2.	West group – Green East group – Blue	6:00AM-6:45AM
Wealth and Prosperity	June 2.	West group – Green East group – Lt. Blue	9:00AM-9:45AM
Recognition and Fame	July 2.	West group – Red East group – Purple	12:00PM-12:45PM
Marriage and Happiness	September 2.	West group – Brown East group – Yellow	3:00PM-3:45PM
Luck of the Children	October 2.	West group – White East group – Gray	6:00PM-6:45PM
Helpful People	December 2.	West group – White East group – Sliver	9:00PM-9:45PM

The **third** day of any month.

Career	January 3.	West group – Black East group – Blue	12:00AM-12:45AM
Education	March 3.	West group – Brown East group – Yellow	3:00AM-3:45AM
Health	April 3.	West group – Green East group – Blue	6:00AM-6:45AM
Wealth and Prosperity	June 3.	West group – Green East group – Lt. Blue	9:00AM-9:45AM
Recognition and Fame	July 3.	West group – Red East group – Purple	12:00PM-12:45PM
Marriage and Happiness	September 3.	West group – Brown East group – Yellow	3:00PM-3:45PM
Luck of the Children	October 3.	West group – White East group – Gray	6:00PM-6:45PM
Helpful People	December 3.	West group – White East group – Sliver	9:00PM-9:45PM

The **fourth** day of any month.

Career	January 4.	West group – Black East group – Blue	12:00AM-12:45AM
Education	March 4.	West group – Brown East group – Yellow	3:00AM-3:45AM
Health	April 4.	West group – Green East group – Blue	6:00AM-6:45AM
Wealth and Prosperity	June 4.	West group – Green East group – Lt. Blue	9:00AM-9:45AM
Recognition and Fame	July 4.	West group – Red East group – Purple	12:00PM-12:45PM
Marriage and Happiness	September 4.	West group – Brown East group – Yellow	3:00PM-3:45PM
Luck of the Children	October 4.	West group – White East group – Gray	6:00PM-6:45PM
Helpful People	December 4.	West group – White East group – Sliver	9:00PM-9:45PM

The **fifth** day of any month.

Career	February 5.	West group – Black East group – Blue	12:00AM-12:45AM
Education	March 5.	West group – Brown East group – Yellow	3:00AM-3:45AM
Health	April 5.	West group – Green East group – Blue	6:00AM-6:45AM
Wealth and Prosperity	July 5.	West group – Green East group – Lt. Blue	9:00AM-9:45AM
Recognition and Fame	Aug 5.	West group – Red East group – Purple	12:00PM-12:45PM
Marriage and Happiness	October 5.	West group – Brown East group – Yellow	3:00PM-3:45PM
Luck of the Children	November 5.	West group – White East group – Gray	6:00PM-6:45PM
Helpful People	December 5.	West group – White East group – Sliver	9:00PM-9:45PM

The **sixth** day of any month.

Career	January 6.	West group – Black East group – Blue	12:00AM-12:45AM
Education	March 6.	West group – Brown East group – Yellow	3:00AM-3:45AM
Health	April 6.	West group – Green East group – Blue	6:00AM-6:45AM
Wealth and Prosperity	June 6.	West group – Green East group – Lt. Blue	9:00AM-9:45AM
Recognition and Fame	July 6.	West group – Red East group – Purple	12:00PM-12:45PM
Marriage and Happiness	September 6.	West group – Brown East group – Yellow	3:00PM-3:45PM
Luck of the Children	October 6.	West group – White East group – Gray	6:00PM-6:45PM
Helpful People	December 6.	West group – White East group – Sliver	9:00PM-9:45PM

The **seventh** day of any month.

Career	January 7.	West group – Black East group – Blue	12:00AM-12:45AM
Education	March 7.	West group – Brown East group – Yellow	3:00AM-3:45AM
Health	April 7.	West group – Green East group – Blue	6:00AM-6:45AM
Wealth and Prosperity	June 7.	West group – Green East group – Lt. Blue	9:00AM-9:45AM
Recognition and Fame	July 7.	West group – Red East group – Purple	12:00PM-12:45PM
Marriage and Happiness	September 7.	West group – Brown East group – Yellow	3:00PM-3:45PM
Luck of the Children	October 7.	West group – White East group – Gray	6:00PM-6:45PM
Helpful People	December 7.	West group – White East group – Sliver	9:00PM-9:45PM

The **eighth** day of any month.

Career	January 8.	West group – Black East group – Blue	12:00AM-12:45AM
Education	March 8.	West group – Brown East group – Yellow	3:00AM-3:45AM
Health	April 8.	West group – Green East group – Blue	6:00AM-6:45AM
Wealth and Prosperity	June 8.	West group – Green East group – Lt. Blue	9:00AM-9:45AM
Recognition and Fame	July 8.	West group – Red East group – Purple	12:00PM-12:45PM
Marriage and Happiness	September 8.	West group – Brown East group – Yellow	3:00PM-3:45PM
Luck of the Children	October 8.	West group – White East group – Gray	6:00PM-6:45PM
Helpful People	December 8.	West group – White East group – Sliver	9:00PM-9:45PM

The **ninth** day of any month.

Career	January 9.	West group – Black East group – Blue	12:00AM-12:45AM
Education	March 9.	West group – Brown East group – Yellow	3:00AM-3:45AM
Health	April 9.	West group – Green East group – Blue	6:00AM-6:45AM
Wealth and Prosperity	June 9.	West group – Green East group – Lt. Blue	9:00AM-9:45AM
Recognition and Fame	July 9.	West group – Red East group – Purple	12:00PM-12:45PM
Marriage and Happiness	September 9.	West group – Brown East group – Yellow	3:00PM-3:45PM
Luck of the Children	October 9.	West group – White East group – Gray	6:00PM-6:45PM
Helpful People	December 9.	West group – White East group – Sliver	9:00PM-9:45PM

The **tenth** day of any month.

Career	January 10.	West group – Black East group – Blue	12:00AM-12:45AM
Education	March 10.	West group – Brown East group – Yellow	3:00AM-3:45AM
Health	April 10.	West group – Green East group – Blue	6:00AM-6:45AM
Wealth and Prosperity	June 10.	West group – Green East group – Lt. Blue	9:00AM-9:45AM
Recognition and Fame	July 10.	West group – Red East group – Purple	12:00PM-12:45PM
Marriage and Happiness	September 10.	West group – Brown East group – Yellow	3:00PM-3:45PM
Luck of the Children	October 10.	West group – White East group – Gray	6:00PM-6:45PM
Helpful People	December 10.	West group – White East group – Sliver	9:00PM-9:45PM

The **eleventh** day of any month.

Career	January 11.	West group – Black East group – Blue	12:00AM-12:45AM
Education	March 11.	West group – Brown East group – Yellow	3:00AM-3:45AM
Health	April 11.	West group – Green East group – Blue	6:00AM-6:45AM
Wealth and Prosperity	June 11.	West group – Green East group – Lt. Blue	9:00AM-9:45AM
Recognition and Fame	July 11.	West group – Red East group – Purple	12:00PM-12:45PM
Marriage and Happiness	September 11.	West group – Brown East group – Yellow	3:00PM-3:45PM
Luck of the Children	October 11.	West group – White East group – Gray	6:00PM-6:45PM
Helpful People	December 11.	West group – White East group – Sliver	9:00PM-9:45PM

The **twelfth** day of any month.

Career	January 12.	West group – Black East group – Blue	12:00AM-12:45AM
Education	March 12.	West group – Brown East group – Yellow	3:00AM-3:45AM
Health	April 12.	West group – Green East group – Blue	6:00AM-6:45AM
Wealth and Prosperity	June 12.	West group – Green East group – Lt. Blue	9:00AM-9:45AM
Recognition and Fame	July 12.	West group – Red East group – Purple	12:00PM-12:45PM
Marriage and Happiness	September 12.	West group – Brown East group – Yellow	3:00PM-3:45PM
Luck of the Children	October 12.	West group – White East group – Gray	6:00PM-6:45PM
Helpful People	December 12.	West group – White East group – Sliver	9:00PM-9:45PM

The **thirteenth** day of any month.

Career	January 13.	West group – Black East group – Blue	12:00AM-12:45AM
Education	March 13.	West group – Brown East group – Yellow	3:00AM-3:45AM
Health	April 13.	West group – Green East group – Blue	6:00AM-6:45AM
Wealth and Prosperity	June 13.	West group – Green East group – Lt. Blue	9:00AM-9:45AM
Recognition and Fame	July 13.	West group – Red East group – Purple	12:00PM-12:45PM
Marriage and Happiness	September 13.	West group – Brown East group – Yellow	3:00PM-3:45PM
Luck of the Children	October 13.	West group – White East group – Gray	6:00PM-6:45PM
Helpful People	December 13.	West group – White East group – Sliver	9:00PM-9:45PM

The **fourteenth** day of any month.

Career	January 14.	West group – Black East group – Blue	12:00AM-12:45AM
Education	March 14.	West group – Brown East group – Yellow	3:00AM-3:45AM
Health	April 14.	West group – Green East group – Blue	6:00AM-6:45AM
Wealth and Prosperity	June 14.	West group – Green East group – Lt. Blue	9:00AM-9:45AM
Recognition and Fame	July 14.	West group – Red East group – Purple	12:00PM-12:45PM
Marriage and Happiness	September 14.	West group – Brown East group – Yellow	3:00PM-3:45PM
Luck of the Children	October 14.	West group – White East group – Gray	6:00PM-6:45PM
Helpful People	December 14.	West group – White East group – Sliver	9:00PM-9:45PM

The **fifteenth** day of any month.

Career	January 15.	West group – Black East group – Blue	12:00AM-12:45AM
Education	March 15.	West group – Brown East group – Yellow	3:00AM-3:45AM
Health	April 15.	West group – Green East group – Blue	6:00AM-6:45AM
Wealth and Prosperity	June 15.	West group – Green East group – Lt. Blue	9:00AM-9:45AM
Recognition and Fame	July 15.	West group – Red East group – Purple	12:00PM-12:45PM
Marriage and Happiness	September 15.	West group – Brown East group – Yellow	3:00PM-3:45PM
Luck of the Children	October 15.	West group – White East group – Gray	6:00PM-6:45PM
Helpful People	December 15.	West group – White East group – Sliver	9:00PM-9:45PM

The **sixteenth** of any month.

Career	January 16.	West group – Black East group – Blue	12:00AM-12:45AM
Education	March 16.	West group – Brown East group – Yellow	3:00AM-3:45AM
Health	April 16	West group – Green East group – Blue	6:00AM-6:45AM
Wealth and Prosperity	June 16.	West group – Green East group – Lt. Blue	9:00AM-9:45AM
Recognition and Fame	July 16.	West group – Red East group – Purple	12:00PM-12:45PM
Marriage and Happiness	September 16.	West group – Brown East group – Yellow	3:00PM-3:45PM
Luck of the Children	October 16.	West group – White East group – Gray	6:00PM-6:45PM
Helpful People	December 16.	West group – White East group – Sliver	9:00PM-9:45PM

The **seventeenth** day of any month.

Career	January 17.	West group – Black East group – Blue	12:00AM-12:45AM
Education	March 17.	West group – Brown East group – Yellow	3:00AM-3:45AM
Health	April 17.	West group – Green East group – Blue	6:00AM-6:45AM
Wealth and Prosperity	June 17.	West group – Green East group – Lt. Blue	9:00AM-9:45AM
Recognition and Fame	July 17.	West group – Red East group – Purple	12:00PM-12:45PM
Marriage and Happiness	September 17.	West group – Brown East group – Yellow	3:00PM-3:45PM
Luck of the Children	October 17.	West group – White East group – Gray	6:00PM-6:45PM
Helpful People	December 17.	West group – White East group – Sliver	9:00PM-9:45PM

The **eighteenth** day of any month.

Career	January 18.	West group – Black East group – Blue	12:00AM-12:45AM
Education	March 18.	West group – Brown East group – Yellow	3:00AM-3:45AM
Health	April 18.	West group – Green East group – Blue	6:00AM-6:45AM
Wealth and Prosperity	June 18.	West group – Green East group – Lt. Blue	9:00AM-9:45AM
Recognition and Fame	July 18.	West group – Red East group – Purple	12:00PM-12:45PM
Marriage and Happiness	September 18.	West group – Brown East group – Yellow	3:00PM-3:45PM
Luck of the Children	October 18.	West group – White East group – Gray	6:00PM-6:45PM
Helpful People	December 18	West group – White East group – Sliver	9:00PM-9:45PM

The **nineteenth** day of any month.

Career	January 19.	West group – Black East group – Blue	12:00AM-12:45AM
Education	March 19.	West group – Brown East group – Yellow	3:00AM-3:45AM
Health	April 19.	West group – Green East group – Blue	6:00AM-6:45AM
Wealth and Prosperity	June 19.	West group – Green East group – Lt. Blue	9:00AM-9:45AM
Recognition and Fame	July 19.	West group – Red East group – Purple	12:00PM-12:45PM
Marriage and Happiness	September 19.	West group – Brown East group – Yellow	3:00PM-3:45PM
Luck of the Children	October 19.	West group – White East group – Gray	6:00PM-6:45PM
Helpful People	December 19.	West group – White East group – Sliver	9:00PM-9:45PM

The **twentieth** day of any month.

Career	January 20.	West group – Black East group – Blue	12:00AM-12:45AM
Education	March 20.	West group – Brown East group – Yellow	3:00AM-3:45AM
Health	April 20.	West group – Green East group – Blue	6:00AM-6:45AM
Wealth and Prosperity	June 20.	West group – Green East group – Lt. Blue	9:00AM-9:45AM
Recognition and Fame	July 20.	West group – Red East group – Purple	12:00PM-12:45PM
Marriage and Happiness	September 20.	West group – Brown East group – Yellow	3:00PM-3:45PM
Luck of the Children	October 20.	West group – White East group – Gray	6:00PM-6:45PM
Helpful People	December 20.	West group – White East group – Sliver	9:00PM-9:45PM

The **twenty-first** day of any month.

Career	February 21.	West group – Black East group – Blue	12:00AM-12:45AM
Education	March 21.	West group – Brown East group – Yellow	3:00AM-3:45AM
Health	April 21.	West group – Green East group – Blue	6:00AM-6:45AM
Wealth and Prosperity	July 21.	West group – Green East group – Lt. Blue	9:00AM-9:45AM
Recognition and Fame	August 21.	West group – Red East group – Purple	12:00PM-12:45PM
Marriage and Happiness	October 21.	West group – Brown East group – Yellow	3:00PM-3:45PM
Luck of the Children	November 21.	West group – White East group – Gray	6:00PM-6:45PM
Helpful People	January 21.	West group – White East group – Sliver	9:00PM-9:45PM

The **twenty-second** day of any month.

Career	January 22.	West group – Black East group – Blue	12:00AM-12:45AM
Education	March 22.	West group – Brown East group – Yellow	3:00AM-3:45AM
Health	April 22.	West group – Green East group – Blue	6:00AM-6:45AM
Wealth and Prosperity	June 22.	West group – Green East group – Lt. Blue	9:00AM-9:45AM
Recognition and Fame	July 22.	West group – Red East group – Purple	12:00PM-12:45PM
Marriage and Happiness	September 22.	West group – Brown East group – Yellow	3:00PM-3:45PM
Luck of the Children	October 22.	West group – White East group – Gray	6:00PM-6:45PM
Helpful People	December 22.	West group – White East group – Sliver	9:00PM-9:45PM

The **twenty-third** day of any month.

Career	January 23.	West group – Black East group – Blue	12:00AM-12:45AM
Education	March 23.	West group – Brown East group – Yellow	3:00AM-3:45AM
Health	April 23.	West group – Green East group – Blue	6:00AM-6:45AM
Wealth and Prosperity	June 23.	West group – Green East group – Lt. Blue	9:00AM-9:45AM
Recognition and Fame	July 23.	West group – Red East group – Purple	12:00PM-12:45PM
Marriage and Happiness	September 23.	West group – Brown East group – Yellow	3:00PM-3:45PM
Luck of the Children	October 23.	West group – White East group – Gray	6:00PM-6:45PM
Helpful People	December 23.	West group – White East group – Sliver	9:00PM-9:45PM

The **twenty-fourth** day of any month.

Career	January 24.	West group – Black East group – Blue	12:00AM-12:45AM
Education	March 24.	West group – Brown East group – Yellow	3:00AM-3:45AM
Health	April 24.	West group – Green East group – Blue	6:00AM-6:45AM
Wealth and Prosperity	June 24.	West group – Green East group – Lt. Blue	9:00AM-9:45AM
Recognition and Fame	July 24.	West group – Red East group – Purple	12:00PM-12:45PM
Marriage and Happiness	September 24.	West group – Brown East group – Yellow	3:00PM-3:45PM
Luck of the Children	October 24.	West group – White East group – Gray	6:00PM-6:45PM
Helpful People	December 24.	West group – White East group – Sliver	9:00PM-9:45PM

The **twenty-fifth** day of any month.

Career	January 25.	West group – Black East group – Blue	12:00AM-12:45AM
Education	March 25.	West group – Brown East group – Yellow	3:00AM-3:45AM
Health	April 25.	West group – Green East group – Blue	6:00AM-6:45AM
Wealth and Prosperity	June 25.	West group – Green East group – Lt. Blue	9:00AM-9:45AM
Recognition and Fame	July 25.	West group – Red East group – Purple	12:00PM-12:45PM
Marriage and Happiness	September 25.	West group – Brown East group – Yellow	3:00PM-3:45PM
Luck of the Children	October 25.	West group – White East group – Gray	6:00PM-6:45PM
Helpful People	December 25.	West group – White East group – Sliver	9:00PM-9:45PM

The **twenty-sixth** day of any month.

Career	January 26.	West group – Black East group – Blue	12:00AM-12:45AM
Education	March 26.	West group – Brown East group – Yellow	3:00AM-3:45AM
Health	April 26.	West group – Green East group – Blue	6:00AM-6:45AM
Wealth and Prosperity	June 26.	West group – Green East group – Lt. Blue	9:00AM-9:45AM
Recognition and Fame	July 26.	West group – Red East group – Purple	12:00PM-12:45PM
Marriage and Happiness	September 26.	West group – Brown East group – Yellow	3:00PM-3:45PM
Luck of the Children	October 26.	West group – White East group – Gray	6:00PM-6:45PM
Helpful People	December 26.	West group – White East group – Sliver	9:00PM-9:45PM

The **twenty-seventh** day of any month.

Career	January 27.	West group – Black East group – Blue	12:00AM-12:45AM
Education	March 27.	West group – Brown East group – Yellow	3:00AM-3:45AM
Health	April 27.	West group – Green East group – Blue	6:00AM-6:45AM
Wealth and Prosperity	June 27.	West group – Green East group – Lt. Blue	9:00AM-9:45AM
Recognition and Fame	July 27.	West group – Red East group – Purple	12:00PM-12:45PM
Marriage and Happiness	September 27.	West group – Brown East group – Yellow	3:00PM-3:45PM
Luck of the Children	October 27.	West group – White East group – Gray	6:00PM-6:45PM
Helpful People	December 27.	West group – White East group – Sliver	9:00PM-9:45PM

The **twenty-eighth** day of any month.

Career	January 28.	West group – Black East group – Blue	12:00AM-12:45AM
Education	March 28.	West group – Brown East group – Yellow	3:00AM-3:45AM
Health	April 28.	West group – Green East group – Blue	6:00AM-6:45AM
Wealth and Prosperity	June 28.	West group – Green East group – Lt. Blue	9:00AM-9:45AM
Recognition and Fame	July 28.	West group – Red East group – Purple	12:00PM-12:45PM
Marriage and Happiness	September 28.	West group – Brown East group – Yellow	3:00PM-3:45PM
Luck of the Children	October 28.	West group – White East group – Gray	6:00PM-6:45PM
Helpful People	December 28.	West group – White East group – Sliver	9:00PM-9:45PM

The **twenty-ninth** day of any month.

Career	January 29.	West group – Black East group – Blue	12:00AM-12:45AM
Education	March 29.	West group – Brown East group – Yellow	3:00AM-3:45AM
Health	April 29.	West group – Green East group – Blue	6:00AM-6:45AM
Wealth and Prosperity	June 29.	West group – Green East group – Lt. Blue	9:00AM-9:45AM
Recognition and Fame	July 29.	West group – Red East group – Purple	12:00PM-12:45PM
Marriage and Happiness	September 29.	West group – Brown East group – Yellow	3:00PM-3:45PM
Luck of the Children	October 29.	West group – White East group – Gray	6:00PM-6:45PM
Helpful People	December 29.	West group – White East group – Sliver	9:00PM-9:45PM

The **thirtieth** day of any month.

Career	January 30.	West group – Black East group – Blue	12:00AM-12:45AM
Education	March 30.	West group – Brown East group – Yellow	3:00AM-3:45AM
Health	April 30.	West group – Green East group – Blue	6:00AM-6:45AM
Wealth and Prosperity	June 30.	West group – Green East group – Lt. Blue	9:00AM-9:45AM
Recognition and Fame	July 30.	West group – Red East group – Purple	12:00PM-12:45PM
Marriage and Happiness	September 30.	West group – Brown East group – Yellow	3:00PM-3:45PM
Luck of the Children	October 30.	West group – White East group – Gray	6:00PM-6:45PM
Helpful People	December 30.	West group – White East group – Sliver	9:00PM-9:45PM

The **thirty-first** day of any month.

Career	January 31.	West group – Black East group – Blue	12:00AM-12:45AM
Education	March 31.	West group – Brown East group – Yellow	3:00AM-3:45AM
Health	April 31.	West group – Green East group – Blue	6:00AM-6:45AM
Wealth and Prosperity	June 31.	West group – Green East group – Lt. Blue	9:00AM-9:45AM
Recognition and Fame	July 31.	West group – Red East group – Purple	12:00PM-12:45PM
Marriage and Happiness	September 31.	West group – Brown East group – Yellow	3:00PM-3:45PM
Luck of the Children	October 31.	West group – White East group – Gray	6:00PM-6:45PM
Helpful People	December 31.	West group – White East group – Sliver	9:00PM-9:45PM

Let's say that this diagram is your home, with your front door in the center of the home facing south. As you walk into your house, the first section that you will encounter will be your "career section". To the right of you will be the section representing "helpful people", and to the left of the front door will be the section for "education". The far back room, opposite the front door, will be the section for your "fame and recognition", and so on. Just to example this further, let's say that your door is to the far right of the center of the house. This means that you will not be walking into your house through your career section, but through the section of "helpful people". The direction or placement of your front door will play an important roll in the energy of the home. Make sure that the direction of the door is in an auspicious direction for your personal feng shui candle lighting. In the event that it is not, take a photo of your entry and place that photo in a section of your home that is in an auspicious section. This will not solve the problems that could arise by have an inauspicious entry but it will lesson the effects.

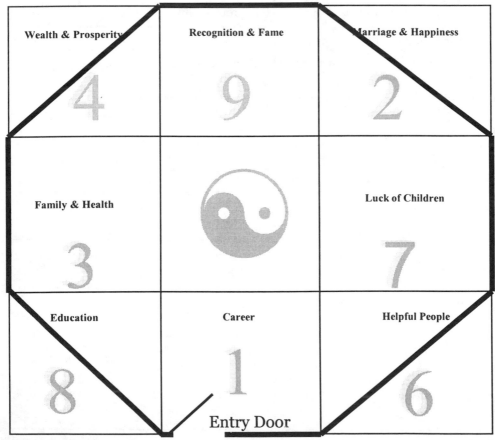

Wealth & Prosperity	Recognition & Fame	Marriage & Happiness
4	9	2
Family & Health		Luck of Children
3		7
Education	Career	Helpful People
8	1	6

Entry Door

I have placed a sketch of our bagua map over the floor plan of a house, so that you can see the different sections as they apply to the entire house.

You can clearly see the importance of keeping a clutter-free home. If you have a garage in your section represented by the luck of your children, you may feel duty-bound to give your children all the help and support that you can, by cleaning your garage.

The same will apply if closets are cluttered in your bedroom, which are located in your wealth and prosperity sections. If your closets are messy and disorderly, your money may try to come in, but will get lost in the confusion and never arrive.

When you have a need to accumulate a lot of things, you must also have a specific place for them in your home. Closets are fine for surplus belongings. However, they must be placed in the closet with care, and in an orderly fashion.

Another important thought to consider "If it does not work – fix it or get rid of it." This concept goes for everything in your life. When you begin to associate broken items with occurrences and feeling that have transpired in your life this philosophy will become very real. Get things fixed before your relationship begins to feel a lot like you're broken refrigerator.

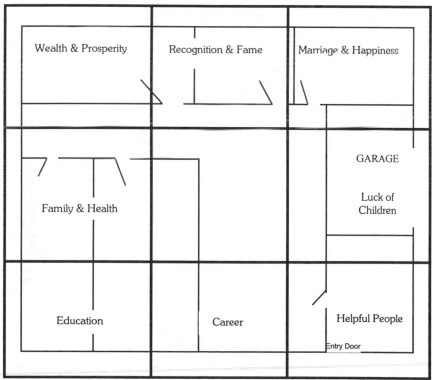

Wealth & Prosperity	Recognition & Fame	Marriage & Happiness
Family & Health		GARAGE Luck of Children
Education	Career	Helpful People Entry Door

Now, we will take the same life map and apply it to just one room. As you can see, we will be entering this room through the education section. To the right is the section for your career, and to the right of that is the section for helpful people.

If this is your bedroom, you may wish to place your bed in the corner represented by your marriage and happiness section, a plant in the corner of wealth and prosperity, and your dresser in the section represented by the luck of children. Perhaps you will place pictures of your children either on the dresser, or hanging on the wall behind it. Never have a mirror in the bedroom facing the bed.

Pictures of people that you feel have been helpful to you should be placed in the section of helpful people. If this is the room in which you will be lighting your candles, pick the section that best represents your desire, and light your candles on that section. By doing so, the added activation of the section of this room will aid you in your desire, so that it will manifest more quickly.

When we purchase or lease a home, we do not have the pleasure of placing closets or storage areas in the most inauspicious directions. With this in mind, you must, and I cannot emphasize this enough, "keep your area clean and free from clutter". You may, in your bedroom, have your closet in the perfect space, but unless it is clean, there will be harmful energy emanating from the closet, causing harassing energy, or at the very least, energy that will keep you up at night.

Wealth & Prosperity	Fame & Recognition	Marriage & Happiness
Health & Family		Luck of Children
Education	Career	Helpful People

Feng Shui masters believe each person, depending on their gender and date of birth, have four auspicious and four inauspicious directions. Your promising directions will be as individual as the group that you belong, either East or West, as determined by your personal kau number. By using your kau number and prescribed directions, you will have all of the energy, encouragement, assistance and motivation needed to reach your personal objectives in this life.

These particular directions will be important when moving into a new home and assigning your children's bedrooms, as well as insuring that your child has the proper seating in the classroom, for success and good grades. This direction for your child will be their fame and recognition direction as per their personal kau number. Positive recognition and fame are important aspects of life, whether you function in the public eye or as a stay-at-home parent.

To some, positive recognition and fame will be the satisfaction of experiencing situations such as raising children, taking care of your health and the ability to make ends meet. It will be the things that you do everyday that need your attention, which, to you, will exemplify the energy of recognition and even fame that will bring you success. The section in your home exemplifying this life experience of "recognition and fame" will be a personal direction as to your specific kau number. This will be just as important as the fame that one might receive out in the world, in a career situation or in a social setting. Fame is fame regardless of its degree!

Notwithstanding, all degrees of fame and recognition are governed by personal standards, and when activated the positive chi in your home, will enable you a greater degree of certainty for success. When your career depends on your ability to gain favorable recognition, activating the chi in this section of your home will be imperative.

There are certain places in your life: cities, towns, or particular countries, where you feel successful, the same as there may be certain place in your home that you feel equally as successful. We don't always take note of our surroundings, or even pay attention to those things that are going on in our homes, once we hit the front door after a long day at work, attention is not on our minds.

Having raised three sons, I found that unless I did something in front of one of them, or asked their help, none of the three would notice something had been changed, or was different, without being prodded to look. You might think that this was a lack of awareness. Yet, I viewed it as them being comfortable at home, and trusting of me, that I would always secure their well being. We now know that it was the comfort of the chi in the home that gave them the peace of mind that all is well!

This is the same thing that I see happening in homes around the world.

Men are coming home after a long day at work, or perhaps being away on business. Totally trusting of the person they had left behind, that, regardless of circumstances, the house and comfort within would be guaranteed upon their arrival. This is positive chi energy at its finest.

However, if your career is not as successful as you might like, and you have not obtained the level of success, fame and recognition that you have expected, then you must activate the chi in this section of your home.

Review the Fame and Recognition chart on page 136. If your personal Kau number is three, you are an East person, and your fame and recognition direction is South. This direction will apply for both men and women. As well this southerly direction will give you additional recognition due to the fact that this is also the direction of fame and recognition for the bagua.

The energy represented on the bagua is indicating to you that the South portion of your home is where you must clean and activate in order for the chi inciting fame and recognition in your life is resonating. In turn by achieving this section you will be manifesting the fame and recognition that you had been looking for. You must make a space for your money to go and you must clear a space for your fame and recognition to settle into. If that space is cluttered, then there will be no room for this new energy to fill.

Find your personal Kau number on the left-hand column in the chart on page 136. Follow that column across to find your fame and recognition direction in your home and in your life.

If your fame section, or direction, is in the Northeast, setup your home office in this direction, position your desk so that you are facing in this direction.

There are several different ways for you to activate your fame and recognition section in your home. To start, Feng Shui does not like clutter. The Chi energy must be free to flow.

Clutter, disorganization and confusion will stop the flow of sheng chi, turning this helpful energy into sha chi, which will destroy the fame and recognition that you are looking to accomplish. So, by cleaning and or-ganizing the section of your home that is entrusted by this fame that you are in search of you will succeed.

Second, the element governing this section is fire. A fireplace here would be wonderful Feng Shui, as long as all other elements in this section are equally balanced. Keep in mind that a fireplace would only emit the fire energy when there is a fire burning in it. This would be a good place for a healthy plant as fire produces earth. Balance of each element in each sec-tion of your home will be essential for the flow of chi.

However, there are certain things that in the western world that we need to watch for. If there is a bathroom that occupies this section of your home, there will be several ways of dealing with this problem. First of all, place the color red in the bathroom, along with white. The red will stimulate the fire energy, and the white will subdue some of the water energy from the tub, shower and toilet. This will as mentioned stimulate the fire element as well as help to balance the other elements in the room.

The reason that you would be doing this is that water puts out fire, so it would not be good to activate the water element in this particular sec-tion. The water is already there, and you will need to insure that it is bal-anced with the other elements so that it does not put out your fire.

A small mirror over the toilet will reflect the concept that the chi energy could be going down the toilet as it is being flushed, sending back the fame and recognition that is being flushed away with the usage of the toilet. A wooden toilet seat will, also, be helpful. There are many feng shui cures that even though may sound ridiculous or even foolish, none-theless have become real over the centuries. This if for no other reason than the energy that the thoughts had instilled. Thus, the reason for such things as the use of so many mirrors in the cures may sound silly but they have worked their way into application because of the amount of energy that has been given to them.

This same necessity to clean to activate, and insure that the elements are balanced concept will hold true when stimulating, sections of your home for love, health, and education, as well as all other important aspects of your life. The following pages will give you the directions to stimulate for these and other meaningful aspects of your life. Keep in mind that you must stimulate your personal chi energy direction for motivation, strength, power and success in each of these different life aspects.

We will be overlapping some life aspect sections, and directions, as we combine the directions using the Lo Shu, Bagua when combined with our personal kau energy.

Recognition & Fame

Personal Kau Number	Direction
1 = East	Southeast – for both men and women
2 = West	Northeast – for both men and women
3 = East	South – for both men and women
4 = East	North – for both men and women
5 = West	Northeast –for men Southwest – for woman
6 = West	West – for both men and woman
7 = West	Northwest – for both men and women (never light a candle in this corner, light this candle in the west)
8 = West	Southwest – for both men and woman
9 = East	East – for both men and women

Just as you may have a Gemini rising in your personal astrology chart, while the natural rising sign astrologically is Aries, there will be a direction representing a life aspect according to the bagua, which are in a different directions for you personally.

In this event you will be stimulating the section that represents your personal kau number direction.

Marriage and happiness: We all know that peace of mind success and happiness will depend on the choice of partners that we choose and the amount of chi we have flowing in our homes.

When you stimulate your relationship section, you are stimulating the emotions for the relationship within your partner, as well as within yourself. Often I hear, "Well, I'm willing to try, but they aren't." By stimulating the chi in this section of your home you will have the opportunity for both of you to be functioning within the same chi vibration at the same time. Thus, both will be focusing on the relationship concurrently. This focus may be unbeknownst to your partner yet this chi energy exist and will compel through its suggestive persuasion that both of you give the relationship another chance for survival, or conversely for the relationship to end through balance and harmony, thus soliciting a amicable separation.

Always remember if you are in a relationship, there is a reason for it. Whether the relationship has ran its course or not, there was a kinship between the two of you that existed in the beginning. Unless you were using your partner for what they had, or for what they could do for you, there was a bond, or passion or some form of love at one time. What ever that feeling was, it is worth your time to gather that energy back up again before making a decision to move on. Everyone deserves another chance, including you.

By activating the chi in this section of your home you will, once again, feel the same energy that brought the two of you together in the beginning. If it were still not what you had aspired, you would have given the relationship every opportunity to be successful. Then, if you choose to move on, you will know that you at least tried. When you go the extra mile for someone else, life will go that extra mile for you.

When sha chi is resonating in the relationship section in your home, you will begin to feel apprehensive, not really knowing if a change is what you are looking for, but knowing that the feeling is apparent and the need for change is inevitable. You may not know in which direction you want to move or what aspect of your life you want to change, but something is going on, because you feel it. If you are experiencing this indecision there are areas in your home especially the relationship section where the chi cannot flow, as a result the shar chi has provoke you to be indecisive.

The chi that we have been referring to in this section is that of Nien Yen. This Nien Yen chi is compassionate, it is strong and demands that it be reckoned with. This chi represents longevity, but not just as it pertains to the length of your life. This longevity is also the same continuance that long-term relationships are made of.

Marriage & Happiness

Personal Kau Number	Direction
1 = East	South for both men and woman
2 = West	Northwest for both men and woman
3 = East	Southeast for both men and woman
4 = East	East for both men and woman
5 = West	(never light a candle in this corner, light this candle in the west) Northwest for men / West for woman
6 = West	Southwest for both men and woman
7 = West	Northeast for men and woman
8 = West	West for both men and woman
9 = East	North for both men and woman

The same correlation will be made between this Nien Yen and your ability to educated yourself to the conditions of your body both mentally and physically as healthy relationships, via Nien Yen chi must be made between two people who are both healthy in body and mind. If not you will experience an unhealthy relationship.

When stimulating this Nien Yen chi in the relationship section of your home, you must also keep in mind – the right choice in whom you choose to engage in a relationship will make all the difference in the world. Maintaining a relationship for all of the wrong reasons, (which would be with the presence of sha chi) will cause all of the wrong things to happen.

Health: When someone says the word belief, we think of religion. This is not always the case, as a belief pattern is anything that you told yourself is worth living for, or that is a way of life or even something that had been told to you by someone that you trust.

One common misconception about belief patterns, that some adults have gown from children to believe as true is, "If it was okay then, it's okay now." "Daddy drank, and hit mommy and me, so it must have been okay, or we deserved it." We all know that this is not correct behavior, and that it is not okay, but when children are brought up under such abusive circumstances, they, by virtue of osmosis, believe that this way of living is right, or okay, or at the very least it is just the way that it is!

The reasons that daddy behaved the way that he did was because there was shar chi, and an imbalance of the elements in the health section of his home when he was, himself, growing up. This past behavior became a belief pattern for him, thus continuing it seemed to be his truth, which he was comfortable with, thus seeing no reason for change.

This was the belief pattern that daddy had, (not my dad by the way), when he was growing up, thus the psychological hypothesis that abuse is a learned behavior is once again seen through the displaced chi and an imbalance of elemental factors.

The chi energy which will resonate within your psyche thus stimulating a healthy body and mind is called Tien Yi chi. Tien Yi translates to "the doctor from heaven direction".

Tien Yi is the chi that, when stimulated, will bring you good health and positive belief patterns. As well, to lessen the effects of sha chi, when stimulated, will allow you to rid yourself of past negative behavioral patterns and dysfunctional beliefs.

We carry with us, by virtue of our psyche, the chi or shar chi conditions with which we grew up. If it was okay to yell in the house, if it was okay not to clean your room, or okay to disobey your parents or to push the envelope of your parents rules, then your belief pattern is that it is still okay to do all of this and more.

Only through the stamina of your Tien Yi chi can you commute the shar into a positive free flowing chi. Tien Yi is the only chi that has the force to transform past patterns, obsessions and addictions into practical, functional and acceptable free-flowing bliss, resulting in good health.

Use your Tien Yi chart to determine the health issues that apply to your

Health

Personal Kau Number	Direction
1 = East	East for men and woman
2 = West	West for men and woman
3 = East	North for men and woman
4 = East	South for men and woman
5 = West	West for men / Northwest for woman
6 = West	Northeast for men and woman
7 = West	Southwest for men and woman
8 = West	(never light a candle in this corner, light this candle in the west) Northwest for men and woman
9 = East	Southeast for men and woman

health direction. You may also consult the back of this book to see which health issues you may have by virtue of your health direction. Always be sure that the elements in this section are balanced, and that the chi is flowing freely, without interference from the engulfing shar chi.

Light your health candles, in this section during the new moon and before the next full moon to stimulate good health and between the full moon and before the next new moon to release poor health thus, stimulating your Tien Yi luck.

We talked enormously about chi and sha chi, balance, yin and yang, as well as harmony and elemental poise within yourself and within your environment. When the elements, as well as the chi, is not balanced, this will disrupt your ability to assimilate information that you, as well as your psyche, are trying to assimilate. This assimilation process must be functioning with clear vision of who and what you are, in order to function properly, which will when your candles are lit activate this Tien Yi chi.

Education: Particularly if your personal kau number is eight, it will be important for you, in this life, to learn as much as you can, about everything that you may be privileged to. As well, you will journey outside of your comfort zone for new horizons, to learn even more. It will be imperative that you stimulate your Fu Wei energy, adding an additional protection to the success that you will obtain through your knowledge, or through your ability to grasp what you are being taught. This will be as mentioned for you with the personal kau number of 8, because your kau direction and your Fu Wei direction are both resonating in the same vibrational direction, which is Northeast.

If you have young, school-age children, it should be essential that you insure that they receive the best possible education available, and for me, personally, it was at any cost. There are some duties and responsibilities bestowed upon us as a parent, such as: that we protect, defend and insure the domestic tranquility for our children, as these rights are bestowed upon us and then to our children once they attain a certain age. Until they do however, it is our responsibility as a parent, to give these rights to our children, and to protect these rights.

Another right as an American, for instance, is that every child under the age of sixteen receives a free and public education in a safe and non-threatening environment. Some people have a problem with "big-brother" dictating the environmental standards, educational doctrine and conditions in which our children learn, and under certain circumstances, I might agree, but my point here is, that even the federal government recognizes that a child's education is vital.

To insure that your child has the ability, as well as the foremost advantages available for his or her ability to comprehend, as well as the ability to retain, you must stimulate, or activate, their Fu Wei energy for education. To do this, first determine their personal kau number. Second, determine what direction is resonating with this energy, by finding their Fu Wei direction for education (see the chart on page 142). If their kau number is six, then their Fu Wei direction is Northwest.

If your child's desk is in their bedroom, you must insure that this room is clean and not cluttered, in addition that there is chi flowing in this room. If there is sha in this room, the child will not study and will not have the ability to retain any of what they may have read.

Their desk chair should not be placed so that your child's back is to the window. This seating position causes distraction, giving the child's psyche the feeling of falling out, thus, taking away their ability to concentrate. For the same reason, they should never sit with their back to the door.

Education

Personal Kau Number	Direction
1 = East	North for both men and woman
2 = West	Southwest for both men and woman
3 = East	East for both men and woman
4 = East	Southeast for both men and woman
5 = West	Southwest for men / Northeast for woman
6 = West	(never light a candle in this corner, light this candle in the west) Northwest for both men and woman
7 = West	West for men and woman
8 = West	Northeast for both men and woman
9 = East	South for both men and woman

Education or the ability to retain knowledge may be your main interests in life. Yet, not everyone will have the same semblance or aspiration to discover, advance in knowledge or the ability to develop mentally.

There will never be anything wrong with individuality. Not everyone was meant to be and Einstein.

But if this is an aspiration of yours you will need to stimulate the direction in your home that represents the knowledge and education section to allow this Fu Wei Luck to be activated so that your ability to retain will be stimulated.

By lighting your candles stimulating this Fu Wei luck you will discover a retention ability for information that you never knew that you had.

Your child's desk should be placed in the Northwest section of their room, to insure their personal Fu Wei power for learning. You should always light the right color candle for this direction, keeping the chi flowing and stimulating this section before important tests.

An important note is that, the colored candles you will be lighting to stimulate this section of your child's room, do not have to be lit in the child's room. They will, however, need to be lit in the West section of the

A child's chair should never be placed in front of a window.

Your child should never sit with their back to the door.

home, or in the West section of the room in which you light your candles. As the West is the candle lighting alternative for Northwest, as our previous example, of a child with a personal kau number of six, and their Fu Wei direction being Northwest. The child's study area must be in the Northwest section of their room, or the Northwest section of the home. There seating must be that they are facing Northwest when at their desk. You will be lighting one yellow candle between the hours of 3:00 AM and 6:00 AM. You will, also, be lighting one white candle between the hours of 6:00 PM and 6:45 PM (see page 214). Both of these candles must be lit, to stimulate the chi necessary to activate the Fu Wei, thereby enhancing your child's ability to learn, concentrate and to retain the information that he or she had been studying. Another important candle that should be lit is the color of candle that will represent your child personally. Using the timing chart on page 92, light the color candle representing the time that your child was born. As well, if their kau number falls in the East group, you will light the second color of candle listed on page 111.

For example, if your child were born between 3:00 AM and 6:00 AM., with a kau number of 3 their personal kau number will fall within the East group, thus you will light a yellow candle. If their personal kau number falls within the West group you will light the color of candle listed under "West Group" which for the same time of birth will be brown. So with our example of the kau number 3 you will be lighting a yellow candle as per page 111 and you will light this candle in the education section for the child which on page 142 for the kau number 3 is East.

Career

Personal Kau Number	Direction
1 = East	North for both men and woman
2 = West	Southwest for both men and woman
3 = East	East for both men and woman
4 = East	Southeast for both men and woman
5 = West	Southwest for men / Northeast for woman
6 = West	(never light a candle in this corner, light this candle in the west) Northwest for both men and woman
7 = West	West for men and woman
8 = West	Northeast for both men and woman
9 = East	South for both men and woman

This candle should also be lit at the same time that the child was born, as well it should be lit between the new moon and the next full moon.

For those who are interested in, or if you depend on, a career for your livelihood, this will be the section that you will need to stimulate, or activate, in order for your career to be successful.

When using the Lo Shu, we see that the career section in our home is North, but if your personal kau number is three, your personal career section, using this career chart shows that your career section is in the East for both men and women.

In this case, you will need to stimulate the East direction in your home in order to stimulate the Fu Wei luck for your career, and to send energy into the career thoughts and aspirations that you might have.

Career: The energy that one needs to sustain a healthy career will be emanating, or vibrating, in the North section of the home when using the Lo Shu.

Depending on your personal kau number, your Sheng chi energy, or career luck, may be in another section of your home. This is not a mistake. There may be two career directions, depending on your kau number.

If your personal kau number is nine, for both men and women, then your career direction is South. As mentioned, the South direction on the Lo Shu represents fame and recognition. This may be fortunate for you because, if you stimulate your personal career section, you will also be stimulating the section, or direction, for fame. Thus, through your career, if your sheng chi is stimulated and flowing freely, you will gain fame and recognition.

You will need to stimulate your career section or direction in your home when or if you feel stagnated or are in need of a boost. The career direction on the Lo Shu is North. You will need to stimulate the sheng chi energy, and the element that is associated with this direction. This direction is ruled by the water element. There are several different ways to stimulate the water element in this direction. One, depending on the size of the room, may be to introduce an aquarium or decorative water fountain (normally not a drinking fountain, but that would work, too).

You will not want to overwhelm the room by using too much water. Too much water will be worse than not having any at all. If your room or office is in this North section and is relatively small, something as simple as a vase of flowers will stimulate the water element, as well as the sheng chi, resulting in the success within your career.

In the western world, the North direction is said to be the direction of the super power. When you want to succeed, and to be victorious over your adversaries, you must approach the situation from the North. This will insure your victory.

It is important in life to guard yourself against adversaries in the business world. As you climb the rungs of the corporate ladder, you must activate the sheng chi to protect your success.

When sha, or shar, chi is active in this section, you will be vulnerable to theft and physical attack. There will, also, be an immense possibility that you will be passed over for the promotion that you had worked hard to receive.

The North section of your home whether representing your career or your nurturing ability to take care of your family can be your best friend or your worst enemy.

Wealth & Prosperity

Personal Kau Number	Direction
1 = East	Southeast for both men and woman
2 = West	Northeast for both men and woman
3 = East	South for both men and woman
4 = East	North for both men and woman
5 = West	Northeast for men / Southwest for woman
6 = West	West for both men and woman
7 = West	(never light a candle in this corner, light this candle in the west) Northwest for men and woman
8 = West	Southwest for both men and woman
9 = East	East for both men and woman

Wealth and prosperity comes about through a copious amount of different means, yet our focus in this section will be money, and your ability to prosper. The Chinese believe that there are three types of wealth luck.

Tien is the first form of luck, which is the luck from the heavens. This luck will be determined, by virtue of your birthright. You will receive a life of prosperity or be doomed to a life of austerity as determined through the Tien. The Tien is a luck that is out of the control of humans. There is little that you can do to stimulate this luck. Chi will not bring it in, and sha chi will not take it away. This luck is determined through the conditions of your birth.

Some people may refer to this as your astrological aspects at birth, or the conditions that you brought with you into this life from the heavens, or another life. It is your birthright.

The second luck is Ti. The Ti luck is earth luck. This luck can be changed. It will give you the ability to prosper; through the conditions or the stimulation of the chi in this section of your home, and through your own personal chi effort, you will prosper. The chi energy that you want to be functioning in conjunction with the Ti luck will be the sheng chi. This is a powerful force of energy, which will contribute to your ability to prosper. This chi will aid you during bad astrological times, that could, under normal circumstances, cause a loss in income.

The third luck is called Ren. This luck here is human luck. This is the energy that will place you in the right place at the right time, and through your efforts to stimulate the sheng chi in your wealth and prosperity section in your home or office you will succeed. When you do not activate this chi, or allow conditions for the chi to flow, inviting sha chi into your life, you will inevitably be in the wrong place at the wrong time, and will not prosper.

The philosophy behind the trinity of luck is that this energy will dictate our destiny. You must have the heaven, earth and human aspects in order to be complete, and to prosper in wealth, and in life.

The Lo Shu direction representing wealth and prosperity is Southeast. The element that governs this direction is small wood. Plants are small wood, so the Southeast corner of your home, or the Southeast room, or section, in your home or office, will be an excellent place to set a few plants. The Chinese Jade plant represents money. This Southeast section of your home will be a great place for a Jade plant.

When choosing your plant, or plants, for this room, it will be imperative that you take care as not to introduce any plants that have long thorns, or anything that might be toxins. You should not place a plant that has no room to grow in this section of your home, or in any section for that matter. Plants represent the small wood element, which will represent your ability to obtain great wealth. If your plant has no room to grow, the message that you are implying is that you have enough, that you have already reached your potential, and that you are satisfied with what you have.

You should always take care that all of your plants are hearty and healthy. If there are brown, or dead leaves on your plants, this is a symbol that you are beginning to stagnate, and there could be a loss of income, if you are not careful in eliminating the shar chi in this direction loss will occur. This is an area of your home that will need plenty of life. Never use dried flowers, or driftwood to stimulate sheng chi luck because driftwood is the epitome of death, and stimulates shar chi and not the sheng chi that you need.

Networking and communication may be a nineties term but the concept has always been acclaimed that, through contact, success will ensue. This chart will give you an indication as to where you must go, and which section in your home or office you will have to activate, in order for you to receive or feel the sheng chi luck that you need to effectively communicate. This will stimulate your ability to communicate with those who are in a position to help you by virtue of their position in life and your desire for success.

The direction represented by virtue of the Lo Shu is the Northwest. It is governed by the trigram Chien that exemplifies inherent and spiritual help. This is the direction that you will need to activate so that the chi will flow, thus stimulating your ability to establish a relationship with a mentor. By stimulating the chi in this direction, there is no end to the ability that you will feel, thus, obtaining whatever guidance or help you need in this life.

The element of the Northwest direction is big metal. Thus, to stimulate the chi in this section of your home or office, you can use anything that is metal, chimes, statuary or perhaps metal lamps are all good chi stimulators, or perhaps a metal fan. The fan would be an excellent mode of stimulating the chi, because, as the fan blades move, they will be stimulating the chi.

This chi that functions in the Northwest direction is kind and proficient. It is not hard to impress the chi in this direction. All that it asks is that it is stimulated. When you are at work, or in your daily environment, and you face this direction, this chi will bless you with its rewards.

If your personal kau number is one, then your networking and communication chien chi will be in the Southeast. If your personal kau number is 2, then you belong to the West group, and your chien chi direction is Northeast. When combining the ken energy from the Northeast with the chien energy of the Northwest, you have a wonderful combination of helpful people, and you will have the opportunity to grow and develop through the company of their knowledge and wisdom. This will lead to no less than success for you. The conditions here are powerful and stable. The chien chi is vital in your ability to communicate successfully. If the chi is stifled, stagnate or engulfed by the shar chi, only adversity can come your way, through arguments, quarrels and fights. It is very important that I mention that you should never have a fire or open flame in the Northwest corner of your home or office. By having an open flame in this direction, or section, it is considered as having a fire at heaven's gate, which will create a tumultuous sensation of shar chi. At the very best, this shar chi energy will enhance and multiply itself on a grand scale. It is well advised that this never happen.

Communication & Networking Helpful People

Personal Kau Number	Direction
1 = East	Southeast for both men and woman
2 = West	Northeast for both men and woman
3 = West	South for both men and woman
4 = East	North for both men and woman
5 = West	Southwest for men / Northeast for woman
6 = West	West for both men and woman
7 = West	(never light a candle in this corner, light this candle in the west) Northwest for men and woman
8 = West	Southwest for both men and woman
9 = East	East for both men and woman

Do not light candles in the Northwest section of your home to stimulate your helpful people section. Use metal to stimulate the chi in the Northwest section, and do not light candles in this section to stimulate your health, or for any other reason whatsoever. The alternative direction will be the West. This important message will apply especially to those who have a personal kau number of seven, as the Northwest section is the networking and communication section for them. If your kau number is seven light your candles for networking and communication in the West. For all others, you will be lighting your candles in the section that represents this energy as determined by your personal kau number.

The luck of the children section, will also, encompass creativity. This section is the West direction, and represents not only the creativity of a child, but that of everyone who lives in the house. When there are quarrels between a husband and wife, there is sha, or shar, chi in this West section of the home.

There is a preoccupation among some people to have children to preserve their family name. Shar chi in this section of the home can, also, prevent you from conceiving a child. This section could be very fertile if filled with the more positive sheng chi.

The West section of the home should be filled with the sheng chi of joy, happiness and creativity. This section of your home is where chi stores its youthful expressions. When your children are happy, and investigate their way through the hidden treasures of their minds, this youthful creativity will emerge. With inquisitive smiles and a watchful heart, there will be excitement in your home to experience.

When you have activated this chi, your children will begin to learn, and you will begin to learn along with them. When your child takes his or her first steps and learns to walk, you learn patience. When they learn to draw, you learn to appreciate. When they learn to ride a bike, you learn first aid. With every step that your child takes, with every lesson that they learn, you will learn, too. When sha chi is active in this section you will view your child as innocent of all wrong doing— the my child would never do that – syndrome, lending to a disorderly child.

When you do not take care to activate the sheng chi you will be taking your parenting responsibilities lightly or begrudgingly. As a result, your child's growth and development, as well as your own, will be stifled. You will be putting yourself on your child's emotional level, and fight with them through their growth, and then through their maturity. You will be viewing your children as competition and not as the tender souls in your care that they are. When this happens there is shar chi and you will suffer the ramifications of bad parenting as a result. As well you may perhaps be dealing with the impending legal issues that your child has caused.

So often I hear, "I'll change! I'll change!" But nothing is ever done to break this cycle of bad behavior. The chi is never activated, and the shar chi continues to persevere. The parent and child fight and bicker as children. Sha chi in this section will destroy relationships, often to the point of no return. You may have several children, but when shar chi is unstable in this section, you only have one chance to be a good parent. This is so often the story with the West direction of one's home. Yet, by stimulating the chi in this section, you will be encouraging the happiest

Luck for the Children

Personal Kau Number	Direction
1 = East	Southeast for both men and woman
2 = West	Northeast for both men and woman
3 = East	South for both men and woman
4 = East	North for both men and woman
5 = West	Southwest for men / Northeast for woman
6 = West	West for both men and woman
7 = West	(never light a candle in this corner, light this candle in the west) Northwest for men and woman
8 = West	Southwest for both men and woman
9 = East	East for both men and woman

section in your home, and through your knowledge of activating the chi, you will experience the happiest memories, and the most gratification, of your life. When you have eliminated clutter in this section, and feel confident that you are taking the best advantage of the space available, the sheng chi will once again commence to flow. Depending on your kau number, light your candles in the appropriate section and at the individual times, to stimulate the flow of chi in this section of your home.

If you want to stimulate the sheng chi – light your candles between the time of the new moon and the next full moon. If you are lighting your candle to lessen the effects of sha chi you will be lighting your candles between the time of the full moon and before the next new moon. Lessening the effects of sha chi is only a quick fix and never a antidote for anything – it only gives you the time that you might need to clean and balance this section of your home.

There will never be a good enough excuse for not doing the right thing, as a parent for your children!

Candle Lighting

Most of us are looking for answers to our questions about happiness, success, love and peace of mind. Many of us are looking for the answers to many other questions, as well. As we move more and more into a spiritual age, an age of inward understanding and outward manifestations, we have become more aware of how these questions are answered, and the desires that go with them are manifested.

In her many books on spirituality and candle lighting, Tina Ketch has opened to us the realm of all things being possible. She is an expert in the field of candle lighting and the new and extraordinary field of Feng Shui Candle Lighting, which incorporates aspects of the ancient Chinese art of Feng Shui with the ancient art of Candle Lighting, to assist us in achieving that which we so desire, and that which is ours to have.

Unbeknownst to our conscious mind, there is a guiding, directing force behind us all. We will refer to this force as an inner wisdom, that we allow to make decisions for us. These decisions, which are made on a subconscious level, aid and guide us to the next level of our growth and development. We might not know why we light a white, or even a yellow candle during our meditations, and we might not give it a second thought when we light pink or purple candles at the dinner table, or a blue candle to read by before we drift off to sleep, but all of these spontaneous and intuitive decisions to light candles set up the energy for manifestation.

Our subconscious knows to what we are aspiring, and what we need to do in order for our desire to manifest. When we become inspired to light candles, it is because of this psychological response within ourselves that imparts the power of manifestation in our lives. Most of us think we are lighting candles because we like them, and we do, but there is a much deeper, subconscious "need" to light, or be drawn to, certain colors, and a definitive subconscious response to the candles' energy once they have been lit. As you begin to discover the power of candle lighting, as well as this subconscious energy within yourself, you might ask, "How does this all happen?"

This happens because the subconscious mind knows much more about what we need than does the conscious mind. This quiet mind knows where our fears and blocks lie, and what it will take to rid us of them. When we consciously say, or feel, that we want something, this inner wisdom will kick into action, guiding us to that which will fulfill those desires, that which has to happen, as well as to put us in the direction that we need to go in order for our desires to manifest. It's the underlying phenomenon of human behavior.

It's psychology, by today's terms, but in its purest form.

The power of candle lighting, the psychology of human behavior, and the dynamics of relationships, all fall into one category when you begin to discover the cycles of your life through the power of candle lighting. This category is referred to as being bio-cosmic.

The motivating energy of candle lighting is based on your relationship to this bio-cosmic universe. The effectiveness of candle lighting is determined by the power of light through its spectrum, and how the eyes translate that color. This color, as it is being emitted from above in-conjunction with the light emanating from within you, reacts with each other bringing about a concentrated amount of activity for manifestation to occur. The time in which you light the candle will dictate the success-fulness of this manifestation. All of this, I might add, is done primarily on a subconscious level, often times unbeknownst to the conscious mind.

We all know that everything vibrates, and that all things have form, color and odor, according to its unique vibrational level. When you look at something, you are seeing it on more than one level at the same time. You are seeing it on a physical level, which is what you "see", on a vibra-tional level, which is what you "feel", and on a spiritual level which is what you "perceive". All of these levels and experiences function simul-taneously.

The correlation between what you are seeing, feeling and perceiving is the same correlation that you maintain between yourself (man), the heavens (cosmos) and the earth (physical). The relationship between you, the heavens and the earth is what we will call the balance of nature. Man is the resonating energy between the heavens and the earth, as he takes the psychic energy from above, and through intent, manifests it be-low.

In order for your candle lighting to be successful, there must be balance. When you try to control your environment, by taking the free will of oth-ers, you are giving up your own free will, thus creating an imbalance in nature, and disrupting the balance within your own universe. You should not manipulate the free will of others by lighting candles for your own selfish gain. Always maintain your dignity when lighting candles. If there is something that you want, you must first ascertain whether or not it is yours to have. Before you light a candle to get "something", you must first confer with your conscious. Your conscious will always be truthful to you. If your conscious tells you that it is not yours to have, and you light candles to obtain "it" anyway, you will get what you desire, but the energy that you create in doing so will come with karmic strings attached. These strings will have long lasting and far-reaching ramifications, thus creating issues and problems in other areas of your life.

Your universe is round, and the karmic issues that you have created are round, and will continue to come back to visit you, thus lending to the common saying, "What goes around comes around." The cycles of the seasons are round, your time is round and so are your eyes, which are the center of your universe. You see and perceive with your eyes. Your eyes allow the light from within you to resonate with the light from above, which for this bio-cosmic universe, is your sun. Without this cycle of exchange, you would not exist. Without your eyes, and your ability to see and perceive, you would, as you know it, not exist. Thus, your eyes, and your ability to emit and emanate light, create the center of your universe. Your eyes are emanating the light, which is vibrating within your being. By doing so, it is showing you the gateway to your soul.

Your intent, desires, hopes and dreams are viewed through your eyes. The light from above, when joined with the light from within, as viewed through your eyes, allows you the energy of manifestation. Your eyes perceive color. Thus, color, as it vibrates, dictates what you will be manifesting. Your intent is the time in which you activate the colored candle with fire, as fire is yet another form of intense light. The combination of the sun, the light from within yourself, and the light of the fire, will stimulate the light of your soul for the purpose of manifestation.

When lighting candles, we allow our eyes to view vibrational level as color. There are six basic colors: red, orange, yellow, green, blue and violet. White and black are not viewed as color, but rather the absence of all color, as in black, or the combination of all colors, which appears as white. There are three primary colors: red, yellow and blue, and there are three secondary colors: orange, violet and green.

Each secondary color is comprised of two primary colors. Red and yellow make orange, blue and red make violet, and yellow and blue make green. When you light two candles, one being red and the other being green, you are lighting one primary color and one secondary color. So, in a sense, you are lighting four color vibrations. This is because the secondary candle is emanating three colors at the same time. The three colors are: first the yellow, second the blue, and the third color vibration is green.

In this case you are lighting one red, one yellow, one blue and one green candle. Your conscious mind is only seeing two candles, which are the red and green. During the same time, the subconscious mind is seeing all four vibrational energies. This is called the Law of Simultaneous Contact.

Each color vibration emanates not only the color, but also, an emotional response. When you close your eyes to visualize a color, that color will stimulate an emotional response with in your psyche. Blue is a color that we often associate with warmth. With the color green, you may feel a nurturing sensation, as we associate the color green with grass, trees and other living plants which are green, when they are thriving and basking in the summer sunlight. As each color triggers this emotional response, these responses will dictate what you will manifest when lighting the different colored candles.

When lighting candles, you will need to determine the exact window of opportunity to manifest your hopes and desires. There are several methods that you can use in order to insure your success.

The first is that of the lunar cycle that we all follow each month. There are 13 lunar cycles within each year. The time of the new moon until the time of the full moon will be the operative time for you to light your candles to incite something new in your life. This cycle will last for approximately two weeks.

The second cycle of opportunity is from the time of the full moon until the time of the new moon. Again, this cycle will last approximately two weeks. This will be the time that you would light a candle to release something, or somebody, from your life.

The second method may be a bit more difficult for some. In this method, you would first determine where within the lunar cycle you were born. Let's say that, at the time of your birth, the moon was in its crescent stage. In this case, your personal "new moon phase" would be every month when the moon returned to that same position. Thus, you would light your candles to bring something into your life during the crescent moon phase.

The full moon phase, for you personally, would be when the moon was in the opposite point of your natal crescent mooning, which is called the gibbous moon. An example of this would be if you were born when the moon was in Gemini, your new moon phase would be every month when the moon is in Gemini. The opposite sign from Gemini is Sagittarius.

Thus, your full moon will be every month when the moon goes into the sign of Sagittarius.

The third method will be one that may appear to be the simplest to follow. Just as the month has a cycle that is attuned to the larger cycle of the year, the month has a lesser cycle that is attuned to itself. This cycle is referred to as the day.

Within each day, there are even lesser cycles that are attuned to all of that of which it is a part, such as the bio-cosmic universe itself. With this in mind, we are going to take our lunar cycle and divide it, one more time, into a daily cycle.

In using the new and full moon cycle, we are going to divide it into twenty-four hour cycles. There will be eight cycles, each will have a corresponding color, and each will last for three hours.

We will start at 12:00 a.m. The color associated with this time is white. White is the encompassing vibration of all colors, and will exemplify the same effects as the new moon. This will be the time of new beginnings. If you have the desire for change, and the courage to accept it, you may light a white candle anytime between 12:00 a.m. and 3:00 a.m. This cycle represents the three hour time frame that will be vibrating on the same vibrational level as the color white, and will hold all of the same promise that comes with the new moon.

The next cycle is from 3:00 a.m. until 6:00 a.m., and is represented by the color red. This is a time of renewed strength and enthusiasm. This is the perfect time to light a red candle for strength, focus and the energy to begin your day, with the enthusiasm needed to conquer your objectives.

The next cycle is from 6:00 a.m. until 9:00 a.m. The color which is vibrating at this time is orange. Orange is the color of consistency. If there is anything in your life that has been inconsistent, or anything that you are having trouble completing, this would be the operative time to light an orange candle, so that the energy vibrating at this time might be enhanced, thus giving you the opportunity to focus on that project or desire in order to bring it to fruition.

The last cycle before your "full moon" for this day will be vibrating at the same vibrational level as the color yellow, and between the hours of 9:00 a.m. and 12:00 p.m. This is the color that represents intellect, and your ability to align yourself with those things that are important to you, so that the success you have been working on, whether it is personal, emotional, financial or spiritual, will be successful.

From the time of 12:00 p.m. to 3:00 p.m., the cycle is the same as the lunar full moon. This is the time that is absence of color, which is represented by the color black. During this time, you will be releasing those things in your life that have been causing you discomfort or disease.

The next cycle is from 3:00 p.m. until 6:00 p.m. This is the cycle that you require in order to reflect on your day, your life and your ability to cultivate your relationships. The color which is vibrating at this time is green. If you feel any anxiety during this time, the universe is telling you that you have too many irons in the fire. Thus, it is time to let go of what does not work, so that you might pay more attention to those things in your life that you have been avoiding, out of your fear of commitment.

The next time cycle is from 6:00 p.m. until 9:00 p.m. The color which is vibrating during this time is the color blue. Mentioned previously, blue is a color of warmth and balance. This color emanates peace of mind and serenity. When you light this candle, you are letting go of issues and problems from your day that have denied you the peace of mind that is so desperately needed in maintaining balance within your universe.

The last cycle of our day is from 9:00 p.m. until 12:00 a.m. This cycle is one of the most important. It is vibrating at the same vibrational level as the color violet, which is a spiritual color. Although the color is spiritual, the time is indicating a need to release, or to let go. During this time, you will be lighting a violet candle to let go of conflicting belief patterns. Society often times dictates our beliefs, where our hearts may be saying something else. Let go of the conflict, sleep easy and awake in the morning refreshed and renewed.

When you use the lunar cycle as it stands, you will be lighting your candles to bring your desires to yourself. You will light your candles between the time of the new moon and the time of the full moon. If you are lighting your candles according to the lunar cycle, and are in need of releasing yourself from dysfunction or problems, you will be lighting your candles between the time of the full moon and the new moon.

The proficiency of lighting candles corresponding with the lunar cycle has been matter-of-fact and accepted for decades. It is hard to beat the tried-and-true methods of candle lighting when implementing the consistency of the lunar cycle, as well as the time of the day, which has, up until January 1, 2000, been consistent to the second.

For the purpose of the information in this book, we will rely heavily on both of these methods of time, the lunar cycle and our daily time. We have, in our Feng Shui section, used the time of day in conjunction with the resonating elements. In the candle lighting section, we will again use a timing guide, the elements and the colors, in conjunction with your personal kau number to successfully light our Feng Shui candles.

We will be using Greenwich Mean Time, GMT, in this book, so that it will be more universally user-friendly. It is for this reason that you will need to adjust the time stated in the book to your local time. I will be giving you clear and precise instructions on how and when to do this in the section titled Timing Guide. I will, also, give you the exact times of the full and new moons, so that you will be able to light your candles and activate your feng shui candle lighting successfully.

Feng Shui needs a clear and precise flow of energy. Just cleaning or rearranging a room in your home does not stimulate the chi in the entire house. This energy must be activated. Lighting your candles properly will do this.

The psychological influences on human behavior, of lighting colored candles, have been studied for decades. The studies have been unwavering, and the inferences have been conclusive. To quote Scientific American, a popular American scientific magazine, "It is no exaggeration to say that the splitting of light into color of its spectrum is man's most powerful tool for investigating the universe...", says it all.

We have all had proof of the importance of light at one time or another, if for no other reason then just by virtue of our age. When feeling suppressed or depressed, and then upon going out into the sunlight, we begin to feel refreshed and renewed. The same principal applies when speaking of suppression. If we stay inside away from the light, as well as the sun, our condition worsens, or at the very most stays the same.

That which is important to life is light, and to light is color. When we use this light and its color to dictate our emotional well-being, we will be in harmony with that which we feel we are trying to consummate in this life. This is not a form of control. It is merely a desire to stimulate ourselves to achieve, and not to stagnate or to submit ourselves into suppression. When lighting colored candles, you are saying, "I want to achieve," and, "I want to be happy."

Just as the chi and shar chi emanate a personality of energy, color through light emanates a personality. Each color will emanate a personality all its own. The personality of red and the personality of pink, even though they are in the same family, do not hold or exude the same persona.

This can easily be explained by saying that not all babies in the same family are alike, and that not all siblings act the same, even though they are in the same family. This example may be in its simplest form, because in this section we will be taking color and explaining its personality in its simplest form.

The concept that we are discussing here is the same philosophy whereas some colors may incite you to feel lighthearted, or even exuberant, while irritating the psyche of somebody else. We will go through the distinct personalities of each of the individual colors, in addition to describing how each color will affect different people in a different way, and for what reason this may occur.

These time periods are based on the lunar cycle of time and not the vibrational energy resonating from the directions.

Tien Lung the most powerful of all of the dragons symbolizes benevolence and nobility

T he simplest way to remember, and to associate with something that is inanimate, is to turn it into a personality with which you might correlate. Just as there are sometimes when you do get along with your friends, and sometimes that you do not, the same holds true about the colors.

This period will be determined by the energy with which you are encompassed. If you are in the company of chi energy, there will be certain colors toward which you will gravitate. When you are in the company of shar chi, colors will appeal to you that perhaps you did not feel comfortable around just a few days earlier.

It is important to keep in mind that balance is essential in life. Shar chi must exist to complement the chi. One is not bad where the other is good, and both must exist in order to promote the balance of life and nature, as yin and yang are the balance of nature, and both represent the opposite of each other.

As we discuss the different colors, giving them a description and a personality, I want you to keep in mind that, when you see someone that brings to mind the personality of the color that you are feeling, there will be a reason for that impression. There is energy that emanates around every living thing. This energy is called an aura, or by the scientific community, optical wavelengths.

Some people who are sensitive to this vibration of vision can see this energy. When you view the energy, you will be seeing color. Each color vibrates at a certain rate of speed, which in turn will dictate its color. This rate of speed is called an Angstrom rate or unit. Some colors vibrate at a higher rate of speed that others, thus again, the difference in color.

Optical wavelengths are very tiny, and thus, the Angstrom is often used. One Angstrom is defined to be 10^{-10} meters, and visible light spans that range from about 4000 to 7000 Angstroms, or a little less than a factor of two in relative wavelengths.

For comparison, the near ultraviolet is usually defined as the region from 2000 Angstroms up to the visible. The far ultraviolet goes down to 912 Angstroms, and the extreme ultraviolet extends down to about 50 Angstroms. Hence, ultraviolet light extends over a factor of about 80 in relative wavelengths!

Red	6000 – 6700 Angstrom	Green	5000 – 5500 Angstrom
Orange	5900 – 6000 Angstrom	Blue	4700 – 5000 Angstrom
Yellow	5800 – 5900 Angstrom	Violet	4300 – 4600 Angstrom

As we have mentioned, each color vibrates on its own unique vibrational level. You will never see the color blue vibrating on the same vibrational level as the color red. If this were to happen, the color blue would then change to the color red.

Just as the colors vibrate on their own vibrational levels, you will see that directions, conditions and all living things such as; people, plants and animals, vibrate on a level unique to themselves. These vibrational levels are not the same as the vibrational levels of color that we measure with the Angstrom, but they do vibrate, nonetheless. These vibrational levels are coexisting levels of vibration.

When you are stimulating the chi in your home, and not lighting colored candles, you will use the colors mentioned representing the directions from page 164, which are dealing primarily with element vibration. When you are lighting candles to stimulate the chi in your home, you will use the Kau number, Direction and Color chart.

Also, when using colors to stimulate the chi, you will be using the chart on page 164. When you are lighting colored candles to excite transformation and comfort from the universe, if your kau number is 8, you will light your candle in the Northeast section of your home and you will be lighting a indigo colored candle.

Although the colors for the directions will be different as they pertain to some of the individual kau numbers, both are functioning at the same time and in the same place. These cycles will be coexisting vibrational levels, or two things happening at the same time.

You must keep in mind that, even though more than one vibrational energy may be functioning simultaneously, they must be balanced in elements for this vibrational energy to produce chi. If not, you will be producing shar chi, thus defeating the purpose which is allowing your desires in life to manifest.

I have written extensively on the different life situations that are dictated by which color vibration in Volume I and then again in volume II of the Candle Lighting Encyclopedias, as well, discussing the time periods that you would need to light your colored candles in order to manifest your desires, and conversely, when to light your candles in order to eliminate certain conditions or dysfunction from your life.

We will not go over that information in this book. However, as it is vital to obtaining chi in your life, I would suggest that you read over, and familiarize yourself with, more of the detail with in each life issues mentioned here, which you will find in the Candle Lighting Encyclopedias.

One important issue that I must bring up is that, if your intent is to release yourself from shar chi, you will need to light your colored candles between the time of the full moon and the next new moon.

If your desire is to promote chi, and to insight new changes and situations into your life, you will need to light your colored candles between the time of the new moon and the next full moon.

One common question that I have often been asked is, "If I light a candle to bring something to myself, such as a new relationship or a new job, and I light the candle during the bring time frame which is as mentioned, between the time of the new moon and the next full moon, and the candle is still lit when the full moon comes, do I have to put the candle out?" The answer to this question is, "No!"

When ever you blow out or snuff out a candle you are stopping that energy from flowing abruptly. In the event that you do not plan ahead know that a seven day candle will be lit for between five to seven days and you light it two days before the full moon, allow the candle to stay lit. It will still resonate with the same energy that it was when you lit the candle, which will solicit your desire of a certain event or thing to manifest. Yet, in the future please plan ahead.

If you are serious enough in changing your life and making it better then you need to be serious enough in planing your candle lighting so that candles lit in order to manifest change will be lit during the two weeks of the "new moon" cycle. And your candles that you light as to rid yourself from undue influence and dysfunctional issues will be lit during the "full moon" cycle.

It is worse to blow out a candle than it is to allow it to stay lit during the wrong moon phase. You light candles to incite change. The candle will begin its task of summons this change as it stimulates the sheng chi in your life. This manifestation of change will begin the moment the flame touches the wick. The longer the candle is lit the more emphases is placed on your desire.

In the event that you are not in a position to allow your candles to stay lit for long periods of time, please light smaller candles, as this will benefit you more that having to blow out a candle.

I have grown accustom to lighting large seven day candles in my research and studies. However when challenging the sheng chi and Sha chi to manifest using small votive candles, this energy did perform and my desire for the study did manifest showing that the votive candles are effective in the manifestation of your desires.

By lighting a candle, you are stimulating your personal and environmental chi. If, for whatever reason, you put the candle out before it had time to burn out by itself, you will be ceasing the chi from flowing. If you have no choice as to whether or not to put out the candle or to leave it lit, then you must put it out. If you do have choices, do not snuff out a burning candle.

You should not leave lit candles unprotected and unattended, for safety reasons. I have found seven-day candles in a glass jar to be safe to leave lit during my absence. However, I only leave them for short periods of time, and only if they are burning on my fireplace hearth, or during the summer, in the fireplace, so my lit candles are never left in a place that could potentially cause my home to catch a flame.

If you do not have a safe place to light your candles, please only light votive candles, which burn for shorter periods of time, giving you the opportunity to be in attendance.

Chi will be stimulated once the flame reaches the wick and the colored wax begins to melt. Bigger candles are not always better, or necessary.

Kau Number	Direction	Color of Candle
1	North	Blue
2	Southwest	Yellow
3	East	Green
4	Southeast	Orange
5	Center	Black
6	Northwest	Purple
7	West	White
8	Northeast	Indigo
9	South	Red

Colored Candles and Your Personal Kau Number

W hen you use a color that compliments your personal kau number, or light the candle that will exemplify the first through the fourth best of your kau numbers, you will be stimulating your personal sheng chi, as well as the positive chi within your home, which is called environmental chi. By doing this, you will be stimulating your capacity to manifest your dreams and aspirations through the medium of the lighting of colored candles.

Use the charts titled "Best Color Personalities for Males" and "Best Color Personalities for Women" to see which colors will compliment your own personality, as well as aid you in your desires to manifest a successful life. If your kau number is 3 and you are female, your color vibration is green.

When lighting a green candle, you will be stimulating your own personal chi that is resonating along the same vibrational level as your innate personality. You will have other colors that will complement your personality, too, as well as enhance your ability to manifest your desires.

As you will see on the chart on page 166, your best color, as well as color of candle to light which will be resonating with your intrinsic personality, if your personal kau number is three, this complimentary color will be red. Red is not the color that you will be resonating with, rather the best color, which will complement your innate vibrational color, which is, again, green. The color red will stimulate the color green only if your kau number is three.

Just as you get along with some people and not others, some colors work well with some other colors, but not all other colors.

As we have mentioned, the best color of candle for you to light to stimulate your ability to manifest your desires will be red. The second best color will be blue. The third best color will be orange, and the last color will be green.

As not to confuse you, yes, green is the fourth-best color to light to stimulate your ability to manifest, and it is also the color of your innate personality. The first candle that you will light will be the green candle to stimulate your kau energy or your innate personality chi.

The second green candle that you will be lighting will represent your desire to manifest a specific aspiration. In simple terms, the first candle will represent "that you want", and the second candle will represent "what you want."

W hen you have determined your personal kau number, use the chart below to light the right color of candle that will assist you in stimulating the chi of which you are in need. You may light these candles in the rooms that you want to stimulate in your home, and if possible, in your office.

If you cannot light candles in your office, determine which direction that you need to have stimulated, or activated, and light the color of candle that will represent that chi in your home before going to work. The chi will find its way to your office. Energy has no boundaries, and there is no distance that is too far for the chi to travel.

If your personal kau number is 4, the best color for you to light to stimulate your personal chi will be blue, as the number below on our chart, next to the kau number 4, under the Best column is the number 1. The color for number 1 is blue.

Your second best color to light will be the number color that represents the kau number 9 which is red. The third best color for you to light will be the kau color representing the kau number 3, which is green. The fourth color will be the kau color represented by the kau number 4, which is the color orange.

Best Color Personalities for Woman					
Color	**Kau**	Best	2nd Best	3rd Best	4th Best
Blue	1	4	3	9	1
Green	3	9	1	4	3
Orange	4	1	9	3	4
Red	9	3	4	1	9
Black	5	2	6	7	8
Yellow	2	8	7	6	2
Purple	6	7	8	2	6
White	7	6	2	8	7
Indigo	8	2	6	7	8

Color	Kau Number	Best	2nd Best	3rd Best	4th Best
Blue	1	4	3	9	1
Green	3	9	1	4	3
Orange	4	1	9	3	4
Red	9	3	4	1	9
Black	5	2	6	7	8
Yellow	2	8	7	6	2
Purple	6	7	8	2	6
White	7	6	2	8	7
Indigo	8	2	6	7	8

Best Color Personalities for Males

I will be giving you my interpretation of each chi color, as well as the same colors, but through shar chi energy. It will also be important for you to meditate on each color, so as to determine your own personalities for each color. When determining the personality of a color you must use the color guides that I will be giving you, and through meditation, begin to identify with the colors as if they were your friends, giving them a personality with which you can identify.

Red

When I visualize the color red, I see a tall lanky woman, a woman that has a sassy personality, and the ability to get anything that she wants. She has good karma, and does not manipulate her way through life, only reaps the rewards of past karma or deeds. Through her ability to pursue her friends, as well as her adversaries, she will never go without.

She is sly and cunning, but she is passionate, and has the ability to save the world through her passion. She has a kind heart. She is always in a hurry, but she will stop to help you, if you ask.

She will not help if you do not ask. She will be the first one at the scene of an accident, and help in anyway that she can. She can render first aid, as well as an encouraging word. When you see these types of behavior, you will know that the Sheng chi energy that is being exhibited here is red.

The color red typically represents the southerly direction of your home. It is, also, the color which resonates with the kau number nine.

When it's fame and recognition that you are looking for, you will need to stimulate the chi in the South section of your home, and by lighting a red candle, you will be activating this chi energy for your success.

Blue

When I see the color blue, I see an innocent child, a small, blonde-haired, little girl that wants everything to be okay. She is sweet, creative and has the ability to make the sun smile when she winks in its direction. She is magic, and can set your world right. All you have to do is acknowledge her presence.

The color blue will bring you balance, and she will, also, help you through any depression that you might be feeling. She is the smile at the end of the day, and the light at the end of the tunnel.

She has a natural beauty that will shine through any conflict. When you are in need of help, for any emotional reason, she can help.

When you have a desire to help somebody through an emotional crisis, you will be exhibiting the chi energy of the color blue. The color blue resonates with the kau number one. The direction which this color represents is North.

When your career is in question, or in need of stimulation, you may light a blue candle, which will stimulate this chi. This will release you of personal shar chi, as well as the shar chi in this North direction, or section, in your home.

Green

When I see the color green, I see a strong businessman that makes decisions based on the facts. He has no time for nonsense. This is a man that can set your world right through his ability to lend a helping hand to a deserving person.

This color personality will open doors for you that you once thought had been closed. Through the help of this color chi energy, you will advance financially. Monetary problems can be resolved through the stimulation of this color, and by lighting a green candle in your most auspicious direction section in your home.

This color represents the natural order of life, going from one progressive stage of development to the next. This is the color that will give insight into your development, and into your life.

When you are in need of advice, and do not see this sheng chi emanating from the person from whom you have sought assistance, they will not be in a position to help you.

The kau number that resonates with this color is three. The direction which is represented here is the East section of your home, or the direction of East.

This direction is dictated by the life aspect of health and family, and the Chen energy. Your desire to stimulate this section in your home will manifest through lighting a green candle in this section of your home, thus stimulating this Chen chi.

Orange

When I see the color orange, I see a tender soul with the wisdom of truth and the ability to make you feel safe, regardless of the situation. When I visualize the color orange, I see the mother of time, with her arms opened wide to rescue and to comfort anyone in need.

I see strength, honor, integrity, and consistency. I see a feeling of safety that has no bounds and no abstract, a quality that no other color can offer.

This color holds no, and sees no, fear. This is the color that can erase past karma that is causing you to be confused, or to have feelings of inadequacy.

The Sheng chi emanating from this color will give you the ability to strengthen your willpower. This is the color of candle that you will need to light if you want to break addictions, or for anything that you want to accomplish that will take a great amount of willpower, or that will take inner strength to accomplish.

When you see someone who seems to have enormous strength, the ability to comfort others and the willingness to help others with no questions asked, you will be seeing the sheng chi of the color orange.

This is a very high energy color, and when it has been activated it should not be challenged.

The Sheng Chi personality of the color black is the all-encompassing color, which is misleading in its appearance. It may appear to be ambivalent to your cause. The sheng chi energy of this color is not uncaring, and it is not unresponsive. Rather, it is a personality possessing a higher form of insight.

When you see a person that seems to be in a fog, inattentive or indifferent to your presence or current situation, you are actually witnessing the sheng chi of the color black.

This personality, as you perhaps have noticed, is not really that they do not care about your situation. It is more that they know their limits, and out of a righteous decision, (subconscious as this decision may have been), choose not to become involved with situations which they cannot alter.

It is not that this color sheng chi personality is not compassionate about your situation, it is more that they comprehend on a much deeper level the meaning of karma and its particulars.

The sheng chi of this color will lend itself to you in the form of detachment. When you need clarity in any situation, you can light a black candle. By doing so, you will have the ability to detach from your present confusion, so that clarity will prevail.

This chi is very positive, enabling you the distance that you need for clarity. The sheng chi emanating through the color black will hold you to your individuality, as through this energy, you will be forced to make decisions for yourself.

This color personality resonates with the kau number 5, which, in actuality, does not exist. A man with the kau number 5 will use the kau number 2, and females with the kau number 5 will use the kau number 8.

This direction is neutral, and in the center of your home. It does not represent a life aspect, but does pose life situations. When, as mentioned above, you are looking for clarity in your life, light a black candle in the center of your home.

Yellow

When I visualize the color yellow, I see the intellect of a mature individual, and the patience and knowledge of a saint. I see a student yearning for the ability just to pass his or her next test. The color yellow represents the ability to obtain great knowledge, but has a frail disposition, almost insecure about the knowledge that he will potentially grasp. The energy personality of the color yellow approaches every new adventure with caution.

The contradictions exemplify the color yellow. The color yellow is a color with many sides, and just as many faces. The color yellow will embellish mental power, and possess the ability to intimidate at the drop of a hat.

The color yellow is almost obsessive over the right thing being done, and the right answer being given. The color yellow represents an over-achiever, a person who fears the wrong answer and a person who seldom ever has the wrong answer, thus, having no justification for having this fear.

The color yellow is one of the only colors that long for the companionship of others. The color yellow represents an energy that seldom stands alone.

When the mind tries to visualize the color yellow, it immediately wants to go to the next color in the spectrum. The color yellow loves company.

The sheng chi of the color yellow represents the kau number 2, and the Southwest direction. When your desire is to stimulate your intellect, and the bagua direction of the Southwest, which represents happiness and marriage, light a yellow candle in the Southwest section of your home.

Purple

When visualizing this color, there will be images of greatness. The color purple is the exemplification of majesty, spirituality and the ability to be humble.

When you close your eyes and create excellence in your mind's eye, you will see the color purple. The color purple is the sheng chi of high-mindedness, benevolence, unselfishness and generosity. When I visualize the color purple, I see an unselfish child that would give you the shirt off his back, when he would have needed it worse. The color purple is an energy that will allow you the ability to grow, develop and live, with design, a life of peace and happiness.

The chi energy of the color purple represents the Northwest direction. It is no wonder, as the Northwest section is referred to as, "Heaven's Gate", that this is where greatness abides. It is known that you should never have a bare flame in this section of your home.

The kau number that is represented here is the number six. To light a purple candle to stimulate this God like sheng chi you will need to light it in the westerly direction of your home. The West section represents the luck of the children, as we are all children in the eyes of the creator.

Indigo

When I close my eyes to visualize the color indigo, I see the truth of the universe, the knowledge of our ancestors and the apprehension they left behind. The apprehension of truth, what that truth will do to those who are willing to except it and the pain that it could cause to those who are not ready for its revelations, is the basis for this apprehension.

I can see into the future through the color indigo. When I close my eyes, I visualize this color as the gateway into the unknown that will set us free from the restrictions that have confined us to the physical body. These are the confines that have not allowed us, until now, to explore all that the universe has to offer.

With the color indigo, I can see the jubilance that the ancients held in their accomplishments. Through my minds eye, I witnessed their zealous approach to knowledge, to know and explore all that they could, as fast as they could, insuring that they took every measure known to mankind to insure that the vibration of truth continued from generation to generation. Their goal was to insure that this knowledge maintained its innocence, unsoiled and untarnished by the doctrines and the dogma of education, and the sovereignty of political and religious discipline.

We should not be surprised that the direction which represents knowledge and education on the bagua is in the Northeast section of our home, as the color indigo, also representing knowledge and your ability to ascertain the truth, resonates in this direction.

If your personal kau number is 8, you will be resonating with this knowledge and direction. There will be a desire in your soul for the truth, and a passion within yourself to learn. When your desire is to activate this section of your home, to promote the sheng chi and release your environment of shar chi, light an indigo colored candle in the northeast section of your home.

If you do not have a conductive candle lighting area in this section of your home, you can light the candle in another section. Remember to take care that you still light the candle in the Northeast corner of the room that you choose.

White

When I close my eyes to visualize the color white, I see the absence of all that the mind can conceive. Although the color white is perceived to be all that is pure, it is all of that, and more. The color white is all that is, in this world, and all that is, out of this world.

The color white has no boundaries and no descriptions, because the color white is all that is. There is nothing that cannot be achieved through the color white. The color white has no limits, no boarders, no blocks and no boundaries.

The color white has perpetual motion; ever cycling and rhythmically touching every inch of our soul. The color white resonates on the same vibrational level as the West section of our home. The kau number that is represented here is the number seven.

If your desire is to stimulate, or to activate, the West section of your home, you will need to light one white candle in the West section of your home. In turn, you will be stimulating the sheng chi of the luck of the children section in your house.

You may, also, if this section is not conducive for candle lighting, light one white candle is the West corner of another room in your home that will represent one of your four auspicious directions. This will stimulate your personal chi, as well as the chi representing this section of your home.

Remember each section of your home will have all eight directions in it. There will be four auspicious directions and four inauspicious directions. As you will have a bagua in each section as well as a bagua that will fill the entire home.

The worst color personalities with your personal Kau number will represent the colors in order from fourth worst to the very worst, but only when they are combined with your personal Kau number. These will be the colors that, when surrounded by Shar chi, will irritate your psyche, and by so doing, will not allow you to manifest your desires. Instead, you will be manifesting things, and situations, into your life that will come to you with shar chi and anger attached. A good example of manifesting using shar chi is called revenge.

When someone does something to upset you, the shar chi will insight you to seek revenge.

When it is obvious that the sha chi exist, you will need to release it by lighting the color of candle that best delineates your personal kau number before you will be able to light any of your worst colors with the success of manifestation. This new energy will, then, give you the insight needed to manifest your desires, and not to seek revenge on unwitting souls.

If your personal kau number is eight, your very worst color of candle to light is orange. The color orange represents the Lo Shu number 4, which is the Southeast direction which represents wealth and prosperity. If your desire is to stimulate this Southeast direction, and there is sha chi present you must first light the color of candle that represents the kau number 8 before lighting the orange candle in the Southeast section of your home. In the event that you do not eliminate the sha chi first you will not be capable of manifesting your wealth and prosperity that you were looking for.   *Personal sheng chi is very important to maintain!*

Worst Color Personalities for Woman					
Color	**Kau**	4th Worst	3rd. Worst	2nd Worst	Very Worst
Blue	1	7	8	6	2
Green	3	2	6	8	7
Orange	4	6	2	7	8
Red	9	8	7	2	6
Black	5	9	1	3	4
Yellow	2	3	4	9	1
Purple	6	4	3	1	9
White	7	1	9	4	3
Indigo	8	9	1	3	4

As you read my insights into the chi color personalities, you might have said to yourself, "I know someone who, if not so mean or negative all the time, could be like that!" The positive sheng chi color personalities vibrate on a level that shar chi cannot reach.

However, the definition of the color is a neutral vibration, which will, through the vibrations of the person taking that color upon him or her self, will pull the vibration up or down, depending on their own personal kau number. Thus, you will have the color vibration functioning on a sheng chi or a shar chi energy vibrational level.

The diagram below will give you a visual of how this happens.

Sheng Chi

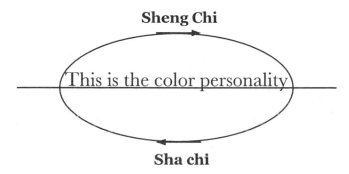

Sha chi

The straight line is the definition of the color. The oval is the sheng chi and shar chi energy cycle. The energy cycles, as will your thoughts and emotions. We all know that, not everybody has the best thoughts or feelings all the time, regardless of how hard they try to maintain their sheng chi or vibrational level.

Worst Color Personalities for Males					
Color	**Kau**	4th Worst	3rd. Worst	2nd Worst	Very Worst
Blue	1	7	8	6	2
Green	3	2	6	8	7
Orange	4	6	2	7	8
Red	9	8	7	2	6
Black	5	3	4	9	1
Yellow	2	3	4	9	1
Purple	6	4	3	1	9
White	7	1	9	4	3
Indigo	8	9	1	3	4

Red

The shar chi of this red color personality is angry, and can be hostile. This color is always in a hurry, and exudes nervous energy. The sheng chi of this color will be the first one on the scene of an accident to render first aid, where the shar chi of the color red will be the cause of the accident.

Everybody will feel the shar and the sheng chi energy at one time or another in their lives, and perhaps daily. The objective of our efforts will be to manifest our desires using only the sheng chi energy. It is to our advantage, when maintaining the sheng chi energy, to light those candles which will stimulate our personal chi. Then, as we manifest change, our hearts and intentions will be pure.

The personality of the shar chi red is aggressive, and can be antagonistic. If you are a West group person with a kau number of two, six, seven or eight, you will be more likely to feel the shar chi of this color than an East group person.

Blue

When I visualize the shar chi that resonates with the color blue, I see depression, or at the very best, a self-complacent attitude. The sheng chi of the color blue will make you smile. The shar chi of the same color will render the opposite effects, or personality traits.

The color blue exemplifies emotions, and not physical activity. The shar chi of this color will aid and assist when your desire is to be suppressed and left alone.

You will only feel the shar chi personality of the color blue if your personal kau number is two, six, seven or eight, and if you are not personally functioning with sheng chi.

This is in no way inferring that only those who are in the West group are prone to depression. It is merely suggesting that, if you are not balanced, and the sheng chi is not stimulated in your home and within your personal chi, you will be more prone to suppression than, perhaps, somebody in the East group.

When you feel this suppressive energy, light the color of candle that best represents your personal kau number. This will activate your personal sheng chi energy, thus releasing yourself from the shar chi of the color blue.

This candle should be lit in the section of your home which is the best direction for your personal kau number. This example is: if your kau number is 3, your best color of candle to light would be green. The direction, or section, in which this candle should be lit, to activate your personal sheng chi energy, is South.

One thing to note here is that the kau number three resonates with the direction of East. Yet, the best direction for this East kau number is South.

Green

When the color green is emanating the shar chi of its personality, you will experience feelings of hesitation toward your financial responsibilities. You may very well have the funds to fulfill your responsibilities, yet a feeling of extreme liability may beset you.

When this shar chi is active, you may feel as if you have no way to dig yourself out of these, often times imaginary, financial problems. It is, also, not uncommon for this shar chi to cause your house plants to wilt.

The shar chi of the color green is a cause of minor health problems, such as the common cold, flu and other short-term health uncertainties. When you feel this shar chi has engulfed your sheng chi, light the color of candle that represents your kau number, in its most auspicious section of your home.

When your desire is to manifest additional income, and if the color green, which is a color to light for financial advantages, is not functioning through the shar energy, you may light the green candle, soliciting the financial help that this color will provide. Remember, you must light the candle that represents your kau number first, as this will better insure your success for financial relief.

Orange

The shar chi of the personality of the color orange is the exact diametrical of its sheng chi counterpart. The sheng chi of this color will release you from fear.

People with cancer will often light orange candles, lessening the fear that this illness may instill. Yet, when the shar chi of this color is functioning, you must light the color of candle that represents your kau number first, before the sheng chi will resonate within you. By doing so, the shar chi of the color orange will not prevail. In the event that this is not done, the shar chi of this color will instill even more fear than you had before.

The shar chi of this color personality will cause you to gain weight. If this is something that you want, it will work. If you are not wanting to gain weight, light your kau number color, so that your weight will not be a problem.

This is often the problem when people want to lose weight. The shar chi of the color orange is putting excess weight on you. Then, it instills the fear that you will never be able to take it off, thus instilling the vibration of the shar chi. If you do not light the color of candle that represents your personal kau number, it will be difficult for you to lose weight.

Light your kau number colored candle in the section that best represents your kau number. If your personal kau number is four as seen on page 164, you will light an orange candle in the North section of your home. Even though the direction that you are resonating with is the Southeast as per the same chart– your very best or complementary direction as seen on page 235 shows your "best" direction as North.

Black

We have all heard the stories of a person with a black personality, a person who is evil, deceptive and unscrupulous.

This may not be the true personality of the person's color personality, but it is the personality of the shar chi of the color black.

When the sheng chi is absent from the color black, it may appear as if there is a black hole in your life. You will feel as if everything that you are looking for has been stolen. You put your car keys on the kitchen counter, but when you returned to retrieve them, they were gone.

It is not that there is a little fairy running around your house, taking your things so as to confuse you. The shar chi of this color is one of confusion and forgetfulness.

You may very well have placed your keys somewhere other than the kitchen counter, forgetting where you put them, thinking only of where you thought you had seen them last.

This color, as seen through shar chi, can be mind boggling. It may be imperative to light the color of candle that represents your personal kau number, so that you do not forget to pick the children up at daycare!

Yellow

When the shar chi personality of the color yellow is being activated within your personality, or in the environment, you will feel a sense of relief that you do not have to perform, as the shar chi of this color is a nonconformist. The shar chi of the color yellow says that they don't really care what the right thing is, or if it ever gets done. This energy will take a law abiding citizen into a "who cares" attitude. The energy that will be resonating, when shar is present in the color yellow, is a high form of non-commitment.

The sheng chi of the color yellow strives to be as good as it can be, where the shar chi of the same color could care less. The typical teenage term, which represents the shar chi of this color is, "Whatever!"

If you begin to feel that your teenager may be right, you will want to light the color of candle which represents your personal kau number. Take care that you light your candle in the best direction which represents your personal kau number, as well.

I might add that you can, also, light a candle for your child, If your child's personal kau number is four, you will be lighting an orange candle in the North section of your home. The sheng chi must be activated, but it does not have to be your child that lights the candle, as we have studied intent in Volumes I and II of the Candle Lighting Encyclopedias.

Purple

In life, as well as in the universe, balance must exist in order for growth to continue. The sheng chi of the color purple is of high-mindedness and greatness. The shar chi of the same color can indicate an almost criminal behavior.

When your child, or even you, seem to be out of control, and you know that their, or your, heart is good, you will need to stimulate the sheng chi of the color purple. This will stimulate that much-needed sheng chi.

The direction that resonates with the color purple is Northwest. You will not be lighting a candle in this section of your home, as it is the "Heaven's Gate" section, so you will be lighting the candle that represents your personal kau number in the West direction, or section, of your home.

White

The sheng chi of the color white presents all that the world has to offer, and often more which we cannot even conceive. It is no wonder that, when the shar chi has engulfed this positive chi, that it leaves the person wondering if they have ever been sane.

The shar chi of the color white lends a feeling of dread, doom and hopelessness. This is not a feeling of depression, but that of questioning; questioning the fate of tomorrow, and the actions and behaviors of yesterday.

During this state of bewilderment, we have a tendency to make hasty and rash decisions that will have long-reaching consequences. Before you make these decisions, light the color of candle that represents your personal kau number, in the best direction that will be resonating with that color.

For instance, if your personal kau number is seven, the color candle that resonates with your kau number is white. The best direction, or section of your home, to light your white candle, will be Northwest so you will be lighting your white candle in the West section of your home as the West is your Northwest alternative.

Remember, you will be lighting the color of candle that represents your kau number, and you will be lighting the candle in the best direction that resonates with the color of your kau.

Indigo

The sheng chi of this color is universal truth. When shar chi from this color is resonating within your personality, or your environment, you will not see or understand the truth of this color.

When you are resonating with the Sha chi of the color indigo you can be argumentative toward people who may be trying to tell you the truth.

Have you ever tried to study a religious or new age subject and regardless of how close attention you paid or how many times you read over the material you just don't see the truth in the subject or retain what you have read. This is not that the subject is wrong, rather you are resonating with the Sha chi of the color indigo. This will leave you ill-equipped for your day to day activities, as this shar chi will permit you only to question yourself and others, distrusting everyone, including yourself.

It will be imperative for you to light the color candle that represents your kau number, in the best direction, as listed on the next page.

I f you are a female and your Kau number is 1, the color vibration that you will be resonating with will be the color blue. Your very best direction will be Southeast. The bagua on page 112 shows us that this Southeast direction represents "wealth and prosperity".

It would not be uncommon for you to be prosperous in this life. Lighting a blue candle in the Southeast section of your home, or in the Southeast section of the room that you most commonly occupy, will stimulate your prosperity.

The Southeast direction will, also, be the most auspicious direction for your success. With this in mind, when attending a luncheon or business meeting, sit facing your most auspicious direction. If this is not possible, you can sit in one of your other auspicious directions.

Do not be confused by resonating directions and the best directions. The direction that is resonating with your personal kau number is the direction that represents your kau number.

The "best" directions, listed on the chart below, will be the four directions, from the best to the fourth best, that you will be lighting your colored candles to activate. This will stimulate the sheng chi within your personality, as well as within your environment.

These four directions will, also, be used when making decisions as to job locations, and where to move if you are so inclined.

Best Colors and Directions for Females					
Color	**Kau**	Very Best	2nd Best	3rd Best	4th Best
Blue	1	Southeast	East	South	North
Green	3	South	North	Southeast	East
Orange	4	North	South	East	Southeast
Red	9	East	Southeast	North	South
Black	5	Southeast	Northwest	West	Northeast
Yellow	2	Northeast	West	Northwest	Southwest
Purple	6	West	Northeast	Southwest	Northwest
White	7	Northwest	Southwest	Northeast	West
Indigo	8	Southwest	Northwest	West	Northeast

This chart will give the four best directions for males, from the best to the fourth best. As men are typically the head of the household, you will want to make sure that the front door of your home faces one of your best directions.

When lighting candles to stimulate your sheng chi, you will need to light them in one of your auspicious directions. This will stimulate your personal chi, as well as the chi in your home.

It is virtually impossible to eliminate the shar chi, entirely and this is not something that you would want to do any way, as there must be a balance between both in order for harmony to exist. We would be serving ourselves well if we allowed the shar chi to live in our garage, storage room or in the closet, and not set up residence in our master bedroom or in the room that our prosperity section already occupies.

If you are a male, looking for a new career and your personal kau number is three, you will light one green candle and one blue candle in the South section of your home. The reason for this is that your kau number is three, and your candle color for this kau number is green. The direction on the bagua representing a career is North, and the color representing North is blue. Your best direction, listed on the chart below, is South. By lighting these candles in these directions, you are stimulating your personal sheng chi energy, the bagua career section through the blue, and you are lighting the candles in your most auspicious direction. *(do not confuse one exercise with another, all are designed to stimulate and to activate personal and environmental chi)*

Best Colors and Directions for Males					
Color	**Kau**	Very Best	2nd Best	3rd Best	4th Best
Blue	1	Southeast	East	South	North
Green	3	South	North	Southeast	East
Orange	4	North	South	East	Southeast
Red	9	East	Southeast	North	South
Black	5	Northeast	West	Northwest	Southwest
Yellow	2	Northeast	West	Northwest	Southwest
Purple	6	West	Northeast	Southwest	Northwest
White	7	Northwest	Southwest	Northeast	West
Indigo	8	Southwest	Northwest	West	Northeast

Kau Numbers and Auspicious Directions for Front Entryways

There are four main chi energies that we will be discussing here. These chi energies will be Sheng chi, Tien Yi, Nein Yen and Fu Wei. These chi energies will bring, depending on your kau number, an array of life experiences, with an underlying sense of gratification.

It was once believed that this chi energy and the descriptions of the kau number, in combination with the direction of the front entryway of your home, only affected the head of the household. I have seen, however, that this chi resonates through every member of the family, affecting each of them differently, depending on their own individual kau number.

Kau Number One

If your kau number is 1, and your front entryway is facing North, the chi energy resonating here is Fu Wei. This chi brings with it luck, in a diversified manner. There will be romantic and financial success. There will, also, be success with children and pets. One might think that pets, children and romance would not fit into the same category. Yet, with the Fu Wei, one never knows which luck is right around the corner.

To activate this luck, allowing the happiness and bliss to continue or emerge, light a blue candle in this North section of your home. Lighting this candle is advisable, as this energy, although not violent, is changeable, and is subject to taking away what it has already given you.

If your front entryway faces South, this Nein Yen chi will bring you many opportunities. This chi loves to be happy, and will encourage you to seek out fame and fortune through its assistance. You may wish to light a blue candle in this South section of your home, stimulating your many opportunities for life's advancements.

If your front entryway faces East, you will be experiencing the Tien Yi chi. This chi energy, combined with your kau number, brings happiness in love and career. If you are ill, then you have moved to the right place, as this chi promotes good health, and will assist you on your road to recovery. You may wish to light one blue candle in this East section of your home, so as to continue the activation of this chi, enabling good health and prosperity, to yourself, as well as other members of your family.

If your front door faces Southeast, you will experience the ecstasy of the Sheng chi. This is the ultimate chi combination for love, honor, integrity and success. There will be many happy unions, both in business and love. Your children will, also, excel in their endeavors. To activate, and to continue to reap the rewards that, this sheng chi has to offer, light one blue candle in this section of your home, thus continuing its exhilaration.

Kau Number Two

If your kau number is 2, and your front entryway is facing Southwest, you will experience happiness, but feel as if there is something missing. There is not. Your apprehension is due to the fact that you have never felt this type of success before, and perhaps feel undeserving. Accept this offer of good luck from the Fu Wei, as you are deserving. Light a yellow candle in this section to release your feeling that the other shoe is about to fall. You are secure.

If your front entryway is facing Northwest, you will experience a smooth and peaceful home life. This is the Nein Yen chi that will allow you, with this kau combination, peace of mind, as well as a successful business life. You should not light a candle or have an open flame in the Northwest section of your home as it is an extraordinary space, and is referred to as "Heaven's Gate". By lighting a candle or having an open flame in this section of your home, it is viewed as being disrespectful to the chi. The alternative direction for you to light your yellow candle will be in the West section of your home.

If your front entryway, and what I mean by front entryway is that your front door is facing West, you will be experiencing the Tien Yi chi. This chi promises, in conjunction with your kau number, extreme luck and satisfaction in your endeavors. You must, also, keep in mind that your home and person must be emanating chi, and not Sha or Shar chi, in order for you to experience this Tien Yi chi. As you activate the chi in your home, and stimulate the chi within yourself, you may light a yellow candle in this West section of your home, thus stimulating the Tien Yi chi to enter your home with its gifts and rewards for a good life.

If your front entryway is facing Northeast, you will be experiencing the Sheng Chi which is the almighty force of manifesting chi. This will be a situation where you may call your own shots for success. Your family luck will be good, and you will feel the luck change in your life upon moving into this home.

Continue to encourage the Sheng Chi in your home by lighting a yellow candle in this Northeast section of your home. This should be done as often, or as seldom, as you feel you wish to reactivate this chi.

Kau Number Three

If your personal kau number is 3, and your front entryway is facing East, you will be experiencing the luck of the Fu Wei. This luck is good, but often unpredictable. Love with in this home will be very good or very bad, as the Fu Wei has a tendency to show you balance through adversity. As this energy changes, and if you can ride the wave of its flow, you will ultimately be very happy. To stabilize the effects of its curve, you may light a green candle in the East section of your home.

If your front entryway faces Southeast, you will be experiencing the Nien Yen chi that promises you the ability to be in the right place at the right time. There is financial, as well as romantic, success resonating with this kau and directional combination. To continue to activate this Nien Yi chi, light a green candle in this section of your home. When lighting candles to stimulate the chi in your home, or to neutralize shar chi, your candles may be lit at any time.

If your front entryway faces North, you will be experiencing the Tien Yi chi. This chi energy will allow you a relationship that is steadfast. In this day and time, this is probably the best chi that you can have, enabling your relationships to survive these turbulent times. Any long-term relationship, whether romantic, family, friend or business-related, will encompass good days and bad days, and good years and bad years. This test in your endurance, and your ability to endure, will come from the Tien Yi chi.

This may not sound like good news, but in starting over, you will only change faces, not places, and you will go through the same thing with somebody else. Your ability to endure the hard times, as well your excitement through the good, will bring about ultimate success. To lessen the effects of any difficult periods, light a green candle in the North section of your home.

If your front entryway faces South, you will be basking in the Sheng chi energy. This is a blissful energy that will enable you to fulfill your hopes and dreams. There is, also, a tremendous amount of clarity that will escort this combination of kau and directional energy to success and financial security. To activate this energy, light a green candle in the South section of your home.

Kau Number Four

If your personal kau number is 4, and your front entryway faces Southeast, you will be living with the Fu Wei energy of luck, which, for you, will bring an innocent and playful lifestyle. Everybody would love to enjoy the childlike aspects in their adult life. This energy will enable you to enjoy your life, as well as be as serious as you need to be as you succeed in the business world. To continue the activation of the Fu Wei, light an orange candle in the Southeast section of your home.

If your front entryway faces East, you will have the company of the Nien Yen energy. This unrelieved and sovereign, flowing energy will smooth out your feelings of uncertainty, as well as release your daily anxiety before you enter your home, thus enabling you to relax stress-free. To preserve this life of rest and relaxation in your home, light an orange candle in this East section of your home.

If your front entryway is facing South, you will feel the Tien Yi energy that will ensure you good health and a good income. This will be a home of prosperity for you. The children will be well-respected, and your ability to provide a positive influence will prevail. To continue to stimulate this direction, and your Tien Yi energy, light an orange candle in this South section of your home.

If your front entry is in the North section of your home, you will be in the company of the Sheng chi that will lend to you creativity in your ability to network yourself, or your business, stimulating your communication skills. There is a immense amount of creative energy that will be present in this home, through your personal kau number. If you had not been communicative in the past, this home will enable you to climb rungs to the top of the ladder of success with ease. To continue the stimulation or activation of the sheng chi, light an orange candle in the North section of your home.

Kau Number Five

There is no kau number 5. If your kau calculation is five, and you are a male, you will use the kau number 2. If you are a female, and your kau calculation is five, you will use the kau number 8. All of the charts and tables in this book have been written to reflect these differences.

Kau Number 6

If your personal kau number is 6, and your front entry is facing Northwest, you will be experiencing the Fu Wei energy. In this direction, with this particular kau number, this energy will still produce luck, but it may be a little harder to come by. Your children will push your buttons and pull your strings, but nothing harsher than that. You may feel that you have to prove yourself, but this aspect of your personality will be an illusion. You are accepted, and it is only feelings of the past, that seem to invade your psyche from time to time, that suppress your disposition. Light a purple candle in the West section of your home to stimulate this Fu Wei, and your luck will improve and your children will behave.

If your front entryway is facing Southwest, you will be experiencing the auspicious Nien Yen, which will give you the feeling that all is right with the world. Major issues will appear as insignificant inconveniences. It will not be that you have a naive attitude, rather that you will know your limits and remain steadfast to your own day-to-day issues. Peace of mind, through this lifestyle, will be easy to attain. Light a purple candle in this Southwest section of your home, so that you will continue to be untainted by the harsh realities of the world outside.

If your front door is facing Northeast, you will be surrounded by the Tien Yi chi energy which will bring you good luck and a happy marriage. Relationships, and romantic, business and casual acquaintances, will be fulfilling and prosperous for you.

With this combination of kau number and the front entry placement, you will succeed in your endeavors, as well as feel luck in every aspect of your life. Remember, you must stimulate this chi energy in order for it to flow freely, and not to be engulfed by the shar chi. To stimulate the Tien Yi chi, light a purple candle in the Northeast section of your home.

If your front entryway faces West, you will be experiencing the ever-powerful Sheng chi. This energy has the ability to move mountains. This kau direction combination is an Aladdin's lamp position. The emphasis will be placed on good health in this home, but prosperity, happiness and success are not far down the list of possible life aspects to accomplish. To maintain your good health, success and prosperity, as well as all other lucky circumstances that this Sheng chi has to offer, light a purple candle in this West section of your home.

Kau Number 7

If your personal kau number is 7, and your front entryway faces West, you will be experiencing the luck of the children firsthand. If you have experienced problems with your children in other homes in which you have lived, those problems are over here. This Fu Wei will bring you luck and prosperity to love and care for your family, and to see to it that your children are happy, and live a full and productive life.

This luck energy is precarious, and will allow you to see the ups and downs of parenting. However, the ups will be higher, and the downs will never be as far down, as they have been in the past. Light a white candle in this West section of your home to continue the stimulation and activation of this Fu Wei energy.

In the event that your front door faces Northeast, you will be enjoying the Nien Yen chi, which will bestow upon you the harmony of which you are in search. This energy is the luck of which fairy tales are made, as when Cinderella finds the handsome prince. If a relationship is something for which you are looking, or if your desire is to live somewhere that your present relationship will be secure, this is the place! Light a purple candle in the Northeast section of this home, and the luck of the Nien Yen will continue to safeguard your home.

If your front entryway faces Southwest, you will be entertaining the energy of Tien Yi. This chi energy is blissful, and brings with it many blessings of success, happiness and an astonishing relationship between you and your family, as well as your extended family. Light a purple candle in this Southwest section of your home, so that the bliss of this chi will continue to flow through your home.

If the front entryway of your home faces Northwest, you will be feeling the Sheng chi that will enhance every aspect of your life. Career success will be enhanced through your ability to place yourself in a situation of prosperity and stability. Health, with this combination of kau number and directional placement, will improve over other homes in which you have lived, thus giving you, once again, the vitality which you desire to live a complete and fruitful life.

You will not want to light a candle in the Northwest section of your home, as we have discussed previously. Therefore, this candle should be lit in the Southwest section. Do not be confused. This candle will not activate the Tien Yi energy that was previously mentioned. That would only happen if your front door was in the Southwest section. You will be stimulating the Sheng Chi, as dictated by the placement of your front door.

Kau Number Eight

If your personal kau number is 8, and your front entryway faces Northeast, you will be experiencing the Fu Wei chi. This energy will bring you good luck by diverting the bad luck that is lurking outside in the world, away from your home. You will undergo a transformation of happiness by living in this home. The energy will be high and low, but the luck will remain, and the home will be happy. To stimulate the Fu Wei in this home, light an indigo-colored candle in this Northeast section of your home. The color indigo is a very, very dark blue.

If your front entryway faces West, there will be career changes during your life in this home. These changes will be better than you could have ever anticipated. There is success waiting for you here, and a secure sense of good health. To stimulate the Nien Yen energy in this section, you will want to light an indigo-colored candle in this West section.

If the front entryway of your home is facing Northwest, you will be experiencing the Tien Yi chi. You will experience exuberant luck within your close, personal relationships. There will, also, be luck, honor and pride between you and any children living in the home.

To stimulate this Tien Yi, light an indigo-colored candle in the West section of your home. This alternative is to honor the "Heaven's Gate" energy in this Northwest direction.

In the event that your front door faces Southwest, you will enjoy the Sheng Chi that you will be experiencing during the time that you live in this home. The energy is warm, safe and inviting. You must safeguard that others do not move in with you, as the house is inviting others to come.

The positive and powerful energy resonating in this home, as per your personal kau number and this direction, will allow you to experience exhilaration in your home-life, and with your family. Light one indigo-colored candle to stimulate this sheng chi, enabling you to continue to feel the excitement that this home has to offer.

Kau Number Nine

If your personal kau number is 9, and your front entryway faces South, you will experience respect from your subordinates, as well as your peers. Others will look up to you for guidance and assistance. You will give good advice, as you keep your emotional distance.

Light one red candle in this South section of your home, as the Fu Wei energy is contingent on its ability to be stimulated and activated. This is the only chi that thrives for attention. For this reason, its luck may be tenuous.

If your front entryway faces North, you will experience a good home life, with good health. You may wish to stimulate this Nien Yi often, as it is insuring your good health, and our environment does not offer the best conditions to maintain a strong constitution. Light one red candle in this North section of your home, insuring the activation of the Nien Yi.

If your front entryway faces Southeast, you will be encountering the exhilaration that only Tien Yen can offer. There is promise with this kau and directional combination that you do not want to pass up.

If your choice is between purchasing this entry door placement, and any other, unless the other includes an East entry, then this will be the best for you. Love, happiness, good health and a financially secure career are what this energy has to offer. Light a red candle in this Southeast section, and you will feel the success that this hope has to offer you.

If your front entryway is facing East, this is the home for you. There is no better placement for your personal kau number. Your ability to manifest your dreams and aspirations, while living in this home, will astound you. To continue this Sheng chi activation in your home, light a red candle in the East section of your home.

Dragon of Fortune will only bestow the pearl of prosperity to those who are worthy of its prosperity. But this dragon will help any one in need.

W hen lighting candles and being aware of your most inauspicious directions, you can see in the chart below the directions of which you will need to stay clear. These are the directions that, if you use them for anything important, or for extended periods of time, your Kau energy will be weakened.

If your personal Kau vibration color is yellow, then your Kau number is two. Your kau number color will be a source of power for you. When you are in a situation where you will be spending an inordinate amount of time in an inauspicious direction, you will need to light the color of candle stimulating your personal sheng chi before you leave. If you must spend time in an inauspicious living situation, place your resonating color prominently in the room, or in your inauspicious direction. By doing this, you will be stimulating your personal sheng chi, even though the section of the home is not an auspicious direction for you personally.

Everyone will have four directions that will "work for them" and four directions that will "not work for them". The directions that will not work for you will be the directions listed in the chart below. It is not wise, if at all possible, to place your master suite in an inauspicious section or direction of your home. The same applies if you have a *choice* between working in a building that is in an auspicious direction for you and a building that is not, than your choice should be simple - work in the one that is.

			Worst Colors and Directions for Females		
Color	**Kau**	4th worse	3rd worst	2nd worst	very worst
Blue	1	West	Northeast	Northwest	Southwest
Green	3	Southwest	Northwest	Northeast	West
Orange	4	Northwest	Southwest	West	Northeast
Red	9	Northeast	West	Southwest	Northwest
Black	5	South	North	East	Southeast
Yellow	2	East	Southeast	South	North
Purple	6	Southeast	East	North	South
White	7	North	South	Southeast	East
Indigo	8	South	North	East	Southeast

The same implications apply to men as they do women, when dealing with the inauspicious directions. When you are contemplating a move, or if your front door faces one of your worst inauspicious directions, the chi energy will cause you discomfort.

Kau Number One

If your kau number is 1, and your front door faces Southwest, this will lead to quarrels, misunderstandings, lawsuits and grave unhappiness. To lessen the effects of this inauspicious direction, light a blue candle in your most favorable direction, which is Southeast.

If your entry faces Northwest, you will experience bad luck and feeling of being a failure. You will need to light a blue candle in your second best Lo Shu direction, and that will be East.

If your front entry faces Northeast, there will be betrayal in your working and personal relationships. To lessen the effects of this bad luck, light a blue candle in your third best direction, as per the chart on page 181, which puts your third best direction as South.

If your front entry faces West, that is your fourth worst direction, and you will experience lost opportunities through your inability to pay attention to your surroundings, as well as to detail. You will need to light a blue candle in your fourth best direction, which is North

Worst Colors and Directions for Males					
Color	**Kau**	4th worst	3rd worst	2nd worst	Very worst
Red	1	West	Northeast	Northwest	Southwest
Yellow	3	Southwest	Northwest	Northeast	West
Green	4	Northwest	Southwest	West	Northeast
White	9	Northeast	West	Southwest	Northwest
Blue	5	East	Southeast	South	North
Orange	2	East	Southeast	South	North
Indigo	6	Southeast	East	North	South
Purple	7	North	South	Southeast	East
Black	8	South	North	East	Southeast

In the event that your front entry faces North, and your personal kau number is 2, this direction could lead to quarrels, grave unhappiness and lawsuits. You may wish to light a yellow candle in your best Lo Shu direction, to lessen the effects of this shar chi energy. Your best Lo Shu direction will be Northeast.

If your front door faces South, the energy of this home will be confusion, anxiety and a feeling that the walls are caving in on you. This is often the reason for professional burnout. You may wish to light a yellow candle in your second best, Lo Shu, direction to lessen the effects of this oppressive shar chi. This Lo Shu direction, listed on your chart on page 181, is West.

If your front entry is facing Southeast, you may have feelings of paranoia, that someone is trying to take your job from you, break into your home, or at the very least, that someone is stalking you. You will need to light a yellow candle in the West section of your home. The reason for this is that you should never light candles in the Northwest section of your home, so your alternative direction is West.

If your front entry is facing East, this energy will solicit feelings of being dishonored by your family, especially your children, and that they have aspirations for you to leave the home altogether. To lessen the effects of this chi, you will need to light a yellow candle in your fourth-best direction, which is Southwest. Once this is done, you will, again, feel the love from your family, especially your children.

Kau Number Three

If your personal kau number is 3, and your front entry to your home is in the West, the chi emanating from this direction will cause you extreme duress, as anything that can go wrong will go wrong. Appointments will be missed, and promises will be broken. In this event, you will want to light a green candle in your best Lo Shu direction, which will be in the South direction, or section, of your home.

If your front entry is facing Northeast, you will suffer from hard-to-diagnose illnesses. There will be emotional problems living with this entry direction, which stress will exacerbate. If you are living under these conditions, you will need to light a green candle in the North section of your home.

If your entryway is in the Northwest section of your home, or facing this Northwest direction, you will experience a profound sense of loss. Loved ones may become ill. You will want to light a green candle in the Southeast section of your home.

If your front entry is in the Southwest direction, this chi will bring to you a feeling of desperation about financial situations. There may, also, be a loss of income. When these feelings are predominant over your normal concerns, you may want to light a green candle in the East section of your home.

Kau Number Four

If your personal kau number is 4. and your front entry door is facing Northeast, you will experience communication problems that could land you in court. There may be financial problems from the past that come back to haunt you. You may wish to light an orange candle in the Southeast section of your home, when these issues begin to surface, to lessen their effects, and for your protection.

If your front entry way is in the West, you will experience problems with your children, or younger children, that cause confusion or confrontations with others that you respect. Light one orange candle in the East section of your home to eliminate, or to lessen, the effects of this chi.

If your front entry is facing the Southwest direction, you will feel an overwhelming sense of betrayal, be it real or imaginary. There will be a sensation of forlornness, or feelings of loss. You will want to light an orange candle, allowing you a clear sense of what is really happening around you in the South direction of your home.

If your front entryway is Northwest, you may experience lost possibilities for advancement in the workplace. You may wish to light an orange candle, in the North section of your home, when you know that there is a promotion coming your way, so that you will not be passed over for the position.

Kau Number Five

There is no kau number 5. If you are a male, and your kau calculation is 5 ,you will use the kau number 2. If you are female, and your kau calculation is 5, you will use the kau number 8. Charts in this book, that do show the kau number 5, are done so for simplicity, but have been calculated to reflect the kau number 2 for men and 8 for women.

If your personal kau number is 6, and the front entry of your home is in the South, you may experience one accident after another. Things that you thought could not break will break. The titanic would sink with this combination. You may wish to light a purple candle in the West section of your home, so that the effects of this chi will be lessened.

If your front entryway is in the North section of your home, you may go through deep bouts of doubt about your career, and your ability to maintain your livelihood. A normally strong person will experience self-doubt with this combination. You may wish to lessen these feelings, when they occur, by lighting a purple candle in the Northeast section of your home.

If the front entryway of your home is in the East, you may experience problems with your health, as well as a retention problem. To stimulate your health, mentally and physically, you might want to light a purple candle in the Southwest section of your home.

If your front door is in the Southeast section of your home, the chi will stimulate uncertainties within your home and family. You will experience feeling as if you cannot do what you had thought that you could. The self-doubt here will leave you questioning every aspect of your life, making rash decisions based out of fear, instead of logic. You may want to light a purple candle, so the effects of this uncertainty will be lessened. This candle should be lit in the West section of your home, as the West direction is the chi alternative for Northwest, when lighting candles.

Kau Number Seven

If your personal kau number is 7. and your front entryway is facing East, you will experience communication problems, as well as control issues, that you have never had in any other home with the same members of your family. This chi will bring out the dictator in you, compelling you to disregard the feelings and thoughts of those whom you care about. To eliminate this shar chi, you may wish to light a white candle in the West section of your home. This will, also, assist you in pulling your family back together.

If your front door is facing Southeast, you may feel that your home is oppressive, confining and suppressive. This will leave you with the feeling that you are paying for nothing, as your home will not bring you the comfort and peace of mind for which you had hoped when you purchased it. You may wish to light a white candle in the Southwest section of your home, so that you might enjoy this, as they say, single most important investment in life.

If your front entry faces South, you may experience countless acts of misfortune. A common saying for this combination is, "A day late and a dollar short", or just plain, "being at the wrong place at the wrong time." To avoid these mishaps, you may wish to light a white candle during those times that you feel your luck has passed you by. This candle should be lit in the Northeast section of your home.

If your front entry is in the North section of your home, there will be problems with your relationship. When these problems arise, it will be important to remember that you loved each other deeply, at one time. Light a white candle in the West section of your home, so that the relationship does not have to end in a dreaded divorce.

Kau Number Eight

If your personal kau number is 8, and your front entry is in the Southeast, you may experience uncertainties, as well as go through an inordinate amount of changes, personally, while living in this home. If you are not one for change, you may wish to light a indigo-colored candle in the Southwest section of your home, so that when changes occur, you will go through them with ease, or if your intent is not to have change, that energy will manifest. The color indigo is a very, very dark blue.

If your front entryway is in the East, you may experience difficult problems with family members, that seem endless. There are, also, health problems and possible periods of being unfaithful. To avoid these and other relating problems, light an indigo-colored candle in the Southwest section of your home. When your front entryway is in the East section of your home, this chi energy will bring you health issues for everyone in the family. (When everyone gets sick at the same time, check for things such as gas leaks or spoiled food). To avoid these health issues, light the indigo-colored candle in the Northeast section of your home.

If your front entry is in the North section of your home, the chi in the home has become stagnant. You must stimulate your sheng chi, so that you will be bringing life back into the house. Light an indigo-colored candle in the West section of the house.

If your front entryway is facing South, your feelings about your home will be tenuous. You will feel in a constant state of, perhaps, readiness, as if you have in the back of your mind that you need to move or that you do not feel welcome in your own home.

To feel safe and secure, light an indigo-colored candle in the Northeast section of your home, when these feelings begin to invade your thoughts.

Kau Number Nine

If you're personal kau number is 9, and your front entry faces Northwest, shortly upon moving into this home ,you will begin to hear from others that your temper and aggressive tendencies are out of control, if anyone dare to tell you. You may, also, feel as if your world is getting smaller, as long-time friends will begin to distance themselves from you. You may even think everything is just fine and under control. Light one red candle in the East section of your home, and the veil that you have had over your perception of your life will be lifted, and life can begin to get back to normal. When you feel friends moving away again, you may wish to redo this exercise.

If your front entry way faces Southwest, there will be feelings of discontentment, that your life is going nowhere. There may be health issues, but a diagnosis will be hard to get. You may light one red candle in the Southeast section of your home, to lessen the effects of this chi and kau commination.

If your front door faces West, you will experience problems with your family. Parents may become ill, and your children will become disobedient, rebellious and unruly. Ex-family members will begin to place guilt and blame on you, to ease their own feelings of inadequacy, but you will be chastised nonetheless. You may light a red candle in the North section of your home, when you begin to feel this chi sneaking up on you.

When your front door faces Northeast, there will be legal problems and health issues, with you and other members of your family. These health issues could take years to detect, and even longer to treat. When legal issues begin to intrude, or when health issues begin to become unmanageable, light a red candle in the South section of your home. This will keep this chi at bay!

An important word of advice! If your front door faces an inauspicious direction and you do not wish to light candles, but are experiencing these house symptoms, take a picture of your front entry and place the picture in one of your more auspicious directions.

I had mentioned briefly the notion that Chi follows generations, and that chi is the life-sustaining breath of the dragon. Now, you may not care about whether the dragon could breathe, but would you if you thought you were the dragon?

As mentioned, there is chi and there is shar chi, but there is also personal chi and shar chi, and environmental chi and shar chi. This concept has been echoed throughout generations, yet the exact interpretation has been unclear.

Some examples of these sayings are, "You are what you eat", "Show me five of your closest friends, and I will show you who you are", and "You can tell by the outside of a persons home the conditions of the inside, as the outside reflects the personality of the family inside." When we talk of balance and something being clutter-free, this brings to mind another common saying, "If you don't go within, then you will go without!"

Environmental chi refers to the conditions of your home, where personal chi speaks of conditions of the body, your personal attitude and health. One might wonder how and if genetics are effected here with the personal chi. We all know that, regardless of whether two children are born to the same parents or not, the body conditions, as well as the demeanor and personality of each child, will be different.

The luck of the children section of your home, as we know, is vitally important to the wellbeing of a child. This, also, shows the importance of maintaining this section of your home, regardless as to the age and disposition of your children. Even if your children are grown and have moved away from your home, this section will still apply to them. This is a classic example of how chi follows generations, and how this chi trickles up, and how it trickles down, from one generation to another. Thus, the balance of environmental chi and personal chi will be imperative.

There is a natural order within the universe. There is a balance within nature. Why should there not be a balance within human behavior and the disposition of families? The earth does not disregard a tree that has fallen, so why would the chi discontinue to flow to your children just because they have moved away from home?

It is true that, once your children set up their own homes, they will have a health section of their own, but the luck of the children section in your home will still apply to them. This can be your saving grace for your children, if they do not maintain good chi in their homes.

Environmental chi, as mentioned, refers to the conditions of your home, the outside of the house and the community in which you live. Now, you might be saying that you have no control over what your neighbor does, and that his yard is disgusting, but at this point I beg to differ with you.

How many times have you gone out to cut your grass, only to find the entire neighborhood soon to follow? How many times have you put on a new roof, and then noticed other homes in the neighborhood getting new roofs of their own? The reason for this is that chi moves. When you clean your yard, the chi will stimulate others to do the same. A good way to look at the energy of chi is to think of chi as good luck. We all believe in good luck, and we all want it. People say if they do something good for somebody, then they will have good luck. This is the same as stimulating the chi, and having that luck come back to you.

The same applies to shar chi. If you do nothing and do not put forth effort, the shar chi will bring you bad luck, agitation and poor health. This is just the opposite of the chi luck, which will promote good health and happiness.

The same applies when we speak of stimulating the chi in our homes by keeping it clean, organized and clutter-free. Everything in life has its own space, and if you have too much clutter in your home, you have too much stuff. If it serves no purpose, and is collecting dust, you may need to find a better home for the stuff.

The same applies to things that you have in your home that are broken. If it does not work, get it fixed. Your broken toaster my very well be representing an organ in your body, that may not be functioning properly either. A simple remedy on your road to good health is to clean up, balance the elements in your home and stimulate positive chi and good luck, enabling you good health. This is environmental chi, and it must be balanced with your personal chi.

We used the luck of the children section as our example, so let's take that example one step further. The west section of your home is "the luck of your children." West is the direction of your children's luck! Look at, for example, the South section in your home. South represents fame, recognition and popularity. Now, standing in the South section, look to the West. What is there? Is this direction in the room clean and free from clutter, because your child's health may depend on it? This is not a good place to put the kitty litter.

The health issues in the South section are problems with the eyes, heart and circulatory problems. Chi is luck, and chi promotes good health.

If your child is sick, and you and your doctors can not determine the cause, look in the West direction in each section of your home. Look to see from where the shar chi coming. When you find the problem, you will, also, find the cause of your child's illness.

Your candle is environmental chi, and by lighting the candle, you will be stimulating your personal chi. By lighting the candle at the time which represents the child's birth time, as well as the health conditions, relief will soon follow.

If you cannot, for some justification, clean an area, thereby eliminating the shar chi, so that the chi or sheng chi will flow, you will need to light the candle to represent this section of your home. This will begin to stimulate the chi, so that this chi will give you the health or the energy that you need to rid yourself of the shar chi.

If for any reason you are physically challenged and cannot stimulate the chi for yourself, you can have somebody light your candles in the West section of your home, as this will be the alternative for the Northwest section which is the direction of helpful people. As mentioned this is the section that resonates with those helpful people in your life. If you have a need, stimulate this section and the help will follow, as the chi will go out and get you what you desire.

The energy between candle lighting and feng shui is symmetry. Equal in balance and proportion, creating balance and harmony within the universe, as well as within our homes, hearts and body, will bring you the success in this life of which that you have been dreaming.

The dragon of Ambitions symbolizes success and achievement

For years, people have lit candles, giving no thought or reason to the different color of candles that they were lighting. Often, people who would light candles did so when they were depressed, or when they had company for dinner. They gave no thought to the time of the day, or even the date, when they lit their candles. When the candles were lit at the wrong time, or if the wrong color of candle was lit, the energy that was produced would solicit shar chi, and not the positive, uplifting chi that they might have hoped.

When a person is in a good, positive mood, they change things around to promote positive Feng Shui, or chi energy. When they are depressed, some people tend to move things around to reflect their mood. This is why, when people get depressed, argue and quarrel with others in the home, it is hard to break the cycle of aggression. They have destroyed the chi, giving way to shar chi. By doing so, this shar chi will continue to reek havoc until they change the energy, again, to assist the flow of chi.

Feng Shui and Candle Lighting are both very complex. We will be breaking both down in easy terms and simple applications, so that it will be simple to understand. Both applications use a basic premise, which is that energy moves. Color emanates energy, time solicits energy, the directions promote the existence of energy and the elements are energy.

There are five elements that will represent the productive and destructive cycles of all living things. There will never be an ending that does not signal a rebirth of something new. Understanding this cycle of life will give you a greater understanding of how life functions, and how the cosmic breath of the dragon, or Chi, will implore positive changes in your life. It will, also, aid in your understanding of how Shar Chi will melt optimism. As this melting of optimism happens, you will develop poor health and a destructive, pessimistic outlook on life.

The five elements are: fire, water, wood, metal, and earth (there is also varying degrees of wood, metal and earth). Each element will complement another element, as well as destroy an element. Each element will complement another color, as well as destroy another color. When the elements are not balanced, this can and will effect your mood, attitude and your health. The specific issues or ailments affecting your health will depend on what element is out of balance.

The easy reference guide will help you determine which section references which life experience, and which element.

Element / Season		Color	Direction	Produces	Destroys	Parts of the body
Fire	Summer	Red Purple	South	Earth	Metal	Eyes & Heart
Water	Winter	Black Blue	North	Wood	Fire	Ears, Blood Kidney
Wood	Spring	Green	East Southeast	Fire	Earth	Feet, Buttocks Throat, Thighs
Metal	Autumn	White Silver Gold	West Northwest	Water	Wood	Mouth, Chest Lungs, Head
Earth Third month of each season		Brown Yellow Tan	Southwest Northeast	Metal	Water	Hands, Fingers Abdomen, Stomach

The directions emanated by the elements are explicit, and should be taken very seriously when lighting candles and promoting the positive chi energy. Each direction will represent an aspect of life experiences.

As we place each element in the direction in which it emanates, we will, also, place the life experience which that element represents. Each section will be placed over the floor plan of your house, so that you can see how each room is emanating a different life experience.

The North direction represents your "career". What is in the North section of your home? Is it your living room? Is it a bathroom, or your kitchen? These will be important factors of which you will need to take note, as we discover our home using Feng Shui and Candle Lighting.

The next direction is Northeast, which will represent the section that dictates the energy of "education". Your true potential as well as your ability to retain and use the intellect that you have obtained will be represented in this Northeast section. This section in your home will also represent the intellect and the ability for the other members of your household to learn.

The East direction in your home will be the section representing your "health and family". This is the direction that prevails over your health and happiness, and the health and happiness of your family.

The next direction is Southeast. This is the direction which emanates, and represents, the "wealth and prosperity" in your life.

South represents "recognition and fame". This will not be a good placement for a storage closet or bathroom, if you are building a new home.

The next direction is Southwest. This will be the energy of your marriage (relationships) and happiness.

Following the compass around, the next direction will be West, which is "the luck of your children". This is the positive chi that will follow your children when you are not there to protect them.

The last direction is Northwest, and the life experience is "helpful people". These are those people in your life to whom you can look up, and who help you through your life experiences.

When using the floor plan of your home, evenly divide it into nine sections, with the center being neutral. Place the life experiences in each direction which it represents. You now have a perfect delineation of what your home is representing, and which rooms are emanating which element, and what life experiences.

As you divide your home into the nine equal sections, unless your home is perfectly square, you will experience missing sections. The missing sections will affect the life experiences that the missing section would represent. Let's use the Southwest corner for our example.

The Southwest section, as mentioned, represents the aspects of marriage and happiness, as well as your ability to attract a relationship, and your ability to maintain that relationship. When this section is missing or incomplete, it will be apparent, as the relationships, and your ability to be happy in relationships, will be compromised.

It is not necessary for you to move out of your home, if you aspire toward a relationship. There are simpler things that you can do to close in the section, as well as other parts of your home that you will be able to activate, in order to attract or keep a relationship, or simply to be happy.

Often times, when this section is missing, one may experience problems with their hands, wrist, and complained of having arthritis and an increase in weight around the thighs. There may, also, be a swelling and stiffness in the your hands and or fingers.

I had a client that seemed to be relatively happy without a long-term relationship. When she wanted a date, she would light a pink candle during the time of the new moon. She knew that the color pink represented passion, and that during the time of the new moon was a good time to attract someone that was new, and from whom she would experience passion.

She would attract a relationship, and then soon after, she would tire of them, ending the relationship even before it had time to grow. She said that she derived more pleasure spending her time wandering through jewelry stores. She had more rings and bracelets than anyone I have ever known.

While working with her, I found that her home had a missing section, which was in the Southwest corner of her house. Knowing what the missing section represented, I asked her about her apparent jewelry fetish. She related that, shortly after she moved into the house, she noticed that her taste in jewelry had changed and that no matter what she liked at the store when she got it home she didn't care for the piece any more rather than taking it back, she just kept buying more. It was clear that the problems with her taste was due to the missing section, and that it was time to fill it in. She could go broke, by never fining anything to fill the emptiness that she was experiencing from the missing section in her home.

The element that was emanating here was big earth, and we knew that this element produces metal, thus her jewelry fetish. In order to balance the elements that are missing, we were going to place a statue made of metal and that is brown in color in the area of the missing section. The color brown would represent the element of big earth thus a balance of the elements. Her over compensation was due to the lack of the big earth element which represented this section of her home.

By doing this, we would be adding the big earth and strengthening it by bringing in the metal element, as the metal element was also weak in the section of the room that she did have. The first thing that we needed to do was to determine where to place the statue, so that the room would appear to be complete or closed in. Measurements needed to be taken.

The first measurement was going to be from the far-left corner of the house out into the yard. Second, we measured from the far-right corner of the house to meet the same point in the yard as the far-left point. This will be the apex in which we will place our brown, metal statue. The statue will be 16 inches tall, as that height will represent the Pun energy, which emanates happiness and abundance. In Feng Shui Candle Lighting, each 2 inches represent a yang or yin energy corresponding to life issues.

This section that we have just filled in will stimulate by virtue of the statue the elements representing the missing section. You will from time to time need to reactivate the energy that you have created within the missing section so that the chi will continue to flow not only within this Southwest section of your home but within you personally. Lighting the right color of candle at the right time will do this activation for you.

We have divided the house into nine equal sections, and determined that the Southwest corner of the house represented the energy of marriage and happiness. Now, we will subdivide each section, again, into nine equal sections, so that we will be lighting our candles in the right place at the right time, and using the appropriate color to solicit our heart's desire, as well as to continue to activate our missing section.

You will notice that, within each section, you have a Southwest corner. Now that you have closed in the section of marriage and happiness in your home, you can use the Southwest corner of the other sections to activate your once-missing section. By doing this, you will be activating the energy and chi flow in your once-missing section, as well as giving detail to the relationship which you are attracting, and the happiness for which you are looking.

For example, if you light a candle to strengthen your marriage and your ability to be happy in the Southwest corner of your career section, the candle would be lit in the Southwest corner of your North section. By doing this, you will be attracting someone who not only has a career, but possibly someone that you meet through your own career. The North section, also, represents the element of water. Perhaps you will be attracting someone who was born under the astrological sign of Pisces, Cancer or Scorpio, since all three are water signs.

The North section, also, resonates with the second son and middle aged men. This is a good section to activate if this, again, is something which you might wish to attract, as you stimulate your marriage section. This is not to say that, if you are male, that you will, by using this section to activate the relationship section that is missing in your home, be attracting a male. You may be a middle aged male, and will be stimulating your own desires for a new relationship.

With this same concept in mind, it should not surprise you, when lighting a candle in the Southwest corner of your "education" section, which would be the Southwest corner of your Northeast section, that someone that you teach helps you find a relationship. Alternatively, they may do something that really makes you happy, sending you down that road to a successful relationship. Either is a strong possibility.

The balance of each element is very important. Equally as important is the activation of each section of your home, so that the chi will be enhanced, stimulating peace, harmony, luck and success. When activating the chi, you must light the right color candle, in the right place, and it must be lit at the right time. This is in order to successfully activate the flow of chi by stimulating the balance between the elements.

Using the example in attracting a relationship, lets look at the elements that are involved. The Southwest corner is represented by big earth. The color being emanated by this element is brown. We will be lighting a brown candle.

Using our chart, we see that the Northwest section is big metal. The time which represents big metal is from 9:00 PM – 12:00 PM. So, we will be lighting a brown candle which will represent the big earth element which will produce the big metal balance between the hours of 9:00 PM – 12:00 PM (your time).

The flame on the candle will represent the fire element. The liquid wax will represent the water element. And when lighting a candle in, or representing, the Southwest section, use a metal candlestick, which will again stimulate the big metal element.   As we do this exercise, we are stimulating the positive flow of chi, thus soliciting our dreams, good health, luck and success.

South/Element Fire	12:00 PM – 3:00 PM	Terracotta
North/Element Water	12:00 AM – 3:00 AM	Wood
East/Element Big Wood	6:00 AM – 9:00 AM	Red Glass
West/Element Small Metal	6:00 PM – 9:00 PM	Crystal
Southeast/ Element Small Wood	9:00 AM – 12:00 PM	Red Glass
Southwest/Element Big Earth	3:00 PM – 6:00 PM	Metal
Northeast/Element Small Earth	3:00 AM – 6:00 AM	Metal
Northwest/Element Big Metal	9:00 PM – 12:00 PM	Crystal

The North direction represents the water element the season represented here is winter.

If your personal Kau number is the number 1., this is the direction that you would be resonating with. (Resonating and vibrating are the same terms within this book.)

If you use candlestick holders you will be using ones that are made of the wood element.

This is the location of the Kan energy, which represents the middle son.

Some of the parts of the body as well as health aspects that we have discussed represented by this direction will be the stomach kidneys, ears, and blood.

You may think that if you do not have a career by spending all of your time, at a dead-end job. To stimulate the career energy light the color of candles listed to the left to the kau numbers under the "career chart". You will be lighting them during the times listed on the same chart.

Yet there are many other ways other than your career that this section applies.

The North direction is one of victory and honor. When you are in a situation that is very important to you, if you approach that situation from the North, you will regardless of the situation win!

If you stimulate your Fu Wei direction you will have the motivation that you need to put your career status into perspective so that you might achieve the success in this life that you had wished for.

If your personal kau number is one, North is also the direction of your personal Fu Wei.

If your kau number is eight then your Fu Wei direction is Northeast (see that chart on page 34). Thus by activating the chi in the Southwest direction and section of your home you will have the energy and the motivation that you need to obtain that career that you had hoped for getting yourself out of the dead-end job.

With the combination of the two directions (North and Northeast) in mind it would not be inconceivable if your main excuse or reason for not having the career that you want would be because of a nervous stomach.

Kau Number	Time	Color of Candles
1	12:00 AM – 3:00 AM 12:00 AM – 12:45 AM	One brown & One blue
2	12:00 AM – 3:00 AM 3:00 PM - 3:45 PM	One brown & One pink
3	12:00AM – 3:00 AM 6:00 AM – 6:45 AM	One brown & One green
4	12:00AM – 3:00 AM 9:00 AM – 9:45 AM	One brown & One blue
6	12:00AM – 3:00 AM 6:00 PM – 6:45 PM	One brown & One white
7	12:00AM – 3:00 AM 6:00 PM – 6:45 PM	One brown & One silver
8	12:00AM – 3:00 AM 3:00 AM – 3:45 AM	One brown & One yellow
9	12:00AM – 3:00 AM 12:00PM – 12:45 PM	One brown & One red

As the stomach is one of the primary organs resonating on the same vibrational level as the section or direction of Northeast which is your Fu Wei energy (as per your #8. Kau number). If this nervous stomach excuse were to actually happen this would be a strong indication that there is sha chi in the Northeast direction of your home.

By stimulating the chi in the North and the Northeast sections of your home you will have the motivation needed to succeed.

If your personal kau number is three your Fu Wei direction is East. Use the chart on page 34 to determine your career Fu Wei direction as you stimulate this North direction.

Even though this section is dictating the conditions of your career there are also health issues represented here.

The parts of the body that we have discussed represented by this direction are the kidneys, ears, and blood.

Kidney infection and dysfunction, loss or problems with your hearing as well as infections in the blood or problems with your immune system are associated with this section. These conditions are caused by sha chi. To lessen or to eliminate any of these issues or problems from your life you will need to stimulate the chi in the North section of your home.

Southwest Timing Guide

The Southwest direction represents the big earth element there is not a season represented here although the Southwest direction does represent the third month of each season.

If your personal Kau number is the number 2., this is the direction that you would be resonating with.

The Southwest direction is one of the directions that make up the West group.

If you use candlestick holders when lighting your candles you will be using the ones that are made of the metal element, when lighting candles to stimulate the chi in the Southwest section of your home.

This is the location of the Kun energy, which represents the mother or wife.

A few of the parts of the body that we have discussed represented by this direction are the hands and feet.

When looking for a relationship if your Kau number is 8, the Southwest direction is where you should go to find the person of your dreams, or at the very least someone that you would have a good relationship with. The reason for this is because if your personal kau number is eight then this is your best Lo Shu direction.

The Southwest direction is representative of marriage and happiness. When there is a problem with your relationship you will need to check this directional section in your home to insure that it is neat and orderly. Once this has been done, light your candles using your timing guide to stimulate the relationship, activating the chi in this room sending newly invigorating energy into your relationship.

The Southwest direction is traditionally referenced as the marriage and relationship section but it is also the direction and section in your home that resonates on the same vibrational level as creativity.

Your ability to be creative, to paint, draw, write, or to be creative with your imagination is in this direction. This is also the section of intuitive abilities as well extrasensory perception, clairvoyant and precognizant abilities which when stimulated resonate in this direction or section of your home. This is the section that you might wish to place a room where you can meditate without interruption.

Kau Number	Time	Color of Candles
1	3:00 PM – 6:00 PM 12:00 PM – 12:45 PM	One pink & One yellow
2	3:00 PM – 6:00 PM 6:00 PM – 6:45 PM	One pink & One white
3	3:00 PM – 6:00 PM 9:00 AM – 9:45 AM	One pink & One blue
4	3:00 PM – 6:00 PM 6:00 AM – 6:45 AM	One pink & One green
6	3:00 PM – 6:00 PM 3:00 PM – 3:45 PM	One pink & One silver
7	3:00 PM – 6:00 PM 3:00 AM – 3:45 AM	One pink & One brown
8	3:00 PM – 6:00 PM 6:00 PM – 6:45 AM	One pink & One white
9	3:00 PM – 6:00 PM 12:00 AM – 12:45 AM	One pink & One blue

You will also want to place pictures representing lovers, families or other paintings that represent relationships on these walls.

This section represents the wife and or mother as both energies represent the female principal of love and the ability to nurture. This might stand to reason as who do you think might have the most health related issues in their lives other than women who spend a great deal of their waking moments worrying about the home, children and their relationships?

When this section of the home has been activated you will not have the anxiety connected with motherhood that has pledged women for centuries. Other health issues that will arise by having sha chi in this section may be health issues such as kidney stones and other kidney related disorders. Colon and bowel problems may also be represented in this Southwest section of your home. There may also be a few blood disorders that may arise if there is not a balance between the sha and sheng chi in this section of your home.

Stimulating the chi in this section and lighting your candles will give you a new lease on your physical and emotional health.

The East direction represents the big wood element. This easterly direction along with the southeasterly direction represents the season of spring.

If your personal Kau number is the number 3., this is the direction that you will be resonating with personally.

This easterly direction is one of the directions that make up the East group.

If you use candlestick holders you will be using ones that are made of red glass which lends to the power of this direction as well as the effectiveness of the candles that you have lit.

This is the location of the Chen energy, which represents the youngest son and youthful people.

This energy is stimulating and motivating. When your goal is to motivate your children you will want to activate this section of your home. If you have a child that has a problem being a self-starter, is hard to motivate, or perhaps lazy, send the child in an easterly direction to find a job.

The energy or life influencing aspect that is resonating in this easterly direction is that of your health and family.

The health issues that are functioning in this section if the presence of sheng chi is missing will be problems with your feet and neck. Now I know that these two body parts are not connected but as the vibration of chi flows through the body both the feet and the throat will be vibrating on the same level of vibration thus the resonating energy between the two will be the same.

This will be a space in your home that you will need to embrace with special care insuring that it is free of excess sha chi. This is your health and family section. When lighting your candles as per your personal kau number you will be stimulating the chi thus eliminating the presence of sha chi. As the sha chi will create health problems for yourself as well as with in all of your family members.

This is the reason that once a family member is ill that the whole family will catch what ever is going around. If for instance you light your candles for the ailing family member as soon as they become ill the infection or disease that they have will not spread throughout the entire family. If you're personal kau number is eight, you will need to light a blue candle

Kau Number	Time	Color of Candles
1	6:00 AM – 9:00 AM 6:00 AM – 6:45 AM	One blue One blue
2	6:00 AM – 9:00 AM 6:00 PM – 6:45 PM	One blue & One yellow
3	6:00 AM – 9:00 AM 12:00 AM – 12:45 AM	One blue & One green
4	6:00 AM – 9:00 AM 12:00 PM – 12:45 PM	One blue & One blue
6	6:00 AM – 9:00 AM 3:00 AM – 3:45 AM	One blue & One yellow
7	6:00 AM – 9:00 AM 3:00 PM – 3:45 PM	One blue & One white
8	6:00 AM – 9:00 AM 6:00 PM – 6:45 PM	One blue & One brown
9	6:00 AM – 9:00 AM 9:00 AM – 9:45 AM	One blue & One purple

between the hours of 6:00 AM and 9:00 AM, and a brown candle between the hours of 6:00 PM and 6:45 PM. By doing so you will be inciting the power of chi promoting good health within yourself and your family.

When lighting candles to stimulate the health of a family member light the color of candles during the time frames that represent the personal kau number of the ailing person.

It is very important that you keep this East section in your home clean and free from confusion.

If you are looking for a new family care physician and your personal kau number is three you will see on page 140 that the best direction to look will be North. If your personal kau number is two then you will need to look in the West direction for a new doctor. Use the chart on 140 to determine the best direction to stimulate or to go for health care, or assistance in health care issues. For specific health issues refer to the health listings on pages 202-209, you must eliminate sha chi from these directions which may be causing your particular ailments.

The Northeast direction represents the small earth element. This Northeast direction along with the Southwest direction represents the third month of each season.

If your personal Kau number is the number 8., this is the direction that you would be resonating with.

This Northeast direction is one of the directions that make up the West group.

If you use candlestick holders you will be using one that is made of metal as earth produces metal.

This is the location of the Ken energy, which represents the youngest son as well as youthful people.

The parts of the body mostly predominate in this section are your finger and your hands.

The influencing life aspect functioning in this northeasterly direction is that of education. Now your early childhood education unless you are still living in the same home is not what we are talking about. Rather, we will be discussing your ability now, to learn and to retain the knowledge that you are currently obtaining. This is the section of your home that you may wish to place your child's' study or even a home office.

Each section in your home as well as each direction has consequences and corresponding health issues that resonate with the directional energy. These health obstacles will not manifest if there is sheng chi radiating within the individual sections. Health issues are a direct result of sha chi in a directional section where the elements are not balanced. Some of the health issues connected with this direction will be problems with your hands and fingers including problems such as Carpal Tunnel Syndrome and arthritis. Frequently health issues in this section are difficult to recognize and miss-diagnosed.

People with a personal kau number of one, three, nine or four who use computers are more likely to develop wrist problems if there is sha chi in this easterly direction than would people with a personal kau number of two, six, seven or eight. For those people who do develop a problem with their wrist from prolonged keyboard use, wrist pads will work. But the better solution would be to stimulate the chi in this section of your home or office so that the

Kau Number	Time	Color of Candles
1	3:00 AM – 6:00 AM 12:00 AM – 12:45 AM	One yellow & One blue
2	3:00 AM – 6:00 AM 3:00 PM – 3:45 PM	One yellow & One brown
3	3:00 AM – 6:00 AM 6:00 AM – 6:45 AM	One yellow & One green
4	3:00 AM – 6:00 AM 9:00 AM – 9:45 AM	One yellow & One blue
6	3:00 AM – 6:00 AM 6:00 PM – 6:45 PM	One yellow & One white
7	3:00 AM – 6:00 AM 6:00 PM – 6:45 PM	One yellow & One silver
8	3:00 AM – 6:00 AM 3:00 AM – 3:45 AM	One yellow One yellow
9	3:00 AM – 6:00 AM 12:00 PM – 12:45 PM	One yellow & One red

problem will not occur in the first place. In the event that you already suffer from this plight – stimulating this chi will lessen its effects.

There are numerous solutions that you can use to stimulate the chi in this section. Keeping this portion of your home clean and organized will stimulate the sheng chi. You do not have to keep this or any other section immaculate but there is a certain semblance of order that you must maintain. Another cure or solution depending on the amount of room that you have in this Northeast direction, is that you should arrange your furniture so that none of the corners on your table's point directly toward you as you sit to relax or watch television. If the room that occupies this direction is a bedroom you should never have a mirror facing the bed. As well never place your headboard up against a window. And never position your bed so that your feet point to the exit door. And never ever sleep on a bed that has a mirror over it, your health will depend on it.

To eliminate sha chi in this section of your home or office, light the specific color of candle during the times schedule above as per your personal kau number to insure good health, your intellect, your ability to retain what you have learned and a positive chi flow.

The Southeast direction represents the small wood element. This Southeast direction, also, represents the season of spring.

If your personal Kau number is the number 4., this is the direction that you will be resonating with. This Southeast direction is one of the directions that make up the East group.

If you use a candlestick holder, when lighting these candles you will be using one that is made of red glass. The red glass (or crystal) will represent the fire element, as wood produces fire. This is the location of the Sun trigram energy, which represents the eldest daughter.

The parts of the body most predominate in this section are the thighs and buttocks. These are just two body parts associated with this trigram, as it also, represents common viruses, such as colds and flu.

When utilizing the Lo Shu directions, this section exemplifies the life aspects of wealth and prosperity. However, if your personal kau number were one, your wealth and prosperity section as per the chart on page 146, would also be this Southeast direction, thus, multiplying the positive and powerful effects of this Fu Wei energy. If your personal kau number is two, then your wealth and prosperity section will be in the Northeast section, this is very positive but not as powerful as the kau number one with the double influence. To determine your personal wealth and prosperity section or directions, as it pertains to you personally, through your kau number, see the chart on page 146, and light your candles during the times listed on the Wealth and Prosperity chart on page 216.

Just as we have discussed co existing vibrational cycles, there is one, main Lo Shu giving you the traditional directions of life aspects, and the directions in which this particular energy vibrates. As well, these aspects and directions are, also, personal to each kau number, giving different directions but they will still resonate with the traditional Southeast direction on the Lo Shu for wealth and prosperity.

When stimulating the chi in this Southeast direction, you will be stimulating the chi for wealth and prosperity. If your personal kau number is three, and your personal wealth and prosperity direction is South, you will be lighting your candles in the South section of your home.

As the Feng Shui masters believe that each person, depending on their gender and date of birth, have four auspicious, and four inauspicious, directions. If your personal kau number were one then this Southeast direction would also be your most auspicious direction.

Kau Number	Time	Color of Candles
1	9:00 AM – 12:00 PM 9:00 AM – 9:45 AM	One green One green
2	9:00 AM – 12:00 PM 3:00 AM – 3:45 AM	One green & One brown
3	9:00 AM – 12:00 PM 12:00 PM – 12:45 PM	One green & One purple
4	9:00 AM – 12:00 PM 12:00 AM – 12:45 AM	One green & One blue
6	9:00 AM – 12:00 PM 6:00 PM – 6:45 PM	One green & One white
7	9:00 AM – 12:00 PM 6:00 PM – 6:45 PM	One green & One silver
8	9:00 AM – 12:00 PM 3:00 PM – 3:45 PM	One green & One yellow
9	9:00 AM – 12:00 PM 6:00 AM – 6:45 AM	One green & One blue

When stimulating the Southeast direction, you will be activating the chi for wealth and prosperity. When you activate the chi in your personal kau direction, to activate your Fu Wei luck energy, you will have the necessary energy to obtain these riches.

Yet, without the incentive and motivation through your chosen career, you will not, perhaps, obtain the goals and objectives for which you had hoped.

By lighting your candles to stimulate this particular aspect of your life you will have the drive and motivation that it takes to succeed. By activating both sections, stimulating the trigram energy of Sun and your personal Fu Wei, you will have fulfilled the correct formula for success.

If you are stimulating the Sun energy to promote good health, you will be lighting the candles in the Southeast section of your home. But only light them between the first time listed and not the second. The second time listed will stimulate the life experience – the first time listed will stimulate the health issues resonating within the Southeast direction.

South Timing Guide

The South direction represents the fire element. The season represented here is summer. Isn't it ironic that everyone thinks about going South for the summer? We inherently know feng shui candle lighting but have just now allowed this informational energy to surface for the new millennium.

If your personal Kau number is the number 3., this is the very best direction for you. If you use candlestick holders, you will be using ones that are made of an earthen element, such as terracotta or ceramic.

This is the location of the LI energy that represents the middle daughter. The parts of the body and health aspects, that we have discussed as being represented by this direction, are the eyes, heart and circulatory system.

One simple definition here is that this section is how you appear to the public at large, the world, your family, friends and neighbors. How, everybody, in some way or another, cares about these people, who exist on the fringes of there life. If you did not care, they would not be in your life. You might not think that the gas station attendant could play an important roll in your life. Yet, every time you buy gas, you must go somewhere, and there is a reason, other than for the gas, that you do. It is because of the way that you are treated when you are there. You may need gas every time that you pull into the station, but if you were treated poorly, you, regardless of the price or your need for the gas, would discontinue going to that particular station.

Another example is, if your children were too young for a career, but spent their time in school or day care. Whether or not your children are accepted, or mistreated, would be determined by this direction. This is the direction that affects everybody who lives in the home, even though it especially affects the head of the household.

When lighting candles to activate and stimulate this aspect of your life, the chart will offer you the colors of candles to light, and the times in which they will need to be lit, in order for the activation to take place. When you light your candles at the right time, and in the proper sections in your home, you will be activating these aspects of your life, as well as stimulating the positive chi in your home, lending to the popularity, fame and recognition that you are looking for. You will, also, find peace of mind. Even though this section is dictating the conditions of your popularity, recognition and fame, there are, also, health issues represented here; conditions relating to your eyes, heart, circulatory system.

Kau Number	Time	Color of Candles
1	12:00 PM – 3:00 PM 9:00 AM – 9:45 AM	One orange & One blue
2	12:00 PM – 3:00 PM 3:00 AM – 3:45 AM	One orange & One brown
3	12:00 PM – 3:00 PM 12:00 PM – 12:45 PM	One orange & One red
4	12:00 PM – 3:00 PM 12:00 AM – 12:45 AM	One orange & One blue
6	12:00 PM – 3:00 PM 6:00 PM – 6:45 PM	One orange & One white
7	12:00 PM – 3:00 PM 6:00 PM – 6:45 PM	One orange & One silver
8	12:00 PM – 3:00 PM 3:00 PM – 3:45 PM	One orange and One yellow
9	12:00 PM – 3:00 PM 6:00 AM – 6:45 AM	One orange & One purple

This will include such things as: near- and far-sightedness, astigmatism, glaucoma, blindness, coronary deterioration and other conditions concerning the eyes and heart. (see page 224 for a more complete listing)
One of the biggest health issues, I might add, that is represented in this section, is congestive heart failure or aorta dysfunction. When stimulating this section, you will be lessening the effects of these illnesses as well as promoting your fame and recognition. This is not to say that, if you have a genetic weakness in one of these areas, they will not surface any way, only that you will be lessening the effects by using proper feng shui candle lighting. Feng shui candle lighting should never be used to replace medical treatment. You should never light a candle instead of taking a medication that your physician says will save your life. Feng shui candle lighting should be used in conjunction with medical treatment, not instead of it.

To strengthen your fame and recognition light your candles between the time of the new moon and the next full moon. To lessen the effects of negative criticism or health issues you will light your candles after the full moon and before the next new moon.

T he West direction represents the small metal element. The season is autumn, or fall.

If your personal Kau number is the number 7., this is the direction your psyche – subconscious or the essence of your being will be resonating with. The west direction is one of the directions that make up the West group.

If you use a candlestick holder, you will be using one that are made of crystal, which will stimulate the energy of sheng chi in this direction. This is the location of the Tui energy, which represents young women and the youngest daughter.

The parts of the body, that we have discussed being represented by this direction, are the mouth, teeth and chest. We all know that our children's luck, or even the luck of any innocent child, is very important. His or her ability to learn, to grow, and to be a healthy, happy, productive little human is, from time to time, on the forefront of everybody's mind.

Healthy, productive children cannot grow without influence. This section of your home sends, to his or her little psyche, the influence which you have placed there. If there is a mess, and shar chi, functioning in this section, the message that the children are receiving is that bad is good. I would think that this is not the message that you are trying to send. When there is a mess or shar chi in this section, the children are left vulnerable in and away from home. When you stimulate the chi in this section of your home, the chi will then send a message that bad is not good, and protect the children from harm or ill-will.

Hyperactivity is a common problem among young children, now more than ever. One thing that you may wish to consider is, "It's not their fault". Children do not enjoy being hyper, anymore than you enjoy being in their company when they are jumping, screaming and bouncing on the furniture. A common architectural design in the 70's through the 90's is to have big, or at the very least open, spaces, with the kitchen on the left side of the home, visible from the front entrance. Also, on the left or west side, or section, of the home, is the garage and, or laundry room. There can be no comfort for a child with this design of home. If you can see your kitchen upon entering the home, this lends to quarrels and arguments. These arguments are not exclusive to the children.

Kau Number	Time	Color of Candles
1	6:00 PM – 9:00 PM 9:00 AM – 9:45 AM	One white & One yellow
2	6:00 PM – 9:00 PM 3:00 AM – 3:45 AM	One white One white
3	6:00 PM – 9:00 PM 12:00 PM – 12:45 PM	One white & One blue
4	6:00 PM – 9:00 PM 12:00 AM – 12:45 AM	One white & One green
6	6:00 PM – 9:00 PM 6:00 PM – 6:45 PM	One white & One silver
7	6:00 PM – 9:00 PM 6:00 PM – 6:45 PM	One white & One silver
8	6:00 PM – 9:00 PM 3:00 PM – 3:45 PM	One white and One pink
9	6:00 PM – 9:00 PM 6:00 AM – 6:45 AM	One white & One blue

As the parents quarrel, the children are put on guard for this aggression to be taken out on them. This is commonly referred to as displaced aggression. Your child has no choice but to kick the dog or pull the cats tail. Place a room divider so that the stove is not visible from the entrance of the home.

This will take care of one problem. Take pride in the appearance of your garage or laundry room, as both are a common place for shar chi, and both have heavy equipment that is intimidating to a child's psyche.

Also, it is not uncommon for a child who is hyperactive to have soft teeth, thus needing attention. Stress is a cause for poor gums and teeth. As well, chest pain is often stimulated out of stress. Shar chi is stress.

If your child's room is in this section and there is an inordinate amount of Sha chi, your child, will take this energy to school causing disruption in the class – disruption issues that you will be forced to deal with. You can avoid these problems by stimulating the chi in the West section.

Northwest Timing Guide
DO NOT light Candles in this Section of your Home

The Northwest direction represents the big metal element. There is not a season represented here. Although, like the Southwest, this direction represents the third month of each season.

If your personal Kau number is the number 6., this is the direction that you will be resonating with. The Northwest direction is one of the directions that make up the West group.

It is vital that you never light a candle in the Northwest section of your home or office. On your chart for helpful people (page 150), there will be a list of directions as per your particular kau number that you will use to light your candles, to stimulate the chi for your helpful people section.

This is the location of the Chien energy, which represents the father or husband. A few parts of the body that are represented by this direction are the head and lungs.

The Northwest section of the home, or the Northwest direction in general, represents the life aspect of helpful people. It is also revered as a sanctified space. Now, a helpful person does not just apply to the man that maintains your yard, or the person who cleans your home. Helpful people, in this regard, also represent the family members that have since departed. As well those people who have left a legacy of insight and knowledge for us to follow. Such as: Albert Einstein, Auguste Renoir, William Wordsworth, Abraham Lincoln, Helen Keller, Sir Walter Scott and people in our history from which you have benefited by virtue of their skills, talents and insights as this leadership continues to live.

How many times have you pondered over issues or situations, and all of a sudden, the solution appears out of nowhere? I am not suggesting that the spirit of a long-departed relative or master has just impressed upon your mind the answer to anything, but these things have been know to happen and this is a sanctified space.

How many times have you thought, "I would love to go on vacation, alone, with my spouse," as by taking the children would be cost prohibitive, when, all of a sudden, the phone rings, it's the grandparents, wanting the children for the week, or even overnight? These things happen. Call it luck, call it magic or call it sheng chi. What ever you call it, when the chi is flowing freely and uninhibited in this direction or section in your home, we must call it positive.

Light your candles in the directional sections below   # Helpful People

Kau Number	Time	Color of Candles
1 **Southeast**	9:00 PM – 12:00 AM 9:00 AM – 9:45 AM	One purple & One Yellow
2 **Northeast**	9:00 PM – 12:00 AM 3:00 AM – 3:45 AM	One purple & One white
3 **South**	9:00 PM – 12:00 AM 12:00 PM – 12:45 PM	One purple & One blue
4 **North**	9:00 PM – 12:00 AM 12:00 AM – 12:45 AM	One purple & One green
6 **West**	9:00 PM – 12:00 AM 6:00 PM – 6:45 AM	One purple & One silver
7 **West**	9:00 PM – 12:00 AM 6:00 PM – 6:45 AM	One purple & One brown
8 **Southwest**	9:00 PM – 12:00 AM 3:00 PM – 3:45 PM	One purple & One white
9 **East**	9:00 PM – 12:00 AM 6:00 AM – 6:45 AM	One purple & One blue

If your personal kau number is 9., to stimulate the sheng chi in this section of your home, to activate the luck of the ancients or helpful people in your life, you will need to light one purple candle between the hours of 9:00 PM and 12:00 AM., between the time of the new moon and before the next full moon. Then, you will need to follow up by lighting one blue candle between the time of 6:00 AM and 6:45 AM. This candle should be lit within 24 hours of lighting the first candle. This will activate the sheng chi in your home. When there is positive chi in your home and within yourself, the benefits will radiate throughout the entire family, benefiting everyone who lives in your home. Chi is contagious. When you stimulate the chi within yourself, it will, in turn, help to stimulate the desire for others to do the same. The health issues in this direction, if there is shar chi, are those relating to your head and lungs, as well as an asunder of other issues listed on page 229. It is common for people with shar chi in this section to suffer such illness as: migraines, dizziness and neuralgia. There is, as well, a host of lung infections. Pleurisy and pneumonia are just two infections that are the most common. It would be to your benefit to always stimulate this healthy chi into your life.

Here are a few aliments and organs that will be in concert with the directions. The body as a whole must be in harmony with the elements of nature. Aliments in the body are a direct result of an imbalance within these same elements and sha chi in the direction sections in your home and in your yard. If there is a huge pile of trash on the West side of your home this will effect your health.

When determining your personal or progressed birth-chi energy you will also need to know which health conditions will be resonating in these sections of your life. When your progressed birth-chi is Yi -Nien Yen the direction that this energy will be resonating will be the Northwest section and in the West corner of that Northwest section.

When lighting candles to rid yourself of these health issues, you will need to light your candle between the time of the full moon and until the time of the next new moon. Light the color of candle that represents the direction that has incited this health issue for you. You will also be lighting this candle in that direction section of your home. By doing so this will once again summons the sheng chi to your home and eliminate the sha chi which has incited the health problem.

North
_____

Alimentary canals
Asthma
Bladders, urinal
Blood, serum
Blood diseases
Breast
Bronchitis
Cancer
Catarrhs of the stomach
Chest cavity
Caught
Diaphragm
Digestion
Digestion organs
Digestion, juices (problems)
Ears
Elbows
Eliminative system

Esophagus
Gall bladder
Gas (stomach)
Gastric juices
Gastric catarrh
Gastritis
Gastronomy
Heartburn
Hiccups
Hypochondria
Indigestion
Liver (upper lobes)
Lungs (lower lobes)
Nausea
Organs digestive
Ovaries
Pancreas
Peristalsis
Reproductive system
Ribs (lower)
Serous membranes
Serous discharge
Stomach disorders
Teeth
Thorax
Thoracic duct
Tumors
Ulcers
Uterus

South

Bones
Bone disease
Bones broken
Bruses
Cancer (melanoma)
Caughts due to colds
Connective tissue
Curculationaly system
Cutaneous disorders
Cuticles
Depression
Eczema
Eyes
Gallstones

Hair
Heart (lower)
Hysteria
Infantile paralysis
Itching
Joints
Knees
Kneecaps
Nerves
Old age
Polio
Rashes
Rheumatism
Rheumatic disease
Scabies
Sclerosis
Skeleton
Skin
Shin diseases
Spleen
Yeast infections

_____ **East**

Adrenaline
Baldness
Blemishes
Brain
Brain disease
Buttocks
Cerebral congestion
Cerebral hemorrhages
Cerebrospinal nervous system
Cerebrum
Coma
Convulsions
Cuts
Diseases inflammatory
Diseases violent
Dizziness
Earaches
Epilepsy
Eye afflictions
Face
Feet (top)
Fevers

225

Forehead
Gums (upper)
Head
Headaches
Heat exhaustion
Inflammations
Insomnia
Iris (eye)
Jaw (upper)
Lip (upper)
Measles
Mouth
Mumps
Neck front
Nerves (optic)
Neuralgia
Nose
Nosebleeds
Operations
Ringworm
Scalp
Skull
Sleeplessness
Smallpox
Teeth (upper)
Temperament
Thighs
Toothaches
Vertigo

West

Adrenal glands
Back lower section
Balance
Chest
Compromise
Diabetes
Ductless glands
Eczema
Equilibrium
Generative organs
Hypogastrium
Kidneys (upper)
Lumbago
Lumbar region
Mouth

Ovaries
Ovarian problems
Renal disorders
Renal stones
Spine lumbar region
Upper teeth
Uremia (toxic blood)
Uremia headache
Uremia coma
Uremia convulsions
Urethra abscesses
Uric Acid
Vagina
Vasomotor system
Veins

<u>   **Northeast**</u>

Abscess (throat and neck)
Angina Aphonic
Apoplexy
Bronchial consumption
Bronchiole (goiter)
Carpal tunnel syndrome
Collapse
Constipation
Croup
Defluxions of rheum
Diphtheria
Epistaxis (nose)
Fingers
Fluxes of rheum (throat)
Esophagus (upper)
Eustachian tubes
Glandular swelling (neck)
Goiter
Gout
Gums (lower)
Heart trouble
Hoarseness (larynx)
Jaw (lower)
Larynx
Laryngitis
Lip (lower)
Melancholy
Neck
Nose bleed

Pains neck, throat, nap of the neck
Obesity
Occipital region
Oral ducts
Palates
Parotids
Pharynx pharyngitits
Poisoning
Polypus
Rheum
Rheumatism scrofula
Septic poisoning
Strangulation
Suffocation
Syphilis
Thyroid gland
Tongue
Tonsillitis
Toothache
Ulcerated throat
Uvula
Vertebrae cervical
Vocal cords
Voice
Wens on the neck

Northwest

Acute fevers
Anemia
Angina pectoris
Apoplexy arterio-sclerosis
Back (upper half and sides)
Baldness
Blood disorders
Blood poisoning
Compassion
Conjunctivitis
Convulsions
Cutaneous affections
Dorsal
Dizziness
Fainting spells
Effusion of blood
Feverish ailments
Forearms
Headaches

Heat exhaustion
Hardening of the arteries
Hydraemia
Hyperemia
Inflammations inflammatory diseases
Nerves middle dorsal
Locomotor ataxia
Lungs (upper)
Meningitis
Mitral disorders
Mitral valve prolapse
Palpitations
Pleurisy
Pneumonia
Ribs (pain)
Spinal (problems)
Spinal cord
Spinal fluid
Spinal marrow
Spinal meningitis
Spine dorsal region
Spleen
Sun stroke
Vertebrae dorsal
Wrist

Southeast

Anaemia ankles, disease in fractures
Ailments of the legs
Blood circulation
Body fluids
Body fluids distribution
Caisson disease
Calves of the legs
Cramps
Colds
Ether
Fractures ankles, shins
Freewill
Hay fever
Heart dropsy
Heart irregularities in heart beat
Legs
Lymph
Lymphatic system

Lymphatic system ailments
Nervous disorders uncommon
Nervous disorders acute
Spasmodic Diseases
Sprains
Super-sensitiveness
Swelling legs, ankles feet
Varicose veins

_____ **Southwest**

Adenoids
Adrenal glands
Anus
Appendicitis
Bile
Bladders urinal
Blood red corpuscles
Blood red hemoglobin
Bow legs
Bowels
Bubo
Calculus caries
Catamenial disorders
Colon
Diphtheria
Elimination origins of elimination
Elimination of urine through bladder
Endocrine system
Epilepsy
Excretory system
Enlarge Prostate
Genital disorders
Gonorrhea
Groin
Hemorrhoids
Iliac regions of the body
Kidney stones
Kidney gravel
Kidney trouble
Kidney diseases
Kidney (lower)
Menses irregularities
Menstruation
Nasal bone nasal catarrh
Pelvis

As I began, I touched briefly on my curious mind. I had always wanted to know as much as I could about everything that I had come in contact. I had studied Psychology, Theology, Law, the Justice System and a number of new age and scientific studies intensely. I hold degrees or certificates in most. All of these studies, taking years, of course, to complete, held more questions for me than answers, even upon completion.

I have recently come to the conclusion that hindsight is, as we all have suspected, 20/20, and it's not the thought, the theory or the concept that matters, but more, it is the result. It doesn't matter about the journey, but rather the destination. Now, I know that this is not the belief that some of you observe, so let me demonstrate my inference.

When dealing with concepts, I have found that the rules may change. When understanding the basis of a belief system, as time progresses, the doctrine may, also, change. When dealing with mental health, the diagnoses will change as society changes, or conversely, cannot accept its findings. We all know that the laws will change, sometimes as fast and as furious as the next election.

There are but a few things in this world that will never change, and it will be those things that, when observed understood and then implemented by society, then and only then, will lend to an unmolested civilization which will provide a safe, non-threatening and conducive place to raise our children, and to live ourselves. When I say that it is not the journey, but the result, I am saying that it is not the end result, or the satisfaction that we might take with us from this life, but rather the satisfaction or the result that we feel at the end of each and every day!

Did you do everything that you wanted to do today? Do you feel a sense of gratification in your life? When you lay your head on your pillow at the completion of another day, is there a sense of love, peace of mind and anticipation for another day, or are your feeling more a sense of disappointment, anxiety or confusion that you could have done more or that there are so many loose ends in your life?

Another important question that you should ask yourself is, "How much of your day did you spend on yourself, your issues and matters that pertain to you, and how much of your day did you spend tormented by the actions or behaviors of others"?

I am not talking about time you spent with thoughts of endearment or making plans, but how much time did you spend thinking, contemplating or wishing that so-and-so would just listen, shape-up or see that what they are doing will not work?

These types of judgments, intruding thoughts or judicious reasoning take valuable time away from your life, and away from your day. These intrusive thoughts fill your life with shar chi, the energy that we spent 200 plus pages to comprehend, and furthermore, how, to the best of our ability lessen the effects of, in our lives.

That brings me back to my point of end-results. When you spend your time, life or energy trying to live to reason with somebody other than you, you will be wasting valuable time, and even more precious energy. If you want, or feel, the need to guide and direct somebody, even your children, if you do not do it through reason, influence or by example, your efforts will be in vain.

Thus, your anxiety, or shar chi energy, will engulf you with sickness and confusion. You will become obsessed with the position of this energy.

This has been my point exactly! Life, your thoughts, opinions and beliefs, are energy. The same shar chi and sheng chi, and even Fu Wei, energy that has been described in this book.

Energy cannot be destroyed. The elements in their natural state cannot be destroyed. Energy cannot be reasoned with. You cannot influence good energy to be bad, and you cannot pursued bad energy to be good.

Only through Feng Shui Candle Lighting may you change your environment so that the "good" energy will prevail. Only through Feng Shui Candle Lighting can you insure that your children will be safe, with the least amount of physical effort, and that you will succeed in this life with the end result being good every day.

I believe that, if a person lived in a home with the perfect Feng Shui, and lit their candles accordingly, they would be wise beyond their innate ability, and live successfully and happily forever!

Ti Lung is said to bring to you prosperity, health and wisdom.

Question: *Tina under the section of Life Aspects the Lucky Chi you have several it looks like different categories and then the chart showing the direction that represents the category, such as, love, career, and health. Well, on the charts for career, education and health with my kau number of 3, it says that the direction is east for all three categories. Is this right? And how can the same direction represent all three different categories?*

Answer: One of the chi energies that should be present in the East section for you is Fu Wei chi. This chi when activated will enhance your abilities to learn and retain i.e., education and career. The third category which is also being represented in the East with a kau number of three is the health section which is where you will be activating the Tien Yi chi for better health.

It is not only possible but probable that more than one form of chi will be functioning in a direction or section of your home at one time. This would be the same as if you had a kau number of 3 and your child had a kau number of 4. The East direction will have Fu Wei chi, Tien Yi chi and possibility Sheng chi or Sha chi where the same direction may have Nien Yi chi stimulating your child's relationships in this same Easterly direction of the home.

Question: *I just read the other question and wonder how does the chi know where it belongs. Is the chi mine or does it belong to my spouse?*

Answer: If you have read the Candle Lighting Encyclopedia volume II you know that the body is basically a four pole magnate and that there are essentially seven mini batteries which are referred to as chakras. That the body is comprised of energy. This is a mild way of saying we are energy and that chi is energy which means if we do not mix semantics we as humans are also a form of chi energy. And that we are what we project and what we create. This is why it is equally important that your personal chi and your environmental chi is balanced. Your chi will not be someone else's chi the same way you will not become them and that they will not become you. Your home is an extension of yourself, thus if you want to maintain a balance within yourself, you must also maintain that balance within your home and your environment.

The world has been dancing around assertions, we are not humans having a spiritual experience in this life. We are spirits having human experiences in this life. The differences between you as a person and you as energy is that you as a person can reason and have a personality, your energy or chi does not have a personality and cannot reason.

Question: *I am a little confused, is the Lo Shu and the Bagua the same thing? And my daughters kau number is 8 where do I light the candles if I want to send her luck.*

Answer: There is a difference between the Lo Shu and the Bauga.

The Lo Shu is the magic square of corresponding kau number vibrational energies, dividing the kau numbers or personalities into two distinct groups of people. Representing also chi and sha chi balance within the universe. Where the bagua is the corresponding chi vibrations as it pertains to life expressions and conditions, with corresponding kau vibrational sheng chi and Sha chi influences.

When you look at the charts on pages 133 –151 it says for example that if your kau number is 8 the direction for "luck of children" is Southwest.

On the bagua the Southwest section represents marriage and happiness.

When lighting candles to assist and to activate the sheng chi of the "luck of children" you will need to stimulate or activate the Southwest direction or corner of the room that occupies the "luck of the children" section of your home.

So this candle will be lit in the Southwest corner of the West section.

This will also help when sitting up a child's room. Regardless of which bagua section your child's room is in, you will want to match their kau number to their individual education directing in their room.

So if the child's kau number is 3 the education direction is East - so by placing their desk in the East corner of the child's room you will be enhancing their educational vibrational energies or sheng chi. You will need to position the desk so that your child will be facing East.

Question: *You showed a chart that had the worst Lo Shu directions for men and women but not one that showed the best Lo shu directions. Is there one or what is the best way to find out which of the Lo Shu directions I should use? If you need it my Kau number it's 2 and my husbands Kau number is 3. What are our best directions?*

Answer: To find the best directions as per your kau number you will be using the Lo Shu on page 32. For a simpler view I have made a chart for you on the next page, titled Best Compass directions for your Kau number.

Best Compass directions for your Kau number.

Kau Number	Very Best Direction	Second Best Direction	Third Best Direction	Forth Best Direction
1	Southeast	East	South	North
2	Northeast	West	Northwest	Southwest
3	South	North	Southeast	East
4	North	South	East	Southeast
6	West	Northeast	Southwest	Northwest
7	Northwest	Southwest	Northwest	West
8	Southwest	Northwest	West	Northeast
9	East	Southeast	North	South

Question: *You did a chart so it was easy to see the kau numbers that were the best for our kau number but you didn't make one for the worst kau numbers for us. Can you put one in the book so I will have it so I don't have to use the Lo Shu to figure it out myself?*

Answer: Well, I guess I can. Thanks for asking. One simple rule to remembers is: if you are in the East group which are kau numbers one, three, four and nine you will be compatible with your own group and incompatible with the kau numbers or people that are in the West group, or those who have a kau number of two, six, seven and eight.

Kau Number	4th Worst Ho Hai	3rd Worst Wu Kuei	2nd Worst Lui Sha	Very Worst Chueh Ming
1	7	8	6	2
2	3	4	9	1
3	2	6	8	7
4	6	2	7	8
6	4	3	1	9
7	1	9	4	3
8	9	1	3	4
9	8	7	2	6

The dragons in this book are my gift to you, they will keep you and hold you, as they bring to you good health, wisdom, prosperity and ambition.

Tina

Tina Ketch's
Candle Lighting
Workbook

The ancient practice of candle lighting to purpose accomplished by the sages long ago has been brought back to life once again by Tina Ketch in her series of books entitled the Candle Lighting Encyclopedias. The ancients mastered the effectiveness of lighting colored candles at certain times for different reasons. This practice was accepted by many people through out the ages as it was defined and refined. **NOW for the first time in print the vibrational definition of each and every minute of every day.** Learn now how to determine which color of candle to light, and at what time to accomplish your specific desires.

It is no exaggeration to say that the splitting of light into color of its spectrum is man's most powerful tool for investigating the universe... Scientific American

This author believes that physical problems are a manifestation of spiritual issues thus, needing to be released... **TIME Magazine**

Tina Ketch's Candle Lighting Encyclopedia

is the most comprehensive, user friendly book ever in print on its subject. This is the perfect book for the novice, beginner or even the most

advanced candle lighters. There is a list of over 1600 different topics in which to light candles to bring to yourself as well conversely to release. Dysfunctions, blocks and obsessions can now be a thing of the past. The universe is abundant and through your use of this magnificent book you as well can be abundant in every aspect of your life.

Retail Price $15.95

Tina Ketch's
Candle
Lighting
Encyclopedia

Tina Ketch's Candle Lighting Encyclopedia Volume II In this

book you will find for the first time in print the vibrational definition of numbers not one through ten but 1 –100. You will find also the vibrational definitions of EVERY day of the year, with corresponding releases, so that you will be able to live free and uninhibited from past life issues that so often have pledged us all. This book will paint a clear picture of the past so that your future will be free and abundant, mentally, physically spiritually and financially. These titles will positively change your life!

TINA KETCH'S
Candle
Lighting
Encyclopedia
Volume II

Retail Price $15.95

Tina Ketch has now be listed in the Who's Who in America For her contribution in the field of writing.